DISCREPANCY EVALUATION

For Educational Program Improvement and Assessment

MALCOLM PROVUS

McCutchan Publishing Corporation
2526 Grove Street
Berkeley, California 94704

ISBN: 0-8211-1508-1
Library of Congress Catalog Card Number: 75-146312
©1971 by McCutchan Publishing Corporation
Printed in the United States of America

Preface

For a long time, school research and evaluation activity has been dominated by the kind of experimental research conducted in universities to confer doctoral degrees on graduate students in psychology. The generation and testing of hypotheses by means of probability sampling, establishing treatment conditions, and drawing statistical inferences about results was in turn based on work done in the biological sciences at the turn of this century.

Countless evaluations of this sort have been conducted in public schools to no effect. Even when statistically significant findings occur, conclusions about a school program's effect on students are generally unwarranted. Yet, as a result of these evaluations, one hears such statements as "the program resulted in increases in student reading scores," or "health has improved at the school because of the prevention program."

What is at issue here is not the establishment of proof of cause and effect relationships (which we know from the philosophy of science is always a matter of doubt); it is the nature of the evidence that leads to a reasonable presumption of cause and effect. It appears that the descriptive methods of the historian or anthropologist and the case study method of the psychiatrist and sociologist are more appropriate to the task of educational program evaluation than the experimental methods of the psychologist or biologist. Discrepancy evaluation, as described here, establishes that both the case study method and the methodology of experimental design, as well as other rigorous techniques, are required to conduct meaningful evaluations. Yet, this book is not so much about methodology as it is about people—their problems, their programmatic efforts at solution, and the evidence they can amass about their successes and failures. The book establishes that educational programs are enormously complex undertakings that must be evaluated in stages relative to the development and stability of the program being investigated. Values, not statistics, are the source of evaluations, and the basis for the values that both shape a school program and influence estimates of its success are carefully explored here.

Discrepancy evaluation is based on a model that has been under formal development for five years and continues to be revised as a function of the experience of practitioners. Although its presentation here and at a 1969 symposium is at times prescriptive, the model is in fact merely a set of notions to be understood and applied by those conducting evaluations and those for whom evaluations are intended. Use of the model should result in improvement of existing school programs, establishment of new and better programs, greater accountability of educators to the public, and wiser decisions by school administrators. In the best of all worlds, the model offers an opportunity to assess and improve local, state, and national education programs through a coordinated effort while at the same time insuring the traditional autonomy of local schools. From beginning to end, the book predicates that educational programs and their evaluation can be no better than the initiative and commitment of local school staffs make them. Here, then, is evaluation combining local initiative with regional or national accountability.

The author is indebted to innumerable coworkers, many of whom contributed both ideas and textual material to the development of the Discrepancy Evaluation Model. Chapter credits are provided as fully as possible at the end of this preface.

Three major groups deserve special recognition: those who were members of my staff in the Pittsburgh public schools; those who supported the work of that staff; and professional colleagues from outside our shop who contributed ideas and criticism. Many from all three groups are specifically mentioned in the parts of the book where their contributions are incorporated.

In addition, contributing members of the Pittsburgh staff include Mary Jan Duda, Edward Lundeen, Esther Kresh, Russell Scott, Glenn

Queer, Richard and Bonnie Fogel, Ethel Patton, Carter Allen, Dave McCann, Donald Bigelow, James Choakey, and Joan Lasky.

The support for our work in Pittsburgh came first and foremost from Superintendent of Schools, Sidney Marland. Board of Education members Mary Hazard and Robert Kibbee also helped at different times. Outside funding was secured with the aid of Nolen Estes, David Pollen, and Donald Carroll.

Finally, friends Benjamin Bloom, Edward Suchman, William Asher, Morris Burkowitz, Douglas Stone, Donald Mertic, and Michael Kirst contributed invaluable ideas over the years. Egon Guba and Dan Stufflebeam asked me in 1968 to join them in the planning and writing of the P.D.K. Evaluation Monograph, and their stimulation as well as that of Walter Foley, Robert Hammond, Howard Merriman, and William Gephart, is reflected in this book.

This work then is a potpourri of the experiences and thoughts of so many people that I can claim its composition but not its origin. In particular, the following persons require special recognition:

Judith McBroom, Gordon Welty, Esther Kresh, and Leonard Glassner for contributions to chapter 3;

Leonard Glassner for the preparation of material used in chapter 4, as a function of his painstaking work as a project evaluator;

Daniel Stufflebeam, Egon Guba, Walter Foley, William Gephart, John Goodlad, Ralph Tyler, Donald Carroll, and Richard Dershimer, for their remarks in chapter 5;

Ralph Walker, James Popham, Desmond Cook, Harry Silberman, Malcolm Richland, Samuel McClelland, Charles Nix, Frank Nelson, and Raymond Sweigert, among others whose spontaneous remarks are recorded in chapter 6;

Lorie Dancy for the preparation of material used in chapter 9;

Frank Morra for the preparation of material used in chapter 10; and

Esther Kresh, Frank Morra, Carter Allen, Bruce Gansneeder, Phyllis Twing, Lew Rhodes, and Lorie Dancy for their contributions to chapter 11.

I appreciate the cooperation of several publishers in allowing the use here of materials of mine that appeared in earlier publications. Chapter 2 draws material from chapter 5 of *Instructional Media and Creativity* (John Wiley and Sons); the *NEA Time to Teach Project Action Report* (National Education Association); and *Teaching for Relevance* (Whitehall Publishing Co.). Chapter 7 draws on material published by the *Journal of Educational Research and Development* (Summer 1970) and includes most of the material originally presented in chapter 11 of the *NSSE Yearbook* (1969). Chapter 12 includes material scheduled for publication in the article "A Public Philosphy of Evaluation," *Journal of the Ontario Institute for Studies in Education,* Spring 1971 (Toronto, Canada).

Finally, let me assure the reader that despite all the help I received, the errors of this book are mine alone.

Contents

Introduction

That new educational programs should be systematically evaluated before they are widely adopted or prematurely discarded is part of the credo of educational research. The prevailing notion of an acceptable evaluation procedure has been relatively simple: Ascertain the educational objectives of the new program, develop evaluation instruments that will provide data regarding the extent to which students have attained these educational objectives, and employ the instruments to collect data from students before they begin the program and at the end or at other points along the way. These same instruments should also be used with comparison groups of students to estimate the effectiveness of the new educational program in relation to the student achievements in "traditional" programs.

On the surface this procedure seems to be uncomplicated and straightforward. However, as long ago as the 1930's, some complexities were identified in this operation. I was then Director of Evaluation for the Eight Year Study, a project involving 30 school systems in the development of new curricula for secondary school students, many of whom were prompted by the absence of jobs during the depression to continue going to high schools originally designed for those who were college bound. Our evaluation staff found that most programs were undertaken without those involved having clearly

1

formulated the educational objectives that the programs were designed to attain. We knew that experienced teachers often have ideas
about topics, materials, learning activities, and teaching procedures
that seem to work with students without having formulated explicitly what they hope students will learn in these situations. Yet, to find
out whether in fact these programs are educationally effective, it is
necessary to determine what knowledge, skills, attitudes, interests, or
habits can be expected to result from participating in the program so
that the student's achievements in these respects can be appraised.
Many meetings of teachers and curriculum specialists were devoted
to identifying and defining the objectives of the programs.

We also found that the achievement tests then on the market did
not furnish evidence regarding many of the most important objectives and that the scales used for measurement were designed for
appraising individual differences among pupils and not for measuring
progress of individuals or groups in learning. We spent most of our
time constructing evaluation instruments relevant to the objectives of
the new programs.

We also learned that naming and roughly describing a new program
was only an initial step in actually having an operative program that
really fulfilled the description. For example, a number of the schools
decided to adopt a core curriculum for the senior high school, but
several years elapsed before any of the schools had a program in
operation that represented even roughly what was in their minds as
they made the decision to adopt it. It became necessary to free
teachers from other responsibilities for part of their time and to
support them in summer workshops so that they might develop and
put into operation the ideas that were initially approved.

These experiences of 30 years ago led those of us involved to
describe evaluation as a continuing process that goes on in cycles as
ideas emerge and are explored; as educational objectives are formulated, defined, and critically examined; as learning experiences are
developed to help students attain these objectives and evaluation
devices and procedures are worked out to appraise the progress of
students toward them; and as the evidence is reviewed regarding both
the problems of implementing the program plans and the achievements of students. We recognized even then that the task of evaluation must be an integral part of curriculum development and instructional improvement.

The passage of the Elementary and Secondary Education Act of
1965, with its provision that projects funded under the act were to
be evaluated, stimulated an unprecedented number of efforts to

appraise educational programs. Most of these efforts were ill-design-ed, failing to recognize the complexity of the task and the lack of available instruments and personnel.

Some institutional personnel were able to survive the initial frustration and to rethink and replan both the development of innovations and their evaluation. Malcolm Provus (then Director of Research in the Pittsburgh public schools) and his staff developed a systematic evaluation method that took account of experiences like those encountered in the Eight Year Study. This formulation of an evaluation procedure to guide program development or to decide to discontinue program efforts goes far beyond any earlier attempts. It was recognized as an important contribution by a number of leaders in educational research and school administration.

This recognition encouraged the Pittsburgh staff to arrange for a postsession symposium in connection with the Los Angeles convention of the American Educational Research Association. The symposium participants, including both those who devised the procedure and those who were asked to review it, spent the major part of the day in interesting, illuminating, and useful presentations and discussion. The description of the procedure itself, the explanatory presentations, and the critical reviews form the kernel of this book which outlines a systematic procedure for evaluating, guiding, and, when necessary, abandoning educational projects. The book fills a serious gap in the techniques of educational research and development and will be of interest and value to anyone concerned with the problems of introducing new educational programs to attack significant educational problems.

Ralph W. Tyler
Director Emeritus,
Center for Advanced Study in the Behavioral Sciences

1

The Need for
Discrepancy Evaluation

A Time for Accountability

America's public schools are presently being asked to redress the social ills of the nation: to reinvolve the disenchanted; to eliminate longstanding prejudice toward racial and minority groups; to select and train future professionals, skilled workers, and menials (with little or no regard to initial aptitude); to correct the effects of child-rearing abuses; to revitalize community agencies and service institutions; to reeducate parents in family building and maintenance skills as well as participatory democracy; and to secure the continous education of all Americans from infancy to grave. As a result, schools are wallowing in a flood of new programs pumped into existence at staggering cost. School boards, government agencies, and the larger public are now asking about the effects of these new programs. Should they be replaced? Can better programs be found? Should more money be spent or less?

For a long time, the public schools of this country were recognized for the success of their work. Immigrants, the disenfranchized, the confused, the inept, and the outrageously boisterous, were more or less taught to read and write. That some never did learn was of little consequence to those responsible for running the schools. All that has changed. At first because of social awareness of education inequities associated with race and poverty and more recently, because of public aspiration for a more broadly based democracy, more responsive institutions, and greater self-determination, the schools have come under critical public scrutiny. Above all, the role of the federal government and our political system in shaping popular expectations and funding massive local efforts has led to a broad base of support for concern about the quality and benefits of this country's most pervasive and expensive enterprise.

Recent federal legislation provided funds for some school programs and required their evaluation. As Sputnik accelerated science education in our public schools, so Title 1 of the Poverty Section of the Elementary and Secondary Education Act (ESEA) gave major impetus to the evaluation of public school programs.[1] It was the first educational legislation in history to call for local determination of the effectiveness of federally funded programs. As such, it created tremendous demands on the recipients of these funds.

Title 1 was put into effect almost overnight with the intent of compensating for the limited experience of poor, deprived, and handicapped children. Most districts had little or no time to plan their ESEA projects, much less to design project evaluations. Research staffs and facilities were inadequate, and staff added later did not have the advantage of early involvement in project planning and development. Basic information about students and program conditions was not available. Much had to be done to define the scope of the evaluation task, to invent useful data-gathering instruments, and to secure information on short notice from those who were deeply engaged in project operations. Yet school personnel were told that evidence of project effectiveness and reports summarizing the evidence were needed in order to ensure public and congressional support for the coming fiscal year.[2]

That evidence has never been obtained, and for three years the Office of Education has been forced to go to Congress with an annual ESEA report that is purely descriptive, even though Congress has constantly asked for information about program benefits.[3] Many state education agencies and local boards of education also want to know whether money is being spent wisely and how the program benefits the children. It is clear that what is known as program accountability or benefits assessment is desired at all levels of government. Those who attempted evaluation with the techniques generally available have discovered what educational researchers have known for a long time: When quasi-experimental designs are applied to the outcomes of new educational programs, generally no evidence of new program advantages over existing program is obtained.[4] This finding may be due to the relative weakness of new programs, or it may be due to the weakness of the evaluation techniques themselves. Indeed, there is considerable evidence that when school programs do make a difference, our evaluation techniques are inadequate to verify their effectiveness.[5]

In September 1965 those of us from university research backgrounds who cheerfully undertook to implement Congress's mandate to evaluate ESEA did so with a sense of relief: "At last," we said, "curriculum evaluation has come into its own." We began our work by oversimplifying the problem: It was, we decided, simply to find out whether new programs were better than the ones they replaced. We did not realize that our first problem was to find out what a new program was. We continued our work by applying the quasi-experimental designs that had served us well in research settings. We soon found that these designs were inapplicable. Finally we settled down to grapple with better statements of program objectives and the design of new instruments to measure these objectives, largely ignoring the constricting influence our evaluation activity was having on the people responsible for making new programs work.

To the school administrator who needs information about the effectiveness of school programs the word "evaluation" conjures up some unpleasant experiences: a report that took "too long" to prepare and overlooked the obvious while concentrating on the trite; a university consultant who proved unintelligible and eventually hostile; an investigator that got in people's way and never seemed able to draw a definitive conclusion. Where does the blame lie?

It is entirely possible that most public school evaluations are meaningless because they reflect the confusion of administrators over educational programs that are equally meaningless. It is also possible that most evaluators don't know their business. No doubt there is a relationship between the weakness of educational programs, evaluation methodology, and the training institutions that spawn both.

The history of recent public school programs is one of lack of documentation, lack of program control, and measured outcomes suggesting that there is greater variation within programs than between programs. A recent unpublished evaluation of team teaching, to be discussed later in this book, revealed 131 different programs in 39 different schools, none of which adhered to the essential principles of team teaching contained in the school system's original understanding of the concept.[6] Is it any wonder that students who had been exposed to this kind of "team teaching" for six years showed no greater growth in academic performance than did a control group? There is a growing belief among practitioners responsible for evaluation and research at local, state, and federal levels that better ways can be found to evaluate the effect of public school expenditures so that necessary program changes can be made.

Shortly after the ESEA was passed, a number of big city school research directors met to consider the requirements of the act and agreed that programs would have to be better planned and more carefully installed if they were to be effective.[7] This group concluded its deliberations with the statement: "Title 1 of the 1965 Elementary and Secondary Education Act may be forgotten as a poverty act, long remembered as the source of systematic self-appraisal in America's Schools." The statement was not prophetic. Today, useful evaluation theory and practice are no better established in public schools than they ever were. However, the need persists.

Public school systems are traditionally monolithic, hierarchical, monopolistic, and, therefore, relatively insensitive to change. Further, if change is to occur, it must be due either to explosive external force or to skillful, internally directed, gradual pressure—a delicately balanced movement that produces within the members of an organization first uncertainty, then awareness of a problem, analysis, self-appraisal, readiness for change, commitment to change, and ultimately the satisfaction of problem solution and self-realization.

The timing associated with ESEA funding has had disastrous effects on program planning and design. In 1965 few school systems were able to make adequate planning arrangements before receiving Title 1 government contracts. Highly restrictive time periods in which to achieve overambitious purposes were universal. When Title 1 programs were renewed at the end of the first fiscal year, most of these defects in planning were not corrected. Although there now appear to be more specialists assigned and administrative staff time devoted to ESEA projects, there is still a lack of program redesign in order to insure feasibility within the very real constraints of time and money.

Even when programs are well designed, there is considerable evidence that the conditions defined as essential to their success are not secured.[8] Typically, the qualifications for teachers are not met, minimal student competence at the beginning of a program is not verified, and essential staff work and inservice training are not carried out during a program. A conservative evaluation of Title 1 programs credits only 25 percent of all programs with serving even their most general purposes.[9]

The evaluation clause of the ESEA established evaluation as a necessary building block in the design of American educational reform. The evaluation implications of ESEA could eventually have greater impact than the program itself. Congress ordered billions of dollars to be spent in new ways to serve new purposes, yet there is reason to doubt that an administrative capacity exists at each level of government to ensure that the money is well spent. Perhaps before we can build effective new programs, we must establish creative new ways to monitor new programs and eventually to judge their effectiveness. Such a capacity must ultimately depend on a management theory that uses pertinent, reliable information as the basis for administrative decisions to improve or reject ongoing programs.

The evaulation concepts spawned by educators several decades ago to help teachers improve classroom instruction and universities to select students are no longer adequate. Local boards, state officers, and agencies of the federal government are desperately seeking new forms of evaluation. A rash of evaluation activity is presently underway, for the most part aimed at taking stock of our present programs but in fact producing little valuable information. Yet today as never before, there is a will to take stock of our efforts, no matter how painful the findings for some individuals, institutions, or professions.

Clearly, the task defined by most federal legislation is to increase education program payloads for the disadvantaged and to prove it. Before this is possible, however, we will have to improve our program development procedures and know that we have improved them. It is important to note that improvement in procedure is not always immediately reflected in performance. For example, as in aviation a change in wing design may be ineffective until coupled with increased horsepower, so in education a change in instructional material may be inconsequential until coupled with a new mix of students or a new teaching technique.

Education may be defined as the art of bringing about predicted changes in human behavior. Because methods are uncertain and conditions are obscure, predictions are often inaccurate. When dealing with underprivileged students, about whom we know even less than the average school client, our predictions are notoriously unreliable. It follows that educational programs devised for the underprivileged are unreliable. Programs with the same name can differ more from class to class than do programs with different names. On inspection, Miss Brown's remedial reading program may turn out to be a group therapy class, and Miss Smith's therapy class may turn out to be a high school psychology lecture series.

To improve educational programs, then, it follows that we must systematically conduct controlled experiments in the course of regular public school instruction. These experiments must employ sound design and must ensure the maximum freedom of the chief investigator: the classroom teacher. To accomplish this difficult task, we must help teachers and other practitioners realize the intimate relationship between evaluation, research, program design, and program development. We must establish creative ways to develop, test, and debug new programs as they operate in the public schools. Such a capacity will ultimately depend on the installation of evaluation systems that generate pertinent, reliable information as the basis for making sound decisions about program development outcomes and needed research.

What Is Program Evaluation?

At the outset, it is obviously important to determine what is meant by program evaluation. At least five definitions are considered:

(1) The judgment of authorities about a program;

(2) The opinions of program staff;

(3) The opinions of those affected by a program;

(4) A comparison of actual program outcomes with expected outcomes; and

(5) A comparison of an executed program with its design.

There is a long tradition in American education favoring the first approach. An example of this type was a ranking in 1968 of Office of Education Regional Laboratories by an independent evaluator. Funding was based at least in part on rank achieved, with the project at the top of the list receiving almost twice as much money as the project at the bottom. Sometimes when there are several parties to an evaluation by judgment, different opinions must be reconciled before an evaluation is rendered. When this procedure is used, a difference in the judges' standards is often revealed, which leads to some uncertainty whether the program or the judges' standards are being evaluated. The second and third kinds of evaluation have the advantage of providing firsthand accounts of program strengths and weaknesses from the perspective of those close to program operations.

The fourth approach, i.e., evaluation of program outcomes, establishes performance criteria for program recipients. This approach is represented by all that is most current and "scientific" in educational evaluation. Starting with the work of Tyler[10] and the perfection of standardized instruments with norms for various populations, and continuing with the present interest in group criterion reference tests, individual situational testing, and unobtrusive measures of performance, the preoccupation of the present generation of evaluators has been and continues to be with microanalysis of a learner's behavior at various times before and after exposure to a lesson, program, treatment, or institution.[11]

These evaluations are generally equated with pre and post measures of the program's clients to test the null hypothesis that no significant change has occurred or that postperformance is not at a predicted level. Here a vast literature of experimental methodology is appropriate, first useful in science and agriculture laboratories and later prescribed for doctoral candidates in the social science divisions of universities.

Most federal programs are new programs in the sense that they are new to the school district employing them and to most of the personnel involved. These programs are in a "becoming stage" for staff. Procedures must change with experience; as procedures change and the possible and impossible are sorted out, goals must also change. However, when goals are fixed and students frozen into experimental and control groups to satisfy rigorous evaluation designs that assume stable treatments, the dynamics of essential program change are constricted out of existence.

Today, much that passes for research in universities is applied blindly as evaluation methodology by school staffs charged with judging programs and justifying their own existence. The irony of this unexpected and slavish devotion of school men to the canons of "good" research is that these techniques are not only singularly unable to document program outcomes but often counterproductive to program success as well. It is not surprising that many school superintendents and boards of education have long ignored research methodology as a way of either improving school practice or estimating its success.

An evaluation that begins with an experimental design denies to program staff what it needs most: information that can be used to make judgments about the program while it is in its dynamic stages of growth. Furthermore, the imposition of an experimental design in the formulative stages of a program inhibits the staff's natural desire to improve a program on the basis of experience. Evaluation must provide administrators and program staff with the information they need and the freedom to act on that information.

The fifth definition of evaluation, which is advanced in this book, holds that every aspect of a program, not just its outcomes, is involved in an evaluation. Evaluation is primarily a comparison of program performance with expected or designed program, and secondarily, among many other things, a comparison of client performance with expected client outcomes. This comprehensive comparison of many aspects of actual events with expected events therefore requires the explication of a detailed picture of an entire program at various points in time as the standard for judging performance. These program standards may arise from any source, but under the Discrepancy Evaluation Model they are derived from the values of the program staff and the client population it serves.

Similarly, when the values employed by persons conducting an evaluation are compatible with those of the staff and program being evaluated, it is generally possible for everyone concerned to both understand and accept a final evaluation report. When value conflicts exist among clients, practitioners, or evaluators, reports are generally characterized by lack of specificity and debatable conclusions.

What we propose here is to suggest an alternative to the two prevailing methods of evaluation in the country today. We will not use the antiseptic assumptions of the research laboratory to compare children receiving new program assistance with those not receiving such aid. We recognize that these comparisons have never been productive, nor have they facilitated corrective action. The overwhelming number of evaluations conducted in this way show no significant differences between "experimental" and "control" groups. In most public school systems, these evaluations consist of preemptive applications of quasi-experimental designs and abortive efforts to improve programs that were poorly designed and installed and remain poorly administered. The second evaluation method, that of the judgments of "experts" who have made on-site visits to projects or have studied public documents, is equally unacceptable to us. Even when the opinion is disinterested and objective, it tends to reflect personal values rather than acceptable evidence, and the method generates few lasting benefits to practitioners or clients.

The Purposes of Evaluation

Evaluation can serve at least three major purposes: (1) to ensure the quality of the product, (2) to ensure this quality at minimal cost, and (3) to help management make decisions about what should be produced and how. Quality control requires the establishment of procedures to monitor and modify programs to ensure uniform products that meet acceptable standards. Cost-benefit analysis examines the relationship between a program's cost and the value of its products relative to the cost of other products of similar value. Finally, improved decisionmaking is possible when new sources of information about either benefits, costs, program quality, or program operations are at hand. The last of these purposes appears to have begun to gain understanding and support from school administrators within the past few years.

There seems to be general agreement from both users and producers of public school evaluation reports that current information about educational program is too minimal to permit even a summary of actual program activity in most American schools. Information about benefits, costs, and program operations is simply not available, and the possibility of comparing programs on a cost-benefit basis is still only a Defense Department dream in the minds of a few Office of Education executives.

The first purpose, to maintain quality control standards for education projects through an evaluation apparatus, appears to be uppermost in the minds of a good many Office of Education staffers, and it is the cause of continual effort and frustration. Generally, Office of Education personnel have sought to ensure program quality by establishing categorical restrictions on fund use and by urging that more sophisticated evaluation designs be incorporated in program proposals.

This approach to evaluation assumes that school districts will be more likely to attend carefully to program operations if they know that program products will be rigorously appraised. Unfortunately, this strategy presently emphasizes the definition of program outputs in quantified terms suitable for use in experimental designs. In this lies an unrecognized paradox: As state and federal government officers seek to encourage program quality by means of rigorous product assessment, they may thwart quality control work at its only effective point —the local level. This local work is usually of the process assessment type in which evaluators systematically collect and weigh data descriptive of ongoing program activity.

The desirability of evaluating both program products and processes to guide policy makers at the national level will find universal support. However, it is our belief that process evaluation for program improvement must occur at the local level before national assessments of federally funded programs can be meaningful.

It follows that if there are types of programs with different developmental characteristics, the development standards for these program types will vary also. Therefore, it is important to attempt to classify

programs of varying developmental characteristics. In the writer's experience there are two types of public school programs with different
patterns of program development that must be evaluated.

The first type is the "instant installation" program. Most federal
programs, especially those funded under Title 1 of ESEA and often
those under Title 3 as well, are of this variety. They have been quick
cast without careful planning or design to utilize available resources.
Also in the quick-cast category are most of the "new" programs mounted by a public school staff determined to do "something better" on its
own initiative. These efforts are rarely planned and defined with sufficient precision to permit an adequate evaluation of the new program. It
is this type of program, designed by the school system itself, that is
most common and most likely to fail.

The second type, less common but still widely used, is the "canned"
program. In this type either a commercial, public, or nonprofit developer has carefully determined a program's standards in advance of its
installation and has provided explicit guidelines for installation, including staff training.

The Discrepancy Evaluation Model is primarily addressed to the first
type of program. Occasionally, school systems manage to organize the
technical skills necessary to create an adequate program design. In the
author's personal experience, however, this has happened only twice,
and both times sizable funds from outside the school system were
needed. Of course, the existence of these funds, even when earmarked
for careful planning and development purposes, in no way ensures that
a program's design will be adequate. It is, therefore, this first type of
program that stands most in need of evaluation. Vast sums have been
lost on American education because of poor design work or the failure
of educators to recognize the necessity for incorporating design activity within the developmental life of a school program when program
specifications are lacking.

Ultimately, programs will improve only if teachers, administrators,
and students in most of America's classrooms become involved in a
comprehensive effort to review and improve their work. Such an effort
requires a careful analysis of the strengths and shortcomings of existing
procedures, a description of desired events and their sequence, and the
designing of a series of small experiments to test the actual effects of
each event.

Shades of action research?[12] Maybe. But there is considerable evidence in both industry and education that only when personnel responsible for conducting a program are involved in its examination and
revision will the program improve and endure. We must therefore use

federal education dollars to give school personnel a sense of freedom to admit error, to revise programs, and to risk failure creatively, secure in the belief that continuous program evaluation will eventually provide them with evidence of success.

In this light, the fact that most federally-funded school programs have not been carefully planned is not as serious as some have claimed. Programs can be planned after they have begun. Program planning "in midstream" has the advantage of providing staff with information based on pragmatic consequence rather than speculation. That is, classrooms can become labs for gathering and distilling program development information. Further, it then becomes possible for an entire staff to contribute to a program design policy decision and thereby feel a sense of responsibility for it. These benefits, of course, ensue only when evaluation is interpreted to mean staff self-evaluation and continuous program assessment.

The broadening of the superintendent's decisionmaking base to include program staff decisionmaking may be viewed by some as a loss of administrative power. On the contrary, one of the most important considerations in an administrator's policy-making deliberations is the amount of staff support a decision will command. For this reason, superintendents often establish committees or councils as a sounding board for policy before enactment. One great disadvantage of these sounding boards is that they must react to a hypothetical issue without benefit of total staff reaction to "the real thing." When a superintendent can involve his entire staff in actual program revision and policymaking experience, his decisions as chief school officer are likely to be realistic and enduring.

When federal program evaluation is used as a mechanism for the development and improvement of school programs, it takes on the appearance of a staff-training strategy. Staff activity includes systematic study of program variables, such as student ability at program entry point, student-teacher interaction, pupil performance on interim tasks, and student and teacher indices of attitude and satisfaction. Evaluation becomes a vehicle for training staff to meet the changing demands of project activity. This training will eventually help to supply data for both process and product evaluation by ensuring that the staff values, collects, and uses data on a continuous basis for program improvement. It reveals new independent variables and helps to stabilize programs, both of which are essential to an eventual analysis of program benefits. Judgment about program benefits can be based on product assessment only when a program is stable—when it continues to be what staff and administration think it is. The products of two or more stable programs with similar benefits can be meaningfully compared only when all the situational factors influencing the product have been identified and taken into account. Therefore, expecting to evaluate a program on the basis of its products before determining its stability and evaluating its processes will generally lead to misinformation and failure.

Clearly, process and product evaluation are not incompatible; they are interdependent and require careful staging. Program development as a function of "midstream" planning and training must come first, however. Experimental design work can be deferred. To expect significant shifts in student criterion performance scores before the final form of a program has evolved is to expect a caterpillar to fly.

When program is defined by a staff as a dynamic that must undergo developmental stages of growth, it becomes possible to understand, measure, and place value on any program at any time without compulsive reference to standardized achievement test scores or other quantified criteria. Scores are not to be discounted in either short term or long term evaluation, but they must lose their sacredness as *the* criterion of program effectiveness. They are meaningful only when applied to the last stages of program development, and then only when they are part of an experimental design providing for many complex factors.

Some officials in the Office of Education are obviously aware of the need to deemphasize short term product assessment so that internal, local evaluation processes may be employed to strengthen programs. Yet pressure from Congress, the Bureau of the Budget, and elsewhere may be too great to resist. Similar pressure may exist at the local level from militant action groups who, in their desire to see immediate, tangible student benefits, do themselves a disservice by ignoring the complex, maturational nature of any new school program.

Most evaluation efforts have been restricted to the collection of information on the success or failure of programs. While the information is of immediate interest, it has little value for planning and ensuring the success of future programs. If a program is successful, educators will be interested in copying it. For this purpose it is essential to know the exact "recipe" of a program so that it can be reproduced. If a program fails, it is important to know why, so that the same mistakes will not be repeated or so that corrective action can be taken. In order to provide adequate management and thereby increase the probability of program success, in order to collect the "why" and "how" of program success or failure, the decision-maker needs the following information:

(1) A statement of goals (Where is the program going?);

(2) A plan of operation (How are you going to get there? What do you have to do to get ready?);

(3) A statement of support systems (How much time, money, and administrative support do you have?); and

(4) A system for monitoring the installation and operation with provision for feedback (Have you started? Are you staying on course?).

A simple analogy will help to emphasize the importance of each of these components. A man (program manager) decides to take a trip. He chooses California as his destination (goal). Next he must decide which of a number of alternate means of transportation to choose (selection of a program to reach the goal). His decision will be based on a number of considerations such as time, money, etc. He decides to go by car. After he decides on a car trip he must plan the precise route that he will follow, how far he expects to go each day, etc. (plan of operation). He will also have to engage in a number of activities to prepare for the trip, such as making sure the car has gas and oil and that all the parts are in working order. He'll also have to make sure that he has proper financial coverage (support functions) and if he is driving a regular shift car when he has already driven an automatic, he may have to learn to drive the car (staff training). Once he has started the trip, he will want to know whether he is making satisfactory progress toward California (monitoring). By reading the road signs he will know whether he is on the right road, and if he reaches his predetermined destination each day he will know that he is on schedule (feedback). If he sees a sign that tells him he is on the wrong road, he can alter his direction and get back on course. If he does not reach his daily destination, he will know that he probably underestimated the time and will want to revise his estimate. However, other events could put him behind schedule, such as a car breakdown (akin to the thousand and one uncontrolled events that can happen in a school system). Our driver will know whether he has reached California if after a period of time he sees predetermined cues such as signs, landmarks, etc. (success criteria).

Consider what could happen if the man did not go through all the important steps. First, if he hadn't decided where to go (goal), it is obvious that he never could have started. Again, he could not have started if he had not selected his mode of transportation and route (plan of operation) and made adequate preparations. Without a precise plan of the route he would wander aimlessly, and the road

signs and his destination each day would provide meaningless information. Finally, without knowing what cues to look for, he would
never know if he reached California, and even if he did, he could
never adequately tell anyone else how to get there.

Suppose the evaluator is waiting in California for the man who
never arrives. All the evaluator can do is duly note that the man has
not arrived; he doesn't know whether the route the man took was
one that didn't lead to California or whether something went wrong
along the way. (It may be that it's just taking him a few more days
due to car failure). If the evaluator had gone on the entire trip, not
only would he know why the man hadn't gotten to California, but
along the way he could have helped him correct any deficiencies and
thereby increased the probability that the man would reach his
destination. He certainly would be in a better position to tell other
travelers how to get to California. He might even write a program
manual on the subject.

The Importance of Local Evaluation

At the 1969 summer meeting of the American Academy of Arts
and Sciences the President's Advisor on Urban Affairs decried the
lack of planning and managerial expertise that has gone into the
design and execution of American public service programs.

Our crime has not been that we have spent vast sums of money to
little effect, but that we have failed to deal with real and noxious
problems in our society. Therefore, we must find new and better
ways to deal with these problems. More important, the federal
government must employ a strategy for identifying people who will
combine local and national resources and then stand accountable for
effecting local changes that are compatible with the national interest.

The ability of the federal government to determine the effectiveness of education agencies or programs created under new legislation
is central to the notion of national accountability and change.
Without a local measuring system, national effects cannot be
documented and the degree of national change cannot be determined.

If the American educational system succeeds in meeting its current
social and economic crises it will be because of the commitment and
responsiveness of local educational agencies to problems exposed by
local constituents. Local citizens are developing new systems that
will hold school administrators more accountable and permit administrators to hold school staff more accountable for the continuous

improvement of education programs. National improvement in American education can never be more than the sum of improvement in local activity.

Local school evaluation serves the same purposes as national evaluation. Both are concerned with improving existing and new educational programs, separating successes from failures, and determining their relative costs and the conditions necessary to their success in varied educational settings. Both can profit from participation in a joint evaluation system. Only the federal government, however, is in a position to provide guidelines for and coordination of locally determined change so that new educational programs will result in a nationally discernible improvement of educational service to parents and children. The coordination and guidelines must eventually be part of a widespread federally funded evaluation network.

The success of a state or national evaluation system depends on winning the cooperation of local agencies as the result of trade-offs between the data needs of the state or nation and the needs of the local district for meaningful, valuable information about their programs. To make sure that payoffs are profitable to both parties, it is probable that any national evaluation capability will ultimately depend on the existence of self-sustaining evaluation systems in each of the fifty states. Methods adequate for local evaluation and a supply of trained personnel capable of executing it are necessary. One of the purposes of this book is to provide an evaluation method as well as a personnel training rationale.

The failure of federal evaluation programs to date can be explained through the analogy of a small man trying to move huge rocks by working on the wrong end of a small lever. Given the scope and variety of local program activity, Office of Education bureaus have mounted understaffed, underfinanced, and underconceptualized evaluation efforts. It is necessary to pool resources not only by obtaining interbureau cooperation, but also by creating a cumulative resource across all levels of program activity: local, state, and national. This resource can be stored and accumulated gradually and constitutes an information data base to which various users contribute at various times. When a great deal of interrelated information is available regarding any local project it will be possible to evaluate that project, and produce meaningful national program evaluations. Another advantage of the information storage or data base concept is that its value to users at all administrative levels is a function of their data contributions to it. Hence, field support for data collection, something sadly lacking in federal efforts to date, becomes more probable.

Further, users may begin the construction of a data base independently of other users as long as a single, common classification system is established first.

Another reason for lack of local cooperation is inadequate conceptualization about the purposes and processes of evaluation. Local program managers are more interested in information that can be used to improve programs than in information analyzing program outcomes. As has been established, both kinds of information are essential to any defensible evaluation procedure, and therefore it is possible for the interests of both local program managers and federal administrators to be served. The process of evaluation requires the continual collection of information about program standards at various stages in the program's development and the collection of information about performance relative to these standards. The discrepancy found between performance and standards constitutes valuable feedback for program change and improvement. This discrepancy information also provides the best basis for estimating the eventual success or failure of a program at an early stage. Hence, this information is as valuable to federal officers with refunding authority as it is to local managers. The value of this evaluation system to local, state, and national administrators is that it ensures trade-offs between participants and sustains the interest of users in maintaining the system.

Data collected under the system must be objective, comprehensive, reliable, timely credible, and valid. These characteristics of the data can be reasonably assured if local agencies preparing proposals are made responsible for data inputs as a condition of submitting a proposal and receiving a grant. Data sets so obtained would be defined relative to the program to be funded, the client population served, and the information already in storage describing client, agency or community factors that might influence the program.

Current Efforts and Some Reasons for Failure

A great deal of disparate evaluation work is going on in the country today at the local, state, and national levels. Very little of this work at any level is aimed at the establishment of a total evaluation system. Several of the big cities are attempting to construct a data base for information retrieval by computer. None of them have yet created even a comprehensive student file. Advisors who are oriented to computer companies may stress the importance of hardware configurations in the solution of technological problems of filing, retrieving, and displaying information, but the basic cause of inoperative computerized student files remains the lack of adequate information definition.

The Iowa Information Center has mounted a successful information system including a well-designed student file by limiting all information to description in major report categories.[13] This file is useful for generating status reports. However, it is inadequate as a resource for measuring the effects of educational programs on students and the larger society. It is also inadequate for describing educational programs and factors that influence their success or failure.

The federal government has established a limited number of efforts aimed at evaluating the effect of some of its programs. One federal program seeks to help more than 20 state departments of education to reach agreement about the terminology of measuring program outputs.[14] Another program seeks to bring states together to identify common problems and possible joint modes of attack.[15] Still another seeks to trace changes in pupil performance to compensatory education programs.[16] These, and others, all have the appearance of highly constrained, narrowly conceived efforts. In no instance do either the purposes or the methods of these evaluation projects represent more than ad hoc attempts to deal with a few of the kaleidoscope of elements that must be understood and controlled in any national evaluation effort. Even those programs with initially defensible rationales have been compromised beyond recognition by the uncoordinated interplay of local, state, and national forces. The National Assessment Study is a good example of such a program.[17] Its obvious potential for the evaluation of educational programs was soon vitiated by the fears of city and state system superintendents.

Several states have themselves embarked on educational evaluation and assessment programs. Pennsylvania has undertaken a multifaceted attack on the identification of state educational goals, their elaboration in measurable terms, and the collection of data aimed at determining student status relative to these goals.[18] The result will be a capacity to describe student performance relative to important goals. Again, however, no information will be available about educational programs or their effect, nor will any inferences about such information be warranted.

A New Way

Ultimately, programs will improve only if teachers, administrators, and students in most of America's classrooms become involved in a comprehensive effort to review and improve their work. The effort requires careful study by school staffs of their program operations, a detailed analysis of program inputs and processes, and the verification that programs are in fact operating as people believe them to be operating.

Administrators need to understand that the installation of school programs, whether innovative or not, involves a high risk of failure. Evaluators need to understand the kind of information administrators need to reduce the level of risk. Both administrators and researchers must see evaluation as a continuous information management process serving program improvement as well as program assessment purposes. The complexity and concomitant high cost of effective evaluation must be recognized as a necessary management expense somewhat similar to high insurance premiums. Everyone concerned with public education must be willing to spend much larger sums for evaluation if we are to have an adequate management system for protecting federal investments under present Office of Education reform strategy.

Those involved in public school reform through new program development must recognize (1) the natural, developmental stages of any new program; (2) the necessity of evaluation activity appropriate to each stage; and (3) the administrator's dependence on information obtained through evaluation for making timely, defensible decisions.

For four and a half years in Pittsburgh a carefully selected staff was engaged in the construction of a new kind of evaluation model. Our mandate from the Superintendent of Schools, Sydney Marland, was clear: Redefine the purposes of evaluation in a manner acceptable to local, state, and federal education agencies and devise and test an operational model.

The major purpose of our original evaluation effort was to obtain enough information about the operation of new programs to change and improve them in their early stages of planning and installation. This purpose was more relevant to local than to state or federal evaluation needs, but obviously an assessment of the longrun effectiveness of programs at all levels would be dependent on the adequacy of their management, their fidelity with program plans, and the soundness of the plans themselves. Hence, because of the long development time of new programs, a second purpose arose, to enable local or state officals to make early predictions about a program's eventual success.

Ultimately, we become concerned with a long list of questions:

(1) What educational outcomes can be expected from any given educational program?

(2) What are the actual educational outcomes of the program?

(3) What are the educational program needs of a given community?

(4) What resources are available to meet educational needs?

(5) What use should be made of these resources?

(6) How can new programs be more adequately designed?

(7) How can new programs be better installed?

(8) Which programs should be revised and improved during development?

(9) What new programs should be terminated during development?

(10) What are the side effects and unexpected outcomes of new programs?

(11) What is the cost (in dollars and other units of value) of programs relative to their outcomes?

(12) How does the cost of a given program compare with that of other programs with similar benefits?

The procedures for answering these questions constitute the evaluation process. The information used by these procedures constitutes a data base that may be formalized in an information system. Any state, local, or federal agency seeking to answer evaluation questions therefore stands in need of the data required to answer these questions and a method of generating that data. The development of an evaluation system must include an information gathering, storage, and retrieval capacity as well as a set of procedures for identifying and using the information. Procedures for identifying and using information will change, subject to research facilitated by the existence of the evaluation system.

The development of an evaluation system requires attention to design based on theory, research based on experience, and instrumentation based on modern techniques. All three areas of work must proceed simultaneously, thereby providing a support condition for each of the areas of work. It is an assumption of the work reported here that the gradual expansion of adequate evaluation theory is predicated on actual evaluation experience.

It is possible to describe America's educational task using the equation $i\,(p) = o$ where i equals input, p equals process, and o equals outputs or benefit. Outputs are viewed here as a function of the interaction of inputs with process. For example, students, teachers, and materials (inputs) interact in such a manner (process) as to produce student reading competence (outputs).

One of the major purposes of program development work is to understand the relationships described by this equation in regard to any program. As more information is obtained about what inputs, processes, and outputs are involved, a program becomes better defined, more easily operationalized, and, ultimately, likely to be more productive.

Educators must realize that they need to improve their knowledge of all three elements of the equation simultaneously. If, for instance, a program manager defines inputs and outputs in great detail but fails to define process, he may be able to demonstrate that a program has achieved its purposes at a given level of cost, but he will be unable to say what the program was and will be unable to reproduce it. If on the other hand, he defines process well but fails to define either inputs or outputs, either he will have created a program whose cost and prerequisite conditions are unknown or he will have inadequate information about the effects of his well-defined process.

In the early design stage of a program, the value of the terms in the equation will normally be minimally defined. As program adjustments are made, these terms will have to be redefined. The most common error of the evaluator is to sharpen the definition of one term without making corresponding adjustments in the other terms. For example, to redefine the process of a reading program by focusing on the quality of student-teacher interaction without giving careful attention to the kind of student response that will be an immediate outcome of the interaction is to perform an evaluation disservice. On such an erroneous basis, the conclusion could be drawn that (a) the specific interaction process is ineffective or (b) the entire program is ineffective.

Corresponding attention should be given to redefining such inputs as teacher qualifications prerequisite to student-teacher interaction. Again, if teachers' ability to engage in this interaction is not carefully defined, the same conclusions ((a) and (b) above) may be erroneously drawn in a situation where process and program are sound and only a change in input is required to keep the program developing nicely.

Once it is recognized that new educational programs inevitably change in time and that their design and implementation must reflect the change, the job of the evaluator is to see that the definitions of i, p, and o are continuously revised at the same level of specificity.

There is a need, then, for an evaluation model that facilitates program design changes in input, process, and output through inevitable stages of program development while at the same time gathering data essential to judgments about the effectiveness of the program and how it may be improved at any stage of its development. The Discrepancy Evaluation Model presented here is explicit about how evaluation may be used for program improvement as well as program assessment. After reading this book, we hope the reader will agree that an evaluation that does not serve both purposes is not worth doing.

Footnotes

1. Both titles 1 and 3 of *Elementary and Secondary Education Act*, 1965 mandated evaluation.

2. Pittsburgh Public Schools, *Big City Title I Evaluation Conference: 1967 Report*, p. vii.

3. Daniel Stufflebeam, "The Use and Cause of Evaluation in Title III," *Theory into Practice* 6 (June 1967): 126-127.

4. Egon Guba, *Educational Researcher* 30, no. 3 (1969): 3-5.

5. U.S., Office of Education, Bureau of Educational Personnel Development, *Do Teachers Make A Difference?* (Washington, D.C.: Government Printing Office, 1970).

6. Esther Kresh, "Pittsburgh Team Teaching Program, 1967 Report." mimeographed (Board of Education, Pittsburgh Public Schools).

7. Pittsburgh Public Schools, *op. cit.*

8. Thomas Ribich, *Education and Poverty* (Washington, D.C.: Brookings Institute, 1968).

9. Ralph W. Tyler, "Report from the President's Commission on the Educationally Deprived," *NCEA Bulletin* 66 (August 1969): 32-36.

10. The basic work of the 1930's and 1940's was Ralph Tyler's *Curriculum Rationale* (Chicago: 360 Syllabus, University of Chicago Press).

11. D.T. Campbell and J.C. Stanley, "Experimental Design for Research on Teaching, *Handbook of Research on Teaching*, ed. N.L. Gage (Chicago: Rand McNally and Company, 1963).

12. Abraham Shumsky *The Action Research Way of Learning: An Approach to In-Service Education* (New York: Teachers College, Columbia University, 1958).

13. Iowa Educational Information Center. "Management Information System," Walter J. Foley, Director (Iowa City: University of Iowa, 1969-1970).

14. U.S., Office of Education, Bureau of Elementary and Secondary Education, "Belmont Project: Joint Federal State Task Force on Evaluation" mimeographed (Washington, D.C., 1969).

15. U.S., Office of Education, Bureau of Elementary and Secondary Education, "505 Project," mimeographed (Washington, D.C., 1969).

16. U.S., Office of Education, Bureau of Elementary and Secondary Education, 465 Project Institute, mimeographed (Washington, D.C., 1969).

17. Ralph Tyler, "Assessing the Progress of Education," *Phi Delta Kappan* 47 (September 1965): 13-16.

18. State Board of Education of the Commonwealth of Pennsylvania, *Quality of Education Project, QEPS: A Plan for Evaluating the Quality of Educational Programs in Pennsylvania*, 3 vols. (Harrisburg, Pa.: 1965).

2

Early Work

1966 Evaluation Conference

Work on the Discrepancy Evaluation Model formally began in the summer of 1966 with two Office of Education grants: one from the Bureau of Elementary and Secondary Education and the other from the Bureau of Research. Both grants were aimed at supporting the development and validation of a useful evaluation model for public school practitioners. As was indicated in the proposals for this support, the validation of any model would ultimately have to depend on the frequency of its adoption and the satisfaction of its users.

The first benefits of the grants derived from a conference in the winter of 1966 at which a number of research directors from large cities expressed their evaluation needs and described their current evaluation activity.[1] These directors, including the author, had just been given large sums of money to evaluate federal programs. We weren't at all sure how to spend the money, much less how to make sure we spent it well. We were tempted to use the experimental techniques that we had all learned during our graduate school training. Yet even at the outset it was apparent that those techniques would not apply.

A few university-based researchers like Egon Guba,[2] Dan Stuffle-beam,[3] Michael Scriven,[4] and Edward Suchman[5] had been provoking a professional dialogue about the shortcomings of traditional experimental design for the purpose of evaluating school programs. Our problem at the 1966 conference was to come up with something better. We tried at least to think through some of the necessary assumptions that an effective and practical evaluation model would meet.

It was apparent that there was very little planning and practically no design work going into new programs. We recognized that evaluation people would probably never be adequately involved in critical administrative decisions to launch new programs. The basis for moving ahead with a new program always seemed to be tinged with political considerations as well as scientific ones, and we could not always be party to the kind of information the decision maker would use to move ahead with the new program. Therefore, we assumed that research and evaluation directors would begin the evaluation of a program after many of the important planning decisions had been made. It seems clear that this assumption still applies.

We also realized that even though programs are generally imposed by an administrative hierarchy on a lower echelon of staff, the staff must be involved early and committed to the program. This had not generally been true. We decided it would have to become true if programs were to be successful.

Finally, it was clear that even if new programs had been carefully planned and somewhat effectively designed, they were rarely implemented as designed. The goal here was to ensure that program specifications were followed.

In 1962, when the author was director of research in the Chicago public schools, we had set out to evaluate the effectiveness of four different modern math programs. Many of them were well defined by publishers, which gave us a good "leg up" on the specifications to be adhered to in each classroom. We drew up an experimental design and went to the considerable trouble of drawing a random and carefully stratified sample. Then we decided to monitor the actual programs as practiced, week by week.

Four weeks into the program there were more differences within each program than between the programs. Clearly the programs were not being implemented as intended and research efforts to trace observed differences in students to differences in programs would be frustrated.

We tried to set up the usual experimental controls and statistical procedures recommended for this type of comparative study,[6] but we knew this evaluation wouldn't be productive. Furthermore, as we looked at these programs, we couldn't even find the critical processes in a good many cases. Therefore, we had neither product nor treatment; experimental designs were not applicable. Obviously, the programs were going to have to be controlled and improved "in process" if there was going to be anything worth evaluating, and unless new evaluation procedures could be found, we faced the prospect of a photographer mounting cumbersome and expensive equipment in the barn to photograph horses that had run into the meadow.

At the 1966 conference we recognized the central notion that there can be no evaluation without a standard (that whenever a thing is judged, it is always compared with something else) and that the explicitness of the standard generally determines the precision of the evaluation. It was obvious that evaluation would have to include a very careful description of the program and that this description would be the program standard.

We recognized that evaluation has to do with a discrepancy between performance and a standard, the conveying of information about that discrepancy, and the use of that information in a feedback loop that would be useful to program managers. Such an evaluation would help program managers adjust their program to adhere to the standard. We agreed, however, that responsibility for execution of the program would be lodged with the program staff. If we were going to have staff commitment to controlling the program, trying to make it work as intended, and using discrepancy information to adjust program operations, the standard for evaluation would have to be the staff's definition of a program rather than ours.

The author's early program research and development experience in the Chicago public schools was useful in other ways in shaping the model. It is hoped that a review of those experiences will convey a broad understanding of the conditions and activities that characterize program development work in a public school. Moreover, it will show how one particular teacher-training project broke down preliminary, academic distinctions between development and evaluation methodology and established a unified approach to research.

Chicago Creativity Study

From 1962 to 1968, some of us in the Instructional Research Office of the Chicago public schools were able to study experimentally the conditions that supported creative problem solving in advantaged and disadvantaged children.[7] The six-year Chicago Creativity Project, as it was called, moved through three major stages of development:

(1) The identification and description of students capable of producing innovative, creative responses to interesting problems presented in the classroom.

(2) The development of instructional materials and methods aimed at increasing the interest and creative response capacity of public school students.

(3) The development of teacher-training materials that increased the teachers' ability to produce positive, creative responses from students in their own classrooms.

Eventually, an inservice training program was developed with the following characteristics:

(1) Teachers work in the normal setting of their own school buildings and cooperate as team members to use their own classrooms as teacher-training laboratories.

(2) The school principal, serving as the instructional leader, is a member of this team so that teachers and their principal work together and train together, capitalizing on their individual abilities and insights.

(3) Curriculum modifications in the school program are achieved. The training program generates new objectives in the major subject areas as well as new learning activities.

(4) Teachers participate in the observation and practice of new teaching strategies aimed at developing high order cognitive processes within an emotionally charged setting. In particular, the training program develops methods of student-directed inquiry and inductive teaching.

(5) Teachers working with their students are able to study the effect of new teaching procedures on their students and are helped to adjust their teaching procedures through assessment of pupil progress and other kinds of "feedback" derived from self-evaluation activity.

(6) Teachers in all major subject areas benefit from the program. However, teachers of language arts and social studies benefit particularly because of the dearth of inductive teaching materials in these fields at the present time.

The training program was designed to influence changes in teachers and students by providing activities arranged to move teachers sequentially through nine levels of affective and cognitive behavior. The scheme for classifying levels of teacher behavior underlying the project was provided by *The Taxonomy of Educational Objectives:*

Affective Domain.[8] The classification was used as a point of departure for generating the following levels of teacher behavior:

(1) Attention to student-teacher interaction phenomena.

(2) Awareness of a wide range of creative problem-solving ability
in teacher's own students.

(3) Understanding a functional definition of a problem-solving
situation.

(4) Awareness of critical student behavior in the problem-solving
situation.

(5) Awareness of critical teacher behavior in the problem-solving
situation.

(6) Sensitivity to variations in specific components of inductive
teacher behavior.

(7) Sensitivity to teacher's own behavior in the problem-solving
situation.

(8) Comparison of teacher's own behavior with a demonstration
model.

(9) Commitment to modifying teacher's own behavior in terms of
inductive teaching models.

The attainment of each level of teacher behavior was determined
by the teachers themselves as was the proper execution of all phases
of their work. Teacher participation was voluntary and the incentive
to remain in the training program was derived entirely from the
intrinsic rewards of participation.

In the early stages of the project, teachers were encouraged to
study their students' responses to interesting nonacademic problems.
As a result, teachers were forced to give careful thought to why some
students, surprisingly innovative in nonacademic situations, were so
passive in the classroom. What was it about nonacademic problem
situations that evoked creative responses from normally indifferent
students? Could some of these factors be introduced into the regular
curriculum?

With guidance, most teachers agreed that the nonacademic problem situations had encouraged (1) use of the student's personal
values; (2) use of these values to define a meaningful purpose or
goal; (3) analysis of obstacles leading to goal attainment; (4) redefinition of the problem by the student himself with a minimum of
information from others; (5) search for a relationship between the
elements of the problem; (6) establishment of new and higher relationships through reorganization and insight; (7) application of the
new relationships or principles to new problem situations.[9]

During the latter stages of the project, all the activities converged on the teacher's role as facilitator of the creative problem-solving process. Teachers were asked to identify factors in their own behavior that facilitated the students' creative response to both academic and nonacademic problem-solving situations. Most teachers agreed that at least five major stages of facilitating activity could be identified. During these phases the teacher (1) encourages divergent perceptions of the problem; (2) tries to get consensus on the definition of a problem and its terms; (3) encourages manipulation, understanding, and reorganization of the problem's elements so that students may discover a solution; (4) encourages the derivation of a general concept from the solution of the problem; and (5) discovers ways in which students can demonstrate their ability to apply the concept to solve new but similar problems. Eventually the following characteristics of the facilitating teacher were listed:

(1) Encourages each student to contribute his own thoughts to the group effort.

(2) Supports what a student is trying to do even though his efforts result in failure.

(3) Attempts to incorporate the student's own beliefs, goals, and expectations into class discussion.

(4) Encourages students to draw on their own past experience as a basis for their beliefs.

(5) Encourages individual conviction and defense of own ideas.

(6) Encourages students to listen critically to what other students and teachers are saying and to pass judgment on their statements.

(7) Encourages students to react directly to the teacher's and other students' comments as long as they can be heard by the group.

(8) Encourages students to persevere in a self-directed course of action in the face of uncertainty and lack of group support.

(9) Asks questions for which there are no specific answers already obvious to the class or, for that matter, to the teacher.

Ultimately, teachers constructed ideal models of the behavior they wished to exhibit in their own classrooms. With the aid of their peers they demonstrated their behavior through classroom lessons, received feedback, and learned how close their actual behavior came to their desired standards. The continuing process of self-evaluation became the vehicle for the improvement of the school program and the self-realization of children as well as teachers.

Evaluation was clearly a means of improving individual behavior and program performance, and if specifications or models of programs and individual behavior had not been developed, it would have been impossible to engage in evaluation. For the purposes of the

Chicago Creativity Study, evaluation and development had been interdependent. The study was, by the way, judged a unique success by most of the teachers and principals who participated in it. [10]

The NEA Time to Teach Project

While the Chicago study was still underway, the author had an opportunity to direct another project, based on the same concept of individual and institutional improvement through modification of behavior based on information describing discrepancies between expectations and actual performance. The new project, sponsored by the National Educational Association, was called Time to Teach, and originally focused on finding ways in which teachers could improve their conditions or work.

When this project was conceived, the mood of classroom teachers throughout the country was one of intense frustration. A continual rain of letters to the NEA from individual teachers, plus surveys and reports from local teacher associations, had revealed a common plea for action on a range of practical problems from status considerations, to instructional and school organization arrangements, to salary and conditions or work disagreements. Clearly, the problems were primarily caused by management-employee disagreements over the allocation of available human and fiscal resources. The way to resolve these problems appeared to be to engage both management and labor in a common search for better, more satisfying ways to use resources, and that goal became the purpose of the project.

School administrators and classroom teachers across the country were then, as they are yet, struggling with a new meaning for the familiar word "innovation." It had come to mean change based on new technology, management science, and learning theory, not only in methods, facilities, and services but also in organizational structure and relationships. The problem of the schools was not simply or primarily *what* new things to do for the nation's children. *How* to do these new things posed more pressing and less familiar questions: How could purposeful, constructive change become an everyday reality in every school? How could new practices take root and spread and endure? Innovation ultimately depended on the redeployment of the classroom teacher himself as the ultimate resource. Schools could not change unless classroom teachers understood, accepted, and adopted changes.

Therefore, the Time to Teach project did not try to suggest solutions to each practical problem raised, for although individual problems would be legion, general methods of solution seemed to apply universally. The project geared up to help local groups of teachers use general problem-solving techniques to find local solutions. If the effectiveness of this procedure could be demonstrated in a few schools—if the constructive power of teacher initiative could be verified—it might become a new force for solving a myriad of problems that exist in schools everywhere.

To develop a problem-solving procedure, the project reexamined such issues as the organizational structure of the schools; the nature of group process and organizational change; the meaning of work; and the influence of stress, involvement, and status. An earlier review of research in these areas had strongly supported the concept that teacher participation in problem solving would improve morale and produce viable innovations for the schools.[11]

The research suggested that at the most general level the issue in the Time to Teach project was the same as that affecting workers everywhere: the personal meaningfulness of work. In a study at Texas Instruments Incorporated, the findings of Frederick Hertzberg and his colleagues appeared as relevant to teachers as to the factory employees to whom the findings refer.[12] For example:

What motivates employees to work effectively?—A challenging job that allows a feeling of achievement, responsibility, growth, advancement, enjoyment of work itself, and earned recognition.

What dissatisfies workers?—Mostly peripheral factors, such as work rules, lighting, coffee breaks, titles, seniority rights, wages, fringe benefits, and the like.

When do workers become dissatisfied?—When opportunities for meaningful achievement are eliminated and they become sensitized to their environment and begin to find fault.

A number of observers had established that involvement in decisionmaking has a positive influence on professional growth, job satisfaction and productivity. Yet, in 1962 Wayland suggested, and experience confirmed, that teachers had little real opportunity to make decisions beyond those of bureaucratic functionaries.[13]

The importance of participation in decisionmaking appears to be not primarily the enjoyment of the status that the expression of authority brings, but the opportunity to confront the sources of stress in one's work and to achieve the self-realization that comes from success in coping with stress. In 1964 Bower pointed out that stress is a necessary condition to much learning and achievement and is used by individuals to expand, differentiate, and integrate personality.[14] On this same point, Thelen had noted that when an organism subject to stress must react on its own initiative, the "whole organism responds to assimilate the stress and in so doing it reorganizes some of its internal structure."[15] If these observations were valid, the opportunity to work on stress-producing problems could have a profound integrative influence on the teacher.

One consequence of this exploration of the literature was a growing conviction that the peer group must be one of man's most powerful agents for support and assistance in dealing with stress and that teachers commonly fail to use their colleagues in the school for this purpose. Teachers ordinarily feel powerless to influence situations beyond their classroom doors, and they assume that their colleagues are equally without influence. To alter the situation would require fundamental changes in the role concepts and relationships of teachers and administrators. One promising experimental approach to the reduction of stress was the same problem-solving process we had used in the Chicago Creativity Study. We defined the process somewhat differently this time as follows: (1) a state of confrontation, (2) social awareness and the emergence of conversation, (3) group goal orientation, (4) inquiry or search activity, (5) reality contact with frequent and reliable feedback information, (6) insight, (7) perceptual reorganization, and (8) resultant change in individual behavior.

To engage in this process of intensely focused professional interaction, teachers would have to be motivated by a revitalized personal initiative and by the desire to meet the enormous challenge of improving instruction. They would have to see themselves as the ultimate teaching instrument and final classroom authority and their personal judgment and resourcefulness as the crucial determinant of the effectiveness of the entire educational process, regardless of exotic technological innovations or innumerable administrative directives. They would have to recognize that they and their colleagues were the prime force for solving school problems.

The principal, too, would have to change his view of himself. He would have to recognize his role as a facilitator of communication and experimentation in a dynamic system of persons, ideas, and equipment. He would have to be a source of information and support to a group exploring difficult problems, so demonstrating his empathy with teachers and his own devotion to a search for solutions that teachers would be encouraged to commit themselves to the problem solving process.

The school superintendent's view of his role would also be at issue. While he would not dismiss his responsibility as guardian of the community's total educational effort, he would have to put new faith in each school staff's ability to originate and maintain creative educational programs. The work of the principal and teachers would depend on a superintendent's recognition that the heart of each school program is the earnest pursuit of professional goals by a competent staff comprised of teachers who can free the uniquely creative capacities of children and a principal who can free the uniquely creative capacities of teachers.

The success of a venture in group problem solving would therefore depend on the combined energy of teachers, explicit administrative support for teacher-initiated change, and open communication in the schools.

Both teachers and administrators were unaccustomed to the kind of interpersonal relations and problem solving prescribed. Experience and training provided them with little reason for faith in the prescription. To mobilize a school—to undertake group effort in behalf of reduced stress and increased efficiency—would therefore require a program that offered direction, support, and a resonable promise of success. Therefore, the Time to Teach project, as ultimately designed had the following characteristics:

(1) Responsiveness to the needs of teachers as expressed by teachers.

(2) Applicability to a wide range of school conditions.

(3) Provision for teachers and administrators to share responsibility for decisions affecting instruction and working conditions.

(4) Involvement of all teachers in a school in the initiation and support of one or more school improvement programs. Group problem solving was the vehicle for problem identification, program development, and program evaluation in each school.

(5) Effectiveness in fostering teacher-initiated innovation. Data was gathered from experimental action programs in order to (a) describe the inevitable complexities and contingencies to be taken into account in unstructured, staff-determined efforts and (b) determine the staff's assessment of this problem-solving activity's ultimate effect on original problems.

In operation, the project initiated staff decisionmaking through a series of structured group meetings aimed primarily at analyzing problems, agreeing on intervention strategies, and considering the consequences of staff activity. It provided specific methods for group self-evaluation and problem-solving activity. These included an initial teacher report system that provided a composite faculty view of the school. This view was periodically compared with new views at various times during the life of the project in any one school. Other reports called for clear statements from teachers about what they expected to see changed in their situation and how they expected to produce these changes. What teachers expected and what they reported they actually did were systematically compared and fed back to them during the project.

Throughout the project, teachers continued to evaluate their progress and indicate future plans. The project staff analyzed staff progress reports and maintained a feedback loop to teachers and administrators on faculty progress as well as on faculty opinion about original intentions and changes in those intentions.

A number of factors emerged as important signals of project success:

(1) Staff freedom to establish its own goals and standards.

(2) Bona fide, voluntary participation of the school staff.

(3) Open communication between principal and teachers about value questions.

(4) Visible support by the chief executive in the system (usually the school superintendent) for the work of the group, even when that work did not appear productive to, or compatible with, the values of the chief executive.

(5) Staff identification of real and noxious problems rather than pseudoacademic conundrums.

Work in Pittsburgh

Work done early in 1965 in the Pittsburgh public schools also contributed to the fund of experience from which the Discrepancy Evaluation Model was constructed. One of the author's first assignments as research director in the Pittsburgh public schools was to evaluate the effect of over five years of an experimental team teaching program. Funding for this experiment—mostly from a private foundation—had been lavish, and management had been careful to control the development of the program in the sheltered environment of a few schools before trying it elsewhere in the city.

The purpose of the evaluation was simply to determine whether the program had fulfilled its mission. An inspection of the planning and design documents used in the formative years of the program revealed that the major initial thrust of the effort had been to develop in every child, regardless of his background, the intellectual competencies needed in today's world. At a later point in its history, the stated aims of the program were to improve instruction through cooperative teacher planning; better use of teachers, space, learning materials, and equipment; flexible scheduling; varying sizes of classes; recruitment of young beginning teachers for poverty schools; and field trips and more materials.

To effect this evaluation, an attempt was made (1) to secure a description of the operating program—its requirements, activities, and outcomes—so that it might be compared with initial and revised staff expectations; and (2) to determine the program's effect on student achievement.

In this later evaluation, measures of student performance were based on a large sample of over 2,000 students exposed to team teaching for at least four years as compared with a smaller sample of students in the same schools exposed to less than one year of team teaching. Because Pittsburgh had been using the same standardized achievement battery for almost eight years, it was possible to compare the growth rates of the experimental and control groups on a year-by-year basis. Rigorous statistical controls were applied to an analysis of longitudinal data for these students. The conclusion drawn from this phase of the evaluation was that students in the team teaching program showed no more academic progress and achieved no higher scores (after appropriate statistical adjustment) than did students who had not been in the experiment.

The other phase of the evaluation—a comparison of actual program activities with planned or anticipated program activity—went a long way toward explaining why student performance was so disappointing. In 39 schools, 131 teaching teams were found to be practicing 131 different varieties of team teaching. In fact, an adequate description of the actual team teaching program could not be found in the entire school system. [16]

Team teaching was quietly phased out in favor of a better-defined program called "Nongraded Instruction." At the time of this writing, the nongraded program is itself being replaced by a still better program: The Early Childhood Education Program (described briefly in Chapter 9), which is eventually supposed to dominate the first five years of curriculum in the Pittsburgh school system. The Early Childhood Education Program, based on the most advanced theoretical work in the country today, as well as the painful but practical experiences of the Pittsburgh public school staff itself, has already produced some clear evidence of student academic success. Most notable are increases in the intelligence test scores of those students enrolled in Pittsburgh's preprimary program. These increases have been sustained at the end of a second year of testing, and the program promises comparable academic gains in the future.

Essential Principles for a New Approach

By the time we held our 1966 conference with big city program evaluators, those of us from Pittsburgh were aware of a number of operating principles derived from earlier program development and evaluation experience. The conference gave us an opportunity to test these assumptions and learn more about the conditions and purposes of a general evaluation model.

Because some characteristics of big cities do not apply to towns and rural areas, we ran the risk of overgeneralization from this conference. On the other hand, we felt that if we could design a model capable of dealing with the complexity and diversity of big city programs and populations, our model would probably be equal to any demands placed on it. Yet, some of the limiting characteristics of big cities must be made explicit. Most of these cities operate with a considerable degree of independence from state and federal authority. Therefore, their freedom to innovate probably exceeds that of smaller districts. Also, the big cities serve a relatively large number of underprivileged students—a matter of particular concern to the Office of Education. Most possess research staffs presumably capable of supporting a serious interpretation of the evaluation clause of ESEA. Also, it is probably more difficult and costly to secure widespread teacher and other school staff participation in program development and evaluation activity in large cities, because of size and organizational complexity.

The result of our 1966 conference was a sharing of evaluation assumptions and operational procedures. All parties to the conference were surprised at their agreement on basic evaluation purposes, although there was great variety in evaluation methods. A position paper was proposed to summarize areas of agreement and document samples of evaluation work in a number of cities.[17] Generally, conference participants argued for

(1) A recognition that there are multiple, intermediate objectives that lead to some ultimate goal and that the complex measurement of these intervening objectives is essential, continuing evaluation work.

(2) The need for early, comprehensive description of the program to be evaluated and the recognition that adequate instruments generally do not exist for this purpose.

(3) The importance of timely, relevant, and readable evaluation

reports that are used by superintendents and others in authority as a basis for decisions affecting programs.

(4) An awareness of the importance of the administrative climate in which an evaluation is made, and the need for an administrative philosophy that supports honest inquiry and is willing to pay for it.

(5) The need for more personnel trained in the conduct of public school research, development, and evaluation.

(6) The need for modern research facilities including high speed scanning equipment and computers for both information retrieval and data analysis.

Finally, conference participants expressed their belief that unless an evaluation was made of the entire public school program, not just that part funded by the federal government, it would be impossible adequately to assess the effects of individual programs and seriously to reform general educational practice.

These recommendations are reflected in the model that was eventually built, as are the insights obtained from the Chicago Creativity Study, the Time to Teach project, and the early team teaching evaluation in Pittsburgh.

From the Chicago study we rediscovered that an organism's standards shape its behavior. When the organism continuously monitors the discrepancy between its performance and its standards, it is in a position to modify its own behavior. In order to get an organism (a person or organization) to modify its behavior, one must change its standards. A rational organism will change its standards if they do not serve a value or are counterproductive to a higher value. An autonomous organism must want to change its standards before it will in fact change its behavior.

Standards can be changed through the analysis and synthesis of phenomena, insight, and the reorganization of a perceptual field, that is, through the problem-solving research process. It is possible to get a person or group to change standards by showing discrepancies where an analysis of performance shows it to be at variance with not only the standard but also the assumptions and values that gave rise to the standard.

In the Chicago study, teacher attention was focused on student performance that exceeded or differed from teacher expectation. As a result, teachers changed their expectations for students. Later in the study, teachers were able to formulate new standards for their own behavior when they recognized the discrepancy between their own performance and an idealized view of the teacher behavior necessary to facilitate creative behavior of students. Hence, in the

Chicago study, we were able to use the power of discrepancy information to shape new behavior and to change the values underlying the standards that regulate behavior.

From the Time to Teach project we learned that teachers display considerable creative capacity if they are encouraged to use their own initiative to deal forcefully with real and frustrating problems. Because group problem-solving was encouraged, new program objectives were established and teachers were able to modify their solution strategies on the basis of self-evaluation of their efforts. As a result, enormous reservoirs of human energy were released for constructive action within the local school.

As in the Chicago project, goal setting, or the definition of one's own standards, was an essential part of the project. In both projects, the ultimate purpose of project activity was to encourage self-directed reform, based on the analysis of discrepancy information feedback.

From our experience in these early projects, it was clear that self-evaluation was a powerful device, perhaps the essential mechanism in changing individual and group behavior. The critical characteristics of this self-evaluation for individual or group change were:

(1) Freedom to define and redefine goals in accordance with existing values.

(2) Goal orientation as the basis for establishing a hypothetical system capable of converting limited resources into desired outcomes.

(3) Explication of this desired system in a set of standards or blueprints that can be used to give shape to future performance.

(4) Collection of descriptive information about actual performance that may be compared with standard.

(5) Modification of performance or standard, depending on (a) an analysis of the compatibility of the value assumptions underlying the standard with the reality in which performance occurs, and (b) the strength of the values underlying the standard.

Hence, evaluation is seen as a decisionmaking process that generates standards, modifies behavior, and, in short, solves problems that are subject to continuous redefinition. In this sense evaluation, problem solving, decisionmaking, and research are inextricably bound up in the process that man has long attempted to unravel and codify under the title "learning theory."

We came to realize that evaluation activity varies with the development of the program being evaluated and that every program must pass through logical stages of development before it can achieve its ultimate success. Roughly, these stages are design, installation, process refinement, and production.

We also found that program planning and design work are functions as much of consensus building as of analysis. The small group process work that Matt Miles[18] and Ron Lippitt[19] have been talking about for a long time is essential for organizational change, and was indeed essential to our work. We had to start working with people in a very sensitive way if they were going to honestly describe their programs and their goals. We had to be responsive to their definitions, not ours, if our feedback of the discrepancies between their program and their standards or definitions was to be meaningful to them. Therefore, a good deal of our time and technique would be concerned with consensus-building activity.

We left the 1966 conference confident that the needed model could be built. Since then we have found that:

(1) It is possible to evaluate many complex programs simultaneously with the model.

(2) It is possible to train staff to do this work if a team approach for evaluation is used. It is possible but unwarranted to expect one person to be an evaluator of an educational program.

(3) Decision makers want and will act on pertinent evaluative information if they understand its value in advance.

(4) It is not only possible, but essential that program evaluation concern itself with the products of a program (both intermediate and ultimate), the processes or activities leading to the products, and the resources and other conditions needed to launch and sustain the program.

(5) To sustain local public school program evaluation, it is necessary to establish a close working relationship between the area university and the public school system.

We could not have done our work in the Pittsburgh public schools without the help of at least two area universities. What is the nature of that relationship? First of all, we need their specialized talents, for example, for designing necessary instruments or doing some type of multivariate analysis. Perhaps more importantly, we need them for what we call the R & D (research and development) aspect of a new program. We always reach a point where program staff identifies a problem whose assumptions are unknown. They have tried everything and have finally realized that their theory is inadequate. At that point, they need the research assistance that only a university can and should provide. The University does not take on program staff responsibility for designing and implementing programs; it responds with those particulars of service or conceptualization that the staff members need to remain effective problem solvers. Thus, when the program staff asks for help, they must be directed to a university consultant who is knowledgeable and able to supply additional resources needed from the university and to help conduct the developmental work based on research that always seems to be required before public school programs are adequately designed.

The next few chapters will go into considerable detail about the Discrepancy Evaluation Model, which was devised against a background of public school experience. Remember that although it has been said that evaluation has to do with a discrepancy between performance and standard, we can never be sure the standard is right. It is always quite arbitrary. This is a value problem that the author will explore again and again in this book. Beneath every standard, no matter how carefully explicated, lies an ultimate criterion akin to Aristotle's First Cause. Few, if any, of us know ourselves or the world well enough to identify absolute values on which to build immutable standards. Therefore, evaluation becomes involved not only in the application of standards but also in their creation and testing. In this lies both the promise and the dilemma of improvement and assessment through evaluation.

Footnotes

1. Pittsburgh Public Schools, *Big City Title I Evaluation Conference: 1967 Report.*
2. Director, National Institute for the Study of Educational Change, Bloomington, Indiana.
3. Director, Evaluation Center, Ohio State University, Columbus, Ohio.
4. School of Education, University of California, Berkeley.
5. (Deceased.) Department of Sociology, University of Pittsburgh, Pittsburgh, Pennsylvania.
6. D. T. Campbell, and J. C. Stanley, "Experimental Design for Research in Teaching," in *Handbook of Research on Teaching,* ed. N. L. Gage (Chicago: Rand McNally and Company, 1963).
7. Malcolm Provus, *Teaching for Relevance* (Northbrook, Ill.: Whitehall Company, 1970).
8. David R. Krathwohl, Benjamin S. Bloom, and Bertram B. Masia, *The Taxonomy of Educational Objectives: Affective Domain* (New York: David McKay Company, 1964).
9. For similar problem-solving paradigms, see David H. Russell's *Children's Thinking* (Boston: Ginn and Company, 1956); Edgar W. Vinache's *The Psychology of Thinking* (New York: McGraw Hill, 1952); and Max Wertheimer's *Productive Thinking* (New York: Harper and Row, 1959).
10. Provus, op. cit.

11. Malcolm Provus, "Collective Action by Teachers," in *Encyclopedia of Educational Research,* ed. Robert L. Ebel (London: Collier-Macmillan Company, 1969).

12. See the articles reprinted in *Leadership in Action,* ed. Gordon C. Lippitt (Washington, D.C.: Washington National Training Laboratories, National Education Association, 1961).

13. Sloan R. Wayland, "The Teacher as Decision-Maker," *Curriculum Crossroads: A Report of a Curriculum Conference,* ed. Harry Passow (New York: Harcourt Brace and World, 1964).

14. Eli M. Bower, "The Modification, Mediation and Utilization of Stress During the School Years," *American Journal of Orthopsychiatry* 34 (July 1964): 116-174.

15. Herbert Arnold Thelen, *Education and the Human Quest* (New York: Harper and Row, 1960).

16. Esther Kresh, "Pittsburgh Team Teaching Program, 1967 Report," mimeographed (Board of Education, Pittsburgh Public Schools).

17. Pittsburgh Public Schools, op. cit.

18. Matthew Miles, *Change Processes in the Public Schools* (Eugene: University of Oregon, 1965); idem, *Innovation in Education* (New York: Teachers College, Columbia University, 1964); idem, *Learning to Work in Groups* (New York: Teachers College, Columbia University, 1959).

19. Ronald Lippitt, Jeanne Watson, and Bruce Westley, *The Dynamics of Planned Change* (New York: Harcourt Brace and World, 1958).

3

Presentation of the Model

Introduction

The Discrepancy Evaluation Model was presented to the professional community of educational researchers and evaluators at the annual meeting of the American Education Research Association (AERA) in Los Angeles, California, in 1969. For almost three years, the staff of the research office of the Pittsburgh public schools had been developing the model as a function of its responsibility for evaluating educational programs in the school system.

At the AERA meeting, it was possible to bring together most of the knowledgeable and distinguished practitioners and theoreticians in the field of evaluation. A panel of "experts" (Ralph Tyler, Egon Guba, Daniel Stufflebeam and Walter Foley) and "reactors" (John Goodlad, Richard Dershimer, William Gephart, and Donald Carroll) was convened to discuss the model and to stimulate reaction from an equally distinguished audience including directors of regional laboratories, R & D centers, public school research offices, state department research offices, and university bureaus of educational research and other interested practitioners.

The meeting was divided into three major parts: (1) presentation of the Discrepancy Evaluation Model by the Pittsburgh staff, (2) reaction to the model by the eight panelists, and (3) open discussion

Chapters 3, 5, and 6 are based on a verbatim transcript, extant notes, and initial drafts of papers given at the AERA postsession meeting. To ensure continuity and consistency, the editor has deleted some material and made clarifying changes in the author's original manuscript. Despite every attempt to retain the speakers' words and meaning, some distortion may have occured—Ed.

45

from the floor. These parts are treated as chapters 3, 4, and 5 in this book.

An Overview:[1]

The Discrepancy Evaluation Model posits five stages of evaluation:
(1) Design
(2) Installation
(3) Process
(4) Product
(5) Cost

At each of these stages a comparison is made between reality and some standard or standards. The comparison often shows differences between standard and reality; this difference is called discrepancy. On the basis of the comparisons made at each stage, discrepancy information is provided to the program staff, giving them a rational basis on which to make adjustments in their program.

Before a comparison can be made, a standard must be set. The standard for Stages 2, 3, and 4 is the design of the program established in Stage 1. The standard against which the reality of the design is compared in Stage 1 is a set of design criteria. The procedure used in Stage 1 to obtain the reality of the design is the program design meeting. Before the design meeting, the evaluator of the program prepares a set of questions designed to elicit specific information about the program. All levels of the program staff attend the meeting, and the large group is broken up into small groups to facilitate discussion of the questions devised by the evaluator. A trained discussion leader from the evaluation unit presents the questions to each discussion group and then reports the answers from his group to the evaluator. Finally, the evaluator synthesizes the information from all discussion groups into the program design which then becomes the basis for further evaluation of the program.

Having derived the program design, we are ready to make the Stage 1 comparison. At this stage the reality—the program design—is assessed according to the criteria of structural and theoretical soundness using the design criteria and the expert opinion of a consultant. The use of these standards will be discussed later in detail. At this point, it suffices to say, that the design is assessed on these two criteria and that discrepancy information is provided to the program staff.

Once the design has been assessed, it can be used as a standard. At Stage 2, we compare the program operation (reality) with the input and process sections of the program design (standard). The purpose of this comparison is to determine the extent to which the program has been installed.

To understand more fully the effect of work in the first two stages of evaluation, let us take an example. Suppose that we want to construct a water pump system. To accomplish this task, we need a very detailed design or blueprint or plan. As is shown in Figure 1, we would want to know specific things, such as the water level, the location of the pump, and all the specifications for the pump. Once we have the design, we can build the water pump system depicted in Figure 2. When we compare operation to design, we note certain discrepancies. These discrepancies may be due to deficiencies in the installation of the system, *e.g.,* the fan belt specified in the design is missing in the operation, or to deficiencies in design, *e.g.,* the water level was specified much higher than it really was. Because of this error of design, the pipe does not extend down far enough to reach the water.

Knowing these things, we would want to make changes of two types. First, we want to alter the design to specify the water level correctly. Second, after adjusting the pipe to extend to the water level in operation, we would want to make sure that all other elements of the design, *e.g.,* the fan belt, were in operation. It is possible in the same way to adjust both the design and the operation of an education program. On the basis of the discrepancy information provided to the program staff, we expect them to continue making adjustments until design and operation are in accord. Once this has been done, we have a stable educational program, and evaluation is ready to move to Stage 3.

At Stage 3, we investigate the relationship between process and interim products. The standard is the hypothesized relationship specified in the program design, and the reality is the degree to which interim products have been achieved. Stage 3 work will be discussed in greater detail later. Once we have established that the Stage 3 relationships specified do exist, we can move to the Stage 4 comparison.

At Stage 4, we compare the degree to which terminal products have been achieved (reality) with the specification of these products in the program design (standard). Thus, we see that both Stages 3 and 4 are concerned with measuring products: at Stage 3, interim goals and at Stage 4, terminal goals.

At Stage 5 we take the cost of the program being evaluated (reality) and compare it with the cost of other programs having the same product or goal (standard). On the basis of this comparison, it

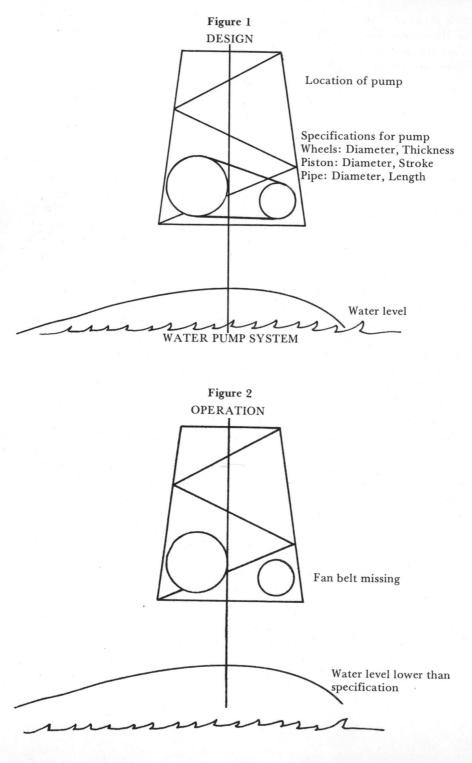

Figure 1
DESIGN

Location of pump

Specifications for pump
Wheels: Diameter, Thickness
Piston: Diameter, Stroke
Pipe: Diameter, Length

Water level

WATER PUMP SYSTEM

Figure 2
OPERATION

Fan belt missing

Water level lower than
specification

is possible to make a policy decision to continue or discontinue the program. Although we do not at the present time have the information to make these comparisons across programs, cost-benefit analysis is the ultimate rational step in the process of program development and assessment by the Discrepancy Evaluation Model. In anticipation of its eventual use, therefore, cost-benefit analysis is posited as Stage 5.

We have now been through the five stages of evaluation and have identified the standard and reality at each stage. From what has been said so far, it might appear that the stages are relatively discrete and are negotiated in sequence. This is not the case. There is a great deal of dynamic interplay and movement between the stages. For example, the comparison between design and standard at Stage 1 may point out so many discrepancies that a great deal of time will be spent working out a sound design. At Stage 2 when program operation is compared to design, there may be so many discrepancies that it takes a number of comparisons, followed by adjustments and new comparisons, to ensure that program operation is reasonably similar to program design. If it is discovered at Stage 3 that a defined set of processes is not producing the specified interim goal, evaluation must move back to the design stage to define a new set of processes. These processes must be installed and checked for installation, and the interim goal in question must be measured again. Thus we see that the first three stages are interactive. Evaluation work will proceed, crossing back and forth between these stages, until all the standards have been met. At Stage 4, although we will continue to monitor program installation to assure that it is at the specified level, the program is fixed, and the terminal product is measured by employing an experimental or quasi-experimental design. Finally, at Stage 5, the results of Stage 4 work will be used to perform the cost-benefit analysis.

In summary, the Discrepancy Evaluation Model uses the first three stages of evaluation for program development and stabilization and the fourth and fifth stages for program assessment.

Stages 1 and 2[2]

It is important to emphasize that the activities discussed here, although presented serially, actually occur concurrently and that the object of evaluation under the model is to compare preformance with a standard and provide feedback on discrepancies. This feedback permits decision makers to change either behavior or the standard and thus equalize the two.

As has been pointed out, the first thing needed in an evaluation is a program design. The design tells us what we're evaluating, what we can expect to find out in the field. Our first task is to gather information for the design.

The traditional way of determining the program's design was to get a copy of the funding proposal. Anyone who has done educational evaluations knows this is not a good practice. A funding proposal has little to do with what's going on in the field. It is designed to get money, not to provide a program design. So we must look elsewhere.

In Pittsburgh we've chosen as the source of program design the people who are actually doing the field work: the teachers, librarians, and so forth. In essence, we ask them "What are you trying to do here?" and when they tell us, we write it down. Specifically, in Pittsburgh we have assembled the various teachers and managers in one spot. (We've tried heterogeneous and homogeneous grouping. We've assembled the whole group and samples of the group.) Then we ask them a series of very specific questions. We might ask, in a remedial reading program, "Do you wish to change reading achievement or do you wish to make a diagnosis of reading difficulties?" The answers to these questions make up the program design.

For example, in evaluating an instrumental music program questions asked of program staff included:

(1) What characteristics does the student have on entering the program that you wish to change before he leaves the program? How do you want them to change?

For example, what kinds of musical ability do you want to develop? What attitudes do you want the child to have toward himself, toward music, toward school? What changes, if any, in his personal characteristics do you want to foster?

(2) What characteristics must the student have in order to enter the program? Are there specific musical abilities or personal characteristics he must have? Do his academic grades have to be kept at a certain level?

(3) What new skills does the teacher develop as a result of this program? What old skills does he improve?

(4) What specific materials are required by the program? (By this we mean such things as method books, music stands, etc., down to extra E strings and repair request forms.) Who chooses the materials to be used?

(5) What facilities are necessary to the program? For example, is there a minimum size for the room in which the lessons are taught? Does it require minimum acoustical properties?

The first question refers to student variables. The third question refers to staff variables. The second, fourth, and fifth questions refer to preconditions for program operation.[3]

The first time around, the design is obviously going to be vague and ambiguous. The teachers, project managers, and other staff employ the usual educational cliches. By the second or third time around, however, more precision is attained, and a clear design gradually emerges.

If the first function of assembling the program staff is gathering information for the preparation of a program design, the second function is consensus building. In 1967, Esther Kresh evaluated the team teaching program in Pittsburgh and reported that there were 131 different programs—a different program for each team.[4] This is what we want to avoid. We want each program in the field to correspond to our program design. Thus the teachers and project managers and other staff must function collectively. All the teachers and managers must internalize the program's concepts as defined in the meetings. For this to happen we must get consensus.

For our purposes, consensus is the establishment of a working agreement, and it is defined as a minimization of variance in rank-ordered objectives. If we have three items (representing three objectives) listed as rows, and three possible ranks listed as columns, we have a square matrix with the rater response entered in the cells as x's and o's for two hypothetical raters.

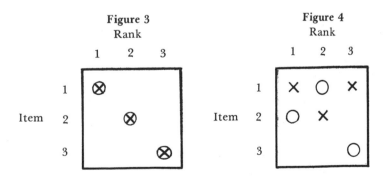

In Figure 3 variance in ranking is eliminated. This is consensus. A working agreement has been achieved. Figure 4 shows dissensus.

These arrays have proved convenient ways of discovering the values to which staff subscribe. Of course, these are all behavioral definitions: in this context consensus does not mean a transcendental unity. As the staff interact together at the meetings, however, problems and conflicts can be worked out and our definition of consensus can be achieved. Then the field operations will correspond to the one and only program design.

When, by gathering information and achieving consensus, we have the program design, the question immediately arises: Is this a good design? As has been pointed out, evaluation is comparison of reality with design. Thus we want to improve the program design. The answer to the question "Is this a good design?" is sought at what we call panel meetings of program staff, outside expert opinion, and evaluation staff. A panel is a mechanism for bringing criticism to bear on the program design.

The program design may be theoretically sound and structurally unsound or vice versa. For instance, a theoretically sound remedial reading program might employ a certain learning program, such as the Sullivan materials, and still be structurally unsound because the dimension of staff qualifications is passed over by the staff as unimportant.[5] Conversely, the program may have a deficient theory but if all its major dimensions are specified, we could say the design of the program is structurally (but not theoretically) sound. Therefore, we must examine two aspects of the program design: the implicit theory and the structure.

To examine the theory, we bring in a specialist in the substantive area of the program. This is an expert who will examine the design and say, for example: "You haven't allotted enough time for this rote-learning activity. You need at least ten minute's practice a day for mastery." These problems are recorded as problems of the design theory.

Unlike the method for examining the theory, in which an outside expert is asked for criticism, to analyze the design structurally, we must compare it with a set of generalized criteria. In general a program consists of *inputs* that go through some *process* and give us *outputs*.

The three elements characterizing *inputs* are (1) variables, (2) preconditions, and (3) criteria. Variables might consist of student performance measures, staff measures, etc. Indeed, anything that is to change as a result of the program is a variable. Preconditions further describe students, staff, and other necessities or overhead items, and do not vary throughout the program. Criteria specify ranges or values of the preconditions and variables. Specifically, criteria on student measures and conditions define the selection of students for a program.

For example, a remedial reading program might specify that the students must have an I.Q. of above 85 to benefit from the remediation. Here the precondition is sufficient student intelligence, and the criterion is that the student's I.Q. (as measured by a standardized test) must be above 85. Or a program might specify that the student be in the third grade to participate. Here the precondition is grade in school, and the criterion specifies third grade.

A program variable could be reading achievement. A remedial reading program, for example, might specify performance at least one year below grade level. Reading achievement is the variable; more than one grade level deficient is the criterion for the variable. Staff measures can be variables when a training program exists within a larger program.

Under *process*[6] there are two characteristic elements:

(1) Variables, including student activities (*e.g.,* the student will read the Sullivan materials) and staff activities (*e.g.,* the teacher will provide positive reinforcement for students reading the Sullivan materials).

(2) Criteria, which might specify, for example, that each student is to spend 80 percent of his time reading Sullivan materials or that the teacher is to spend 90 percent of his time positively reinforcing the child using the Sullivan materials. The process criteria must be sufficient to ensure transformation of the input variables from their initial value into the terminal or exit value of the output variables.

Output involves the same three elements as input: variables, preconditions, and criteria. The variables and preconditions remain the same, but the variables are defined by a new set of criteria to specify the goals of the program. For instance, in a remedial reading program a goal could be specified by the criterion that reading achievement (specified as one year below grade level at the beginning of the program) be at grade level. It is, of course, possible that reading achievement will not be brought to grade level. The student's reading may stay at the same one year deficient level all the way through the program. At the end of the year he violates the precondition criterion of being in the third grade (which, unlike the variable criteria, does not change), and he's eliminated from the program. Obviously, success has not been achieved in this case.

To summarize this discussion of design criteria, let us examine the kinds of problems we can uncover by systematic comparison of the design with the generalized design criteria. In terms of the design criteria we might look at the program and ascertain that a preliminary program requires teachers' aides. Under input preconditions the criteria for staff qualifications must explain what it means to be a teacher's aide. Under process variables, you must be able to determine the activities of a teacher's aide. If the program design doesn't include these items there is a deficiency in the program with regard to the definition of the teacher's aide. In the absence of such information, it is impossible to know in what respects the program has not been implemented, and thus it is impossible to use product data findings for program change and improvement.

Therefore, examining design criteria enables us not only to explicate the structure of the program design, but also to facilitate valid measurement of process and product. This approach is similar to the functional analysis of program planning and budgeting, in which each function is broken down into other smaller units, always under the criterion of sufficiency to realize the larger functions. For example, with regard to staff activity under process, if the staff activity specifies that teachers positively reinforce students' reading, this function could be analyzed at the level of a whole program. In this manner we can pull subprograms from the process area of the design, make them into complete programs, and break them down in turn into further subprograms for analysis.

When the design's implicit theory is criticized and its structure is compatible with the design criteria, all the data, including the original design, the criticisms, and the new design structure, is given back to the program manager as a Stage 1 report. This report provides the basis for another staff meeting to redefine the program.

While this Stage 1 activity is going on, the evaluator is looking around in the field to see what is actually going on there. Part of this is compatibility testing to pinpoint conflicts in facilities, use of media, and so forth. Of particular importance are conflicts of space and human resources. The other part of the fieldwork is Stage 2, which is the congruence testing part of evaluation.

Congruence testing is the comparison of an observed aspect of the program in the field, with the standard provided for that aspect by the program design. The evaluator might find, for example, that the teacher is individualizing instruction about 10 percent of her time while the program design stipulates that she should be spending about 60 percent of her time in individual interaction. In this aspect the program is clearly off target.

The evaluator proceeds item by item through the program design considering each variable for a congruence test. His decision about which variables to test is based on (a) researchability, and (b) the possibility of finding significant discrepancies. These criteria are

introduced because of the limited resources available to the evaluator. A tradeoff is effected between those aspects of the program
easiest to look at and those aspects most important or most likely to
be amiss.

In Stage 2, then, we are trying to find problems in the program. As
anyone who has undertaken educational research knows, it does no
good to find insignificant differences in treatment if a lack of effects
cannot be attributed to some specific failure in the program. The
only certain result of an aggregate statement of "no effects" is a
cutback in program resources. On the other hand, a statement that
the lack of effects was caused by malfunction of a specific component is the basis for program change and improvement.

When the evaluator has completed his study of discrepancies
between program operation and design, he reports his findings to the
program manager. The decision maker can either make changes in the
program operation or take the discrepancy information back to a
staff meeting for redefinition of the program design. By this means,
we see how a rationally managed program proceeds to equalize
operation and design. In Stage 1 the program design is refined, and in
Stage 2 congruence between the standard and operation is increased.
There is a constant interplay between the two stages.

Stages 3 and 4[7]

In Stage 3 we examine the relationship between processes and
interim products. In order to explain the work at Stage 3, some
elements of Stages 1 and 2 must be reiterated. The first step of Stage
1 is to specify the major goals or products of the program. For any
given program only a limited number of major goals will be specified.
An analysis is then made of these major goals to identify their
components or criteria. The technique of components or task analysis is appropriate here and an example of this technique appears in
Figure 5, which shows an analysis of a program with one major goal
(the same analysis would be applied to any number of goals).

Assume, for example, that the goal of the program is to produce a
higher rate of reading achievement growth in students who are below
grade level. In order to achieve this goal, we ask what activities or
conditions will produce this goal. For this program, two sets of
conditions are identified, a set of individualization techniques and a
set of acquired skills on the part of the students. These two sets are
designated Interim Product Sets 1 and 2. The arrow between them
indicates that the first set of conditions must be established before

Figure 5: Diagram of Components Analysis of Program with One Major Goal

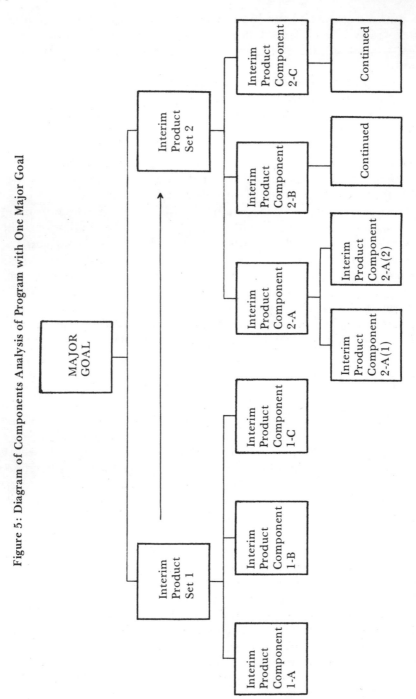

the second set can manifest itself. Now it is necessary to specify the components of each set of conditions. For this example the following three teacher behaviors are identified as the components of the set of individualization techniques: (1) The teacher will be able to write meaningful individual prescriptions based on pupil needs; (2) the teacher will be able to make a diagnosis of test results in order to assess individual needs; and (3) the teacher will be able to use appropriate tutorial techniques with individuals or small groups. These behaviors are designated on the diagram as Interim Product Components 1-A, 1-B and 1-C. The same procedure is used for the area of student behaviors. Here we have identified three sub-sets of skills: (1) structural analysis, (2) phonetic analysis, and (3) comprehension. These are represented in the diagram as Interim Product Components 2-A, 2-B, and 2-C. In turn, then, each of the sub-sets of skills can be analyzed for their components. For example, under structural analysis the behaviors might be specified as: (1) Given a contraction, the student will be able to identify the two words that form it; and (2) given a list of singular words the students will be able to form the appropriate plurals. On the diagram these are Interim Product Components 1-A (1) and 2-A (2).

The components of each sub-set of skills continue to be specified until all the components have been identified. It can be seen from the diagram that the components in any row taken together produce the components of the row above until finally the two interim products sets produce the major goal. The next step, still at Stage 1, is to specify for each component or box on the diagram the procedure or process which will produce that component. For the example in Figure 5 we would specify two sets of processes—one for each interim product set—Process Set 1 and Process Set 2. Together, the two process sets produce the systems design or process criteria for the program.

In Stage 3 we are concerned with assessing the extent to which the process sets and components are producing the interim product sets and components. Obviously it would not be possible to assess the extent to which a process component produces an interim product component unless we have first ascertained that the process components do exist at the operational level specified in the design. Therefore, implementation of Stage 3 depends on meeting the test for congruence that ends Stage 2. Even at Stage 3, however, we do not take for granted that the process components have remained at the operational level; the continuous monitoring of the process components begun in Stage 2 continues through Stage 3.

In Stage 3 the first measures of product are taken. (It must be emphasized that these measures are measures of the interim product components, not measures of the major goal or product.) If we find that a particular interim product component has been produced by its specified process component, the process component has met the final test for acceptance into the system and is no longer subject to revision. However, if the process component has not produced the interim product component, then it returns to Stage 1. In a remedial reading program the process component might be a set of lessons designed to teach contractions. If it is returned to Stage 1, the result could be either revision of the lessons or addition of some lessons. The revised process component would then go through Stage 2 and finally end back at Stage 3 once again. As each process component produces its interim product component, it is accepted into the final system. Finally, all process components are accepted, the entire system is complete and no longer subject to revision, and Stage 3 ends.

At Stage 4 we investigate whether the combination of the interim product sets produce the major product or goal. Stage 4 is not yet fully developed in our model. However, it will resemble traditional evaluations using appropriate experimental or quasi-experimental designs.

Stage 5

Stage 5 is the cost-benefit analysis stage. In 2½ years, however, we have had no opportunity to take any of our programs to a stage where cost-benefit analysis would be appropriate. We believe that it will be many more years before anybody can submit educational programs to the type of rigorous analysis outlined above as a precondition to meaningful cost-benefit analysis.

There are some practical steps that can be taken now in the area of cost analysis. One of the things that program planning and budgeting specialists talk most about is forcing decision makers to define their programs more clearly by submitting them to functional cost accounting. Through the procedures described in this chapter, we, too, force decision makers to define their programs more clearly. In some programs it may be possible to look at cost increments relative to output increments. We are beginning to do that now. However, the comparison of programs with similar goals and varying costs is not going to produce anything but distortion until we have much greater knowledge of program conditions than is now generally available in public school settings.

Footnotes

1. Presented by Mrs. Judith McBroom of the Pittsburgh Public Schools Evaluation Staff. Mrs. McBroom's report largely based on *The Discrepancy Evaluation Model*, written by the staff of the Research Office of the Pittsburgh Public Schools, (1969).

2. Presented by Gordon Welty of the Pittsburgh Public Schools Evaluation Staff. Mr. Welty's report is taken largely from *The Discrepancy Evaluation Model* cited above.

3. I would like to thank Laurie Dancy (Project Evaluator, Office of Research, Pittsburgh Public Schools), who is evaluating the Instrumental Music Program, for this information.

4. Esther Kresh, "Pittsburgh Team Teaching Program, 1967 Report," mimeographed (Board of Education, Pittsburgh Public Schools).

5. On the *dimensional* approach, see A. W. Melton's "Learning" in *Encyclopedia of Educational Research*, ed. W.S. Monroe (New York: Macmillan, 1941), pp. 667-686.

6. On process, see Melton, op. cit., p. 667.

7. Presented by Esther Kresh, Pittsburgh Public Schools, Office of Research Staff. Miss Kresh's report is based largely on *The Discrepancy Evaluation Model* cited in note 1.

4

An Application:
Standard Speech Program

The Standard Speech Development Program

The history of the evaluation of the Pittsburgh Public Schools' Standard Speech Development Program shows how the discrepancy evaluation model can systematically identify deficiencies in a program. The program was originally designed for seventh and eighth grade students in poverty neighborhoods. Until recently it was taught by 92 teachers to approximately 5,000 students in 37 schools as an integral part of the regular English curriculum. The recommended procedure calls for a daily pattern drills lesson of 15 minutes on a particular phonetic or grammatical structure of standard spoken English. In the program the use of nonstandard speech is in no way discredited. On the contrary, its preferability is conceded for many daily situations in the students' lives. However, it is realized that success in middle class social and business activities requires control of the standard language that serves as the currency of communica-

---

This chapter is based on several reports prepared by Leonard Glassner in the course of his work as a program evaluator in the Pittsburgh Public Schools.

tion in the larger world. Pattern drills were therefore developed to equip adolescents with phonetic and grammatical structures that will enable them to achieve this control. With this rationale, the program qualified for federal funding under Title I of the Elementary and Secondary Education Act of 1965, and initial planning began that year. The evaluation staff of the Office of Research did not become involved in the program until it was already underway. Once this involvement had become a fact, program and evaluation activity began to influence each other.

The first step in evaluating the program was to determine whether a design existed in accordance with the design criteria. The evaluation staff assumed responsibility for seeing that this was done. The evaluator prepared a set of questions to be used as the basis for a program design meeting. Nine of the 13 teachers who were teaching pattern drills at that time accepted an invitation to participate in a half-day session in which they would derive the basic design. They were randomly assigned to one of two discussion groups. In addition to the teachers, each group included two administrators or supervisors from the central office who were actively concerned with the planning and instructional aspects of the program.

A day or two before the meeting the evaluator oriented two discussion leaders, briefing them on the background of the program and mapping out a general procedure for conducting the groups and recording the proceedings. They decided to use the circular response technique in which each participant has a chance to make a statement in his turn; in this way no one can dominate the entire discussion and each individual has an opportunity to get his ideas into the record.

A description of the differences between groups and the interaction of participants is enlightening. Despite the random assignment of individuals, each group took on its own unique characteristics. One of the groups was much more open than the other, with each participant willing to talk in his turn and eager to comment and respond to the leader's nondirective guidance. The other group seemed noticeably less secure. New teachers in both groups avoided making comments whenever possible and looked to their more experienced colleagues to give them clues. Even more noticeable was the difference made by the presence in one group of the program director. Although not known as an authoritarian figure, she was obviously perceived as the ultimate decision maker. Even the older teachers in this group tended to look to her for clues to her intent, and were generally content to echo her ideas. Thanks to the ability of each of the discussion leaders, the data from the two groups proved to be reasonably similar.

The evaluator now became a recorder of consensus. By categorizing the responses and fitting them into the broad dimensions of the input, process, and output categories of program design criteria, he developed the formal program design (see Appendix A). Every member of the pattern drills staff received a copy of this design as formal feedback.

The next step in the evaluation process was to hold a panel meeting to assess the adequacy of the design. A linguistics consultant served as the technical expert on the panel; the program director and her supervisor represented the program staff; and the coordinator of evaluation, the evaluator, and a staff psychologist made up the evaluation component of the meeting. For several hours this team put each statement in the program design under the microscope. The evaluator had several responsibilities at the panel meeting. Besides arranging the meeting, he answered questions about evaluation of the program and fed into the record information he had elicited from teachers in school visits before the meeting.

Before distributing the report of the panel proceedings (see Appendix B), the program evaluator conferred with the program director, explaining the findings in an effort to prepare her for the discrepancy report. With her approval, the proceedings were sent to the entire program staff with an accompanying letter of explanation. This distribution constituted formal feedback.

We had now completed a full cycle of evaluation, all of which pertained to Stage 1 activity. Even though the evaluation panel felt that the program was not yet adequately designed and thus required further Stage 1 work, it had raised several questions about operations feasibility and had supplemented the design sufficiently to provide a standard for measuring operation. We were now ready for a new cycle of evaluation, which would examine Stage 2 concerns and at the same time clarify some Stage 1 definitions.

The principle source for identifying specific areas of performance to be studied was the program design itself, which the evaluator examined item by item. However, in the panel meeting, there had been agreement that "outputs" needed clarification. This in turn raised the question whether teachers understood the objectives of pattern drills instruction. Similarly, it was clear that time constraints were a probable source of difficulty in the field. In this connection it was noted that the time dimension was closely related to staff functions and duties.

An ad hoc interview instrument was designed for collecting data on these areas of program performance. See Appendix C. A random sample of pattern drills teachers was drawn, and interviews were conducted in the schools by the evaluator and an assistant from the Office of Research. Analysis of the data revealed the following findings:

(1) A discrepancy *did* exist between desired and actual performance in the time devoted to pattern drills instruction.

(2) A majority of the teachers thought that the drills should not be taught as often as the consultant had recommended. Teachers explained the discrepancy between standard and reality by stating that other curriculum demands left insufficient time for pattern drills and that many students, especially in the eighth grade, found the content too juvenile to engage their serious attention.

(3) Teachers lacked understanding of the program's objectives, with 39 percent mistaking inappropriate objectives for legitimate ones.

These findings were reported both formally and informally to the program director. She was willing to take action regarding the confusion over valid and invalid objectives. It is believed that this willingness was one of the factors that led to a stepped-up inservice program for all pattern drills teachers. She questioned the concern over time constraints, disagreeing with the consultant's recommendation that the drills should be taught for at least 15 minutes every day. This difference of opinion, although somewhat ameliorated recently, is still short of complete resolution. The report containing these findings (see Appendix D) was distributed to all members of the program staff. It should be noted here that the model deliberately makes no provision for forcing program staff to act on evaluation findings. Rather, the initiative for program change is encouraged in administrators through the feedback of evaluation information.

Implicit in the Stage 2 findings of the program was the need to further design the "process" of the pattern drills instruction. To accomplish this, the evaluator drew up a flow chart to show how the teaching of the grammar and phonetic drills was designed to lead to students' control of standard English speech. See Appendix E. This chart indicates the relationships of objectives at various levels of specificity and is an instance of Stage 2 work pointing the way to increased design specificity, which in turn makes Stage 3 work possible. After enabling objectives had been identified, it was possible to begin construction of a Stage 3 instrument. A copy of this instrument is shown in Appendix G.

Influenced by Stage 2 findings, the program director instituted the previously mentioned inservice program for all teachers. A skilled instructor was sent into each school to conduct a half-day workshop in methods and objectives. Her goal was to equip teachers to handle pattern drills with greater understanding and effectiveness. Citing her own experience, she stated that reality did not permit a daily lesson of 15 minutes. She suggested a minimum of three 10-minute lessons weekly.

The inservice program became the focal point for the next cycle of evaluation, which would attempt to measure the effect of the training on classroom practice. Substantially the same instrument was administered as was employed for the previous evaluation, and the same procedure was used to collect data. Although respondents were asked virtually the same questions as before, the rationale underlying the data collection had a somewhat different emphasis. The previous interviews were conducted to determine the degree of initial correspondence between design and teacher performance in the field. The second set of observations was designed to examine the effectiveness of an intervening staff training activity on two key program variables: understanding of objectives and time constraints. Indirectly it also provided a measurement of the effect of earlier feedback on program operation.

The following was noted: The discrepancy between guidelines and practice in time allocation had not been reduced in the period between the two observations. This was reported to program staff. See Appendix F.

Teachers still did not see the need for daily presentation of drills, which was not surprising in view of the instructor's conception of time requirements. Nor were they realizing the reduced time allotment they themselves thought desirable. There was a slight improvement in their understanding of objectives, but not enough to conclude that this was no longer a serious departure from design specifications. The report that provided feedback on this series of evaluation activities listed several alternatives that might improve understanding of objectives and resolve the time conflict. This report has been discussed with the program director and has been distributed to department chairmen in the schools as well as to other key members of the staff.

In this case history we have seen how the evaluation model provided an initial design for the Standard Speech Development Program and how actual classroom practice was compared with that design. This history has shown that the program as designed is not operating successfully because teachers do not understand its objectives and are not devoting enough time to the teaching of pattern drills. The report of these findings has led to several recent decisions. The program has been markedly reduced; it will no longer be offered in grade eight. As of January 1969 it has been limited to four schools, chosen by the director on the basis of availability of skilled instructors. In addition, federal funding has been withdrawn from the program.

This contraction is an instance of how discrepancy evaluation can halt the expenditures of resources, which in the absence of evaluation might continue indefinitely to support a malfunctioning program. More important, perhaps, this history also shows how the model sets up procedures for getting a misdirected program back on course. A redefinition meeting is scheduled to modify the design of the contracted program. When the program has been stabilized in terms of the new design, Stage 3 work can begin.

There is a good chance that the Standard Speech Development Program, under new conditions, will prove its worth. If it does, future evaluation reports will document its success.

Appendix A: Pattern Drills Program Definition

General

I.   Overall Statement of Objectives and Rationale for the Program

The principal objective of the Pattern Drills Program is to provide adolescents who ordinarily speak nonstandard English in all situations with the ability to speak the standard English of Western Pennsylvania when the occasion calls for its use. The rationale for the program acknowledges the place of both nonstandard and standard speech.

II.   Scope

A.   Number of Pupils and Schools Involved

At the end of the 1966-1967 school year, the program served approximately 5,100 students in 20 qualifying secondary schools.

B.   The Grades or Ages of Participants

Students served by the program include all those enrolled in grades seven and eight in participating schools.

C.   General Description of Staff

The staff for the Pattern Drills Program is made up of all teachers of

English in grades seven and eight in participating schools. Supervision is provided by the Supervisor of English regularly assigned to the schools involved.

Outcomes

I. Major Objectives—the changes that are expected to take place in the program participants as a result of their experiences in the program. There are two types of major objectives.

    A. Terminal Objectives: As a direct result of the Pattern Drills Program, it is expected that students will have the following skills:

        1. Ability to communicate clearly with all speakers of English; and

        2. Ability to shift automatically from nonstandard to standard speech and vice versa as the situation requires.

    B. Ultimate Objectives: In the long run it is expected that the Pattern Drills Program will contribute to its participants:

        1. Increased job opportunities;

        2. Increased self-confidence;

        3. Increased opportunity for participation in the activities of middle class society;

        4. Increased enthusiasm for participation and achievement in English classes; and

        5. Increased ability and willingness to communicate with speakers of standard English.

II. Enabling Objectives: In order to bring about the major objectives listed above, the student must first accomplish several things through the program:

    A. Be aware of the importance of standard speech in appropriate situations;

    B. Respect the appropriateness of nonstandard dialects in specific circumstances;

    C. Be able to produce the sounds and syntax of standard spoken speech;

    D. Be able to imitate different patterns of standard English; and

    E. Be able to hear and distinguish between standard English and nonstandard dialects.

III.   Other Benefits: Benefits expected to accrue to the community as a result of the Pattern Drills Program are:

A.   A general upgrading of the community as its citizens are able to participate increasingly in economic and social activities brought about in part by newly acquired control of middle class speech; and

B.   A gradual elimination of nonstandard speech as today's nonstandard speakers extend their knowledge and use of standard English.

Antecedents

I.   Students

A.   Selection Criteria

The Pattern Drills Program was in effect in two of twenty qualifying secondary schools from May 1 through the end of the 1966-1967 school year. All seventh and eighth grade students in these schools participated, the total number coming to 1250. The only prerequisite mentioned for the program, aside from being enrolled in either the seventh or eighth grade in these schools, was "an understanding of English vocabulary." This sole requirement points up two significant observations:

1.   A principal difference between the use of pattern drills in foreign language and standard English instruction lies in the fact that in learning a foreign language the student must be taught to receive as well as transmit the patterns; but in learning standard English the nonstandard speaker already has a passive understanding of the patterns to be mastered.

2.   Hence, in the present program, total energies can be focused on giving students control of phonological and grammatical patterns with which they are already at least passively familiar. This means that it is not generally necessary to avoid the use of lexical items for fear that they would be unknown to the children. This observation supports the consultant's previous finding in analyzing the tapes of students' speech that lexical items were "so minimal as to be negligible."

B.   Entering Behaviors

The students involved in the Pattern Drills Program, though far from a homogeneous group, have in common many observable characteristics that must be taken into consideration when planning instructional activities.

1.   A majority of the students entering the program cannot control standard English.

2. Many students come from homes in which standard English is neither spoken nor accepted.

3. Many students feel that they would be ridiculed if they used standard English in their community.

4. Some students resist standard English because, in the opinions of others, they fear that its acquisition will lead adults to expect too much of them.

5. Many students expect language instruction to offer them a practical tool for communication.

II. Staff

The most important persons in the Pattern Drills Program are the individual classroom teachers, who must have as basic qualifications the ability to speak standard English and at least minimal knowledge of the purposes and techniques of pattern drills. In addition, they should be enthusiastic and convey a lack of prejudice toward dialect differences.

III. Support

A. Administrative Support

Teachers look to the principal (and at Westinghouse to the department chairman) to provide the day-to-day support for the program within a school, such as scheduling pattern drills classes in the language laboratory. As for overall city-wide support, the central office staff is expected to provide the materials, funds, and communication necessary to initiate and maintain a successful program.

B. Human Resources: The following persons' services are important to program implementation:

1. The linguistics consultant has the following major roles:

a. To develop and explain the philosophy of pattern drills instruction;

b. To identify the patterns of standard and nonstandard speech that are to form the content of the pattern drills;

c. To help the pattern drills writing committee with the production of the drills;

d. To demonstrate the techniques of teaching the drills; and

e. To provide analysis and feedback to pattern drills teachers.

2. The instructional leader of English at Westinghouse coordinates the program with the larger English curriculum in the school.

3. Other teachers can facilitate the objectives of the Pattern Drills Program by stressing the same structures and pronunciations that are covered in the formal drills.

C. Media: The four most valuable materials and items of equipment and their purposes are the following:

1. The *pattern drills,* which provide the actual instructional content for the program and assure that a particular pattern is correctly presented with respect to rhythm, continuity, and purity;

2. *Charts* prepared by the Office of Research and the pattern drills writing committee, which are used for motivation and visual cues;

3. A *tape recorder* so that students may hear and evaluate their speech; and

4. The *language laboratory,* which effectively aids development of oral language skills.

Process

I. Student Activities

The drills prepared for the present program are based on a careful comparison between the grammatical and phonological patterns of the nonstandard and standard varieties of English spoken in the Pittsburgh area, because it is in this region that the vast majority of the students will live and work. The very nature of pattern drills, which utilize the aural-oral techniques also employed in modern foreign language instruction, leads to two basic student activities:

A. Listening to the standard English sound or grammatical form; and

B. Repeating the standard sound or grammatical form in a variety of drill practices in large groups, small groups, and individually.

Several observations were made about the second of these two basic activities:

1. Each separate drill must be limited to a specific sound or grammatical form.

2. In order to reinforce and provide for eventual automatic control of the standard pattern, frequent substitution drills are

presented in which students concentrate on nonessential substitutions in phrase or sentence content while they are repeating the desired pattern unchanged.*

3. Occasional drills are designed for testing, but their primary use for students is for pattern practice, reflecting the major objectives of the program.

II. Staff Functions and Activities

A. Staff Functions and Duties with Respect to Specific Positions: The specific functions and duties of the pattern drills teacher are the following:

1. Teaches pattern drills

a. Motivates student for drills (Method varies with individual drills, teacher, and class)

b. Presents drills and guides responses by use of oral and visual cues

2. Plans for coordinating pattern drills with the total English curriculum

a. Allots time for drills within the total English curriculum

b. Incorporates knowledge and skills into rest of English program

3. Evaluates student progress

Conducts test drills

4. Serves on writing committee if appointed

Produces drills for classroom use

---

*For example, in a drill devoted to the standard use of "he doesn't," the students might repeat the following series of sentences, each time focusing their attention on the changing direct object of the verb, while the pattern the teacher wishes to reinforce ("he doesn't") remains constant and seemingly of secondary significance:

He doesn't see the elephant.
He doesn't see the giraffe.
He doesn't see the tiger.
He doesn't see the hippopotamus.
etc.

5.   Communicates with others regarding pattern drills experience

Provides feedback to writing committee

B.   Intrastaff Communication and Coordination: The following intra-staff activities provide for communication about and coordination of pattern drills:

1.   At Westinghouse, teachers are kept informed of developments by the instructional leader of English and the department chairman.

2.   There is informal contact among teachers of pattern drills.

3.   Meetings are held between teachers and the Associate Director of Instruction for English and the English Supervisor.

4.   Inservice sessions are conducted in the schools and at the administration building by the associate director, the supervisor, and the linguistics consultant.

Appendix B: Report of Panel Proceedings

PROJECT PATTERN DRILLS

REPORT OF PANEL PROCEEDINGS

Section of Taxonomy OUTCOMES

Specific Dimensions	Program Definition	Judgments
I. Major Objectives—the changes that are expected to take place in program participants as a result of their experiences in the program		
A. Terminal Objectives	As a direct result of the Pattern Drills Program, it is expected that students will have the following skills:	
	1. Ability to communicate clearly with all speakers of English	Because of the many varieties of standard English, the objective as it is worded may not be too realistic. The consultant suggests restatement as "Ability to communicate clearly with those people with whom they come in contact in Western Pennsylvania."
	2. Ability to shift automatically from nonstandard to standard speech and vice versa as the situation requires	There are two separate objectives here: a. Ability to speak standard speech when appropriate

PROJECT PATTERN DRILLS

REPORT OF PANEL PROCEEDINGS

Section of Taxonomy OUTCOMES

Specific Dimensions	Program Definition	Judgments
A. Terminal Objectives (cont'd)		b. Ability to shift from nonstandard to standard speech when the situation requires Have criteria been developed for terminal objectives? The program has not made it clear that it is not devaluating the nonstandard English spoken in the home and the community.
B. Ultimate objectives—things that the Pattern Drills Program is expected to contribute to its participants in the long run	1. Increased job opportunities 2. Increased self-confidence 3. Increased opportunity for participation in the activities of middle class society 4. Increased enthusiasm for participation and achievement in English classes 5. Increased ability and willingness to communicate with speakers	These are valid Ultimate Objectives, but might logically be rearranged as follows: 1, 2, 5, 4, 3. Perhaps this is a terminal, rather than an ultimate objective. The

Specific Dimensions	Program Definition	Judgments
	of standard English	concept of "willingness," is not really related to the program's objectives.
II. Enabling Objectives: In order to bring about the major objectives listed above, the student must first accomplish several things through the program:	A. Be aware of the importance of standard speech in appropriate situations	The recording "Our Changing Language" (McGraw-Hill, 1967) could be used to implement this objective.
	B. Respect the appropriateness of nonstandard dialects in specific circumstances	
	C. Be able to produce the sounds and syntax of standard spoken speech	This could better be stated as: "Be able to produce the phonological and grammatical patterns of standard spoken speech."
	D. Be able to imitate the different patterns of standard English	This might be more clearly stated as: "Be able to discriminate among the different patterns of standard English." Logically, D should precede C, since discrimination precedes the ability to produce a sound or structure.
	E. Be able to hear and distinguish between standard English and nonstandard dialects	Some specific examples for clarification and guidance of teachers could be included.

PROJECT PATTERN DRILLS

REPORT OF PANEL PROCEEDINGS

Section of Taxonomy OUTCOMES

Specific Dimensions	Program Definition	Judgments
II. Enabling Objectives (cont'd)		Program staff may want to determine how the enabling objectives are related to desired outcomes and how they can be measured. What are the specific activities for each enabling objective?
III. Other Benefits—benefits expected to accrue to the community as a result of the Pattern Drills Program	A. A general upgrading of the community as its citizens are able to participate increasingly in economic and social activities brought about in part by newly acquired control of middle class speech	"Standard" is a more accurate description of the speech referred to than is "middle class."
	B. A gradual elimination of non-standard speech as today's non-standard speakers extend their knowledge and use of standard English	If this concept is internally inconsistent (i.e., in conflict with the program's objectives), it should be eliminated from the definition.

PROJECT PATTERN DRILLS

REPORT OF PANEL PROCEEDINGS

Section of Taxonomy ANTECEDENTS

Specific Dimensions	Program Definition	Judgments
I. Students		
A. Selection Criteria	The Pattern Drills Program was in effect in two of twenty qualifying secondary schools from February 1 through the end of the 1966-1967 school year. All seventh- and eighth-grade students in these schools participated, the total number coming to 1250. The only prerequisite mentioned for the program, aside from being enrolled in either the seventh or eighth grade in these schools, was "an understanding of English vocabulary." This sole requirement points up two significant observations:	
	1. A principal difference between the use of pattern drills in foreign language and standard English instruction lies in the fact that in learning a foreign language the student must be taught to receive as well as trans-	The following could be added: "Students who do not speak some form of English natively are not expected to benefit from the program."

PROJECT   PATTERN DRILLS

REPORT OF PANEL PROCEEDINGS

Section of Taxonomy   ANTECEDENTS

Specific Dimensions	Program Definition	Judgments
A. Selection Criteria (cont'd)	mit the patterns; but in learning standard English, the nonstandard speaker already has a passive understanding of the patterns to be mastered. 2. Hence, in the present program, total energies can be focused on giving students control of phonological and grammatical patterns with which they are already at least passively familiar. This means that it is not generally necessary to avoid the use of lexical items for fear that they would be unknown to the children. This observation supports the consultant's previous finding in analyzing the tapes of students' speech that lexical items were "so minimal as to be negligible."	
B. Entering Behaviors	The students involved in the Pattern Drills Program, though far	

Specific Dimensions	Program Definition	Judgments
B. Entering Behaviors (cont'd)	from a homogeneous group, have in common many observable characteristics that must be taken into consideration when planning instructional activities.	
	1. A majority of the students entering the program cannot control standard English.	This could be added as the first item under Entering Behaviors: "All students speak some form of English natively."
	2. Many students come from homes in which standard English is neither spoken nor accepted.	
	3. Many students feel that they would be ridiculed if they used standard English in their community.	
	4. Some students resist standard English because, in the opinion of teachers, they fear that its acquisition will lead adults to expect too much of them.	
	5. Many students expect language instruction to offer them a practical tool for communication.	It is not made clear that students are also concerned with communication outside of the school. Consideration has not been given to ways of measuring this expectation.

PROJECT   PATTERN DRILLS

REPORT OF PANEL PROCEEDINGS

Section of Taxonomy   ANTECEDENTS

Specific Dimensions	Program Definition	Judgments
II. Staff	The most important persons in the Pattern Drills Program are the individual classroom teachers, who must have as basic qualifications the ability to speak standard English and at least minimal knowledge of the purposes and techniques of pattern drills. In addition, they should be enthusiastic and convey a lack of prejudice toward dialect differences.	What are the specific functions and duties of the program staff?
III. Support A. Administrative Support	Teachers look to the principal (and at Westinghouse to the department chairman) to provide the day-to-day support for the program within a school, such as scheduling pattern drills classes in the language laboratory. As for overall city-wide support, the central office staff is expected to provide the materials, funds, and communication necessary to initiate and maintain a successful program.	

Specific Dimensions	Program Definition	Judgments

B. Human Resources	The following persons' services are important to program implementation:
	
	1. The linguistics consultant has the following major roles:
	
	  a. To develop and explain the philosophy of pattern drills instruction
	  b. To identify the patterns of standard and nonstandard speech that are to form the content of the pattern drills
	  c. To help the pattern drills writing committee with the production of the drills
	  d. To demonstrate the techniques of teaching the drills
	  e. To provide analysis and feedback to pattern drills teachers
	
	2. The instructional leader of English at Westinghouse coordinates the program with the larger English curriculum in the school.
	
	3. Other teachers can facilitate the objectives of the Pattern Drills	

PROJECT PATTERN DRILLS

REPORT OF PANEL PROCEEDINGS

Section of Taxonomy ANTECEDENTS

Specific Dimensions	Program Definition	Judgments
B. Human Resources (cont'd)	Program by stressing the same structures and pronunciations that are covered in the formal drills.	
C. Media	The four most valuable materials and items of equipment and their purposes are the following:	
	1. The *pattern drills*, which provide the actual instructional content for the program and assure that a particular pattern is correctly presented with respect to rhythm, continuity, and purity	
	2. *Charts* prepared by the Office of Research and the pattern drills writing committee, which are used for motivation and visual cues	
	3. A *tape recorder* so that students may hear and evaluate their speech	

Specific Dimensions	Program Definition	Judgments
	4. The *language laboratory*, which effectively aids development of oral language skills	

PROJECT PATTERN DRILLS

REPORT OF PANEL PROCEEDINGS

Section of Taxonomy PROCESS

Specific Dimensions	Program Definition	Judgments
I. Student Activities	The drills prepared for the present program are based on a careful comparison between the grammatical and phonological patterns of the nonstandard and standard varieties of English spoken in the Pittsburgh area, because it is in this region that the vast majority of the students will live and work. The very nature of pattern drills, which utilize the aural-oral techniques also employed in modern foreign language instruction, leads to two basic student activities: A. Listening to the standard English sound or grammatical form	"Listening to and discriminating the standard English sound and grammatical patterns (minimal

PROJECT PATTERN DRILLS

REPORT OF PANEL PROCEEDINGS

Section of Taxonomy PROCESS

Specific Dimensions	Program Definition	Judgments
I. Student Activities (cont'd)	B. Repeating the standard sound or grammatical form in a variety of drill practices in large groups, small groups, and individually	pairs)" would be a more accurate and complete statement of this activity.
	Several observations were made about the second of these two basic activities:	
	1. Each separate drill must be limited to a specific sound or grammatical form.	"Contrast" would be better here than "form."
	2. In order to reinforce and provide for eventual automatic control of the standard pattern, frequent substitution drills are presented in which students concentrate on nonessential substitutions in phrase or sentence content while they are repeating the desired pattern unchanged.	The definition might logically be expanded to establish specific connections between enabling objectives and student activities.

Specific Dimensions	Program Definition		Judgments
I. Student Activities (cont'd)	Occasional drills are designed for testing, but their primary use for students is for pattern practice, reflecting the major objectives of the program.		How is the time dimension evaluated? In the opinion of the linguistics consultant, not enough time is alloted for pattern drills instruction, nor is continuity adequate to realize the program's objectives. This is seen in the program's present definition.
II. Staff Functions and Activities			
A. Staff Functions and Duties with Respect to Specific Positions	The specific functions and duties of the pattern drills teacher are the following:		What is the relationship between teacher functions and activities and program objectives?
	Functions	Duties	
	1. Teaches pattern drills	a. Motivates students for drills (method varies with individual drills, teacher, and class)	
		b. Presents drills and guides responses by use of oral and visual cues	
	2. Plans for co-ordinating pattern drills with the total English curriculum	a. Allots time for drills within the total English curriculum	
		b. Incorporates knowledge and skills into rest of English program	

PROJECT PATTERN DRILLS

REPORT OF PANEL PROCEEDINGS

Section of Taxonomy: PROCESS

Specific Dimensions	Program Definition		Judgments
	Functions	Duties	
A. Staff Functions and Duties with Respect to Specific Positions (cont'd)	3. Evaluates student progress	Conducts test drills	
	4. Serves on writing committee if appointed	Produces drills for classroom use	
	5. Communicates with others regarding pattern drills experience	Provides feedback to writing committee	
B. Intrastaff Communication and Coordination (cont'd)	The following intrastaff activities provide for communication about and coordination of pattern drills:		
	1. At Westinghouse, teachers are kept informed of developments by the instructional leader of English and the department chairman.		
	2. There is informal contact among teachers of pattern drills.		
	3. Meetings are held between teachers and the		

Specific Dimensions	Program Definition	Judgments
B. Intrastaff Communication and Coordination (cont'd)	Associate Director of Instruction for English and the English Supervisor. 4. Inservice sessions are conducted in the schools and at the administration building by the associate director, the supervisor, and the linguistics consultant.	

Appendix C: Pattern Drills Program Interview Schedule

Rationale

The rationale for administering the cycle 2 pattern drills instrument is quoted from the program's cycle 2 plan, dated January 11, 1968:

Program Dimensions	Question	Rationale
Staff Functions and Duties	How consistently and uniformly are pattern drills being taught? Are all teachers using pattern drills?	... The panel stated that staff duties and functions were not specified in the definition. The first step in specifying duties and functions of the teacher is to determine what he/she is doing in the classroom.
Major Objectives and Enabling Objectives	Are teachers aware of (a) major objectives?	If teachers are to present drills properly, they should be able to (a) state program's overall objectives ...

It should be further noted that at a panel meeting on May 3, 1967 the linguistics consultant stated that in order for students to achieve automatic control of standard speech (a key terminal objective), pattern drills should be taught for at least 15 minutes a day. Part One of the instrument will determine to what extent this recommendation is currently being honored.

The data will be tabulated so that separate analyses can be made for elementary school and secondary school respondents.

Procedures for Administering

Before beginning the interview, the interviewer will either ask the respondent to read the introductory paragraph or he will orally explain the purpose of the interview, making the same points as are contained in the opening paragraph.

Part One—Time Dimension

1. The questions on this page will constitute an oral interview, with the interviewer recording responses as they are obtained.

2. Any discrepancies noted between questions 1 and 2 should be summarized in brief anecdotal form in the space below question 3; any discrepancies noted between questions 4 and 5 should be similarly summarized in the space below question 6. If no discrepancies are noted, write "None" or "No discrepancy."

3. At the top of the page the interviewer will record the teacher's name and school together with the amount of inservice training the teacher has had for pattern drills to the nearest half day.

Part Two—Objectives of Pattern Drills

1. This part of the instrument is a questionnaire, which is to be completed by the respondent in the interviewer's presence.

2. In the first column to the left of the page the respondent will check all the objectives that he considers valid for pattern drills.

3. In the second column the respondent will rank-order the five objectives that he considers to be the five most important, with the number 1 indicating the highest priority.

Cycle 2 Pattern Drills Instrument

In the continuing development of the Pattern Drills Program, it is desirable to determine the viewpoints of teachers at periodic intervals. With this in mind, we are requesting your appraisal of Pattern Drills at this time in terms of your experience with them in your own classroom. The Office of Research guarantees the anonymity of all respondents.

PART ONE—TIME DIMENSION

1. How many times each week do you feel pattern drills should be presented in:

Grade 6 _____ Grade 7 _____ Grade 8 _____ Grade 9 _____ ?

2. How many times each week do you ordinarily teach pattern drills in:

Grade 6 _____ Grade 7 _____ Grade 8 _____ Grade 9 _____ ?

3. If there is a difference between your answers to questions 1 and 2, to what do you attribute the discrepancy?

4. How much time do you feel should be devoted to each pattern drills session in:

Grade 6 _____ Grade 7 _____ Grade 8 _____ Grade 9 _____ ?

5. How much time do you ordinarily devote to each session in:

Grade 6 _____ Grade 7 _____ Grade 8 _____ Grade 9 _____ ?

6. If there is a difference between your answers to questions 4 and 5, to what do you attribute the discrepancy?

PART TWO—OBJECTIVES OF PATTERN DRILLS

A. Which of the objectives listed below do you feel genuinely apply to pattern drills? Indicate your opinion by placing a check mark before those objectives you believe pertain to the program. Please mark the check in the first of the two blank spaces that precede the item.

As a result of participation in pattern drills instruction, students should better be able:

_____ _____ To eliminate most gross errors in written composition

_____ _____ To communicate clearly with all English-speaking persons with whom they come in contact

_____ _____ To generalize to standard speech forms in contexts other than those presented in the formal drills

_____ _____ To substitute formal acceptable words and phrases for overused slang expressions

_____ _____ To spot errors in their friends' pronunciation and grammar

_____ _____ To use appropriate speech patterns automatically

_____ _____ To increase their formal vocabulary

_____ _____ To reproduce the sounds and grammatical constructions of standard English

_____ _____ To achieve success in the study of a foreign language

_____ _____ To differentiate between situations for which standard or nonstandard speech is appropriate

_____ _____ To shift from nonstandard speech and vice versa as the situation requires

_____ _____ To instruct their parents and other adults in correct usage

_____ _____ To speak standard English in all situations

_____ _____ To overcome noticeable speech impediments not requiring the services of a speech therapist

B. Now indicate the importance you assign to the objectives you checked as legitimate ones for pattern drills instruction by rank-ordering those you have checked. Start with number 1 for the most important and continue until you have recorded a number for all the objectives you checked. Write your figures in the second of the two blanks preceding the objective.

Appendix D: Cycle 2 Report

An evaluation report of the Pattern Drills Program was issued in September 1967. The findings indicated that the program was generally compatible with the English program and the overall school program, although teachers seemed confused about the relative priorities in the use of class time. The definition of the Pattern Drills Program was found inadequate in four areas. (For an elaboration of these findings the reader is referred to the previous document. Investigation by the evaluation staff has produced no evidence of action by the program staff as a response to these findings.

The current second cycle of evaluation took place during the first semester of this school year. The study was undertaken to determine the degree to which the operating Pattern Drills Program is consistent with the specifications of the program definition.

Program Operation

The evaluation focused on two questions:

(1) How are teachers using the drills, *i.e.*, how often are the drills taught and for what length of time at each session?

(2) Do teachers understand the purposes of pattern drills instruction?

The findings are presented under separate headings below.

(1) Use of the drills. Using two points of reference, it was found that a discrepancy exists between desired and actual performance in the use of the drills. When actual performance was compared with what teachers themselves perceived as desirable, it was found that a substantial number of teachers were neither using the drills as frequently as desired nor holding drill sessions of the desired length. When actual performance was compared with the standards recommended by the program consultant, the vast majority of teachers were found not to be performing in accordance with the recommended standards.

(2) Purposes of the program. In general, teachers do not understand the purposes of pattern drills instruction. When they were asked to select "correct" and "incorrect" items from a list of possible objectives for the program, 39 percent of their responses were inappropriate. Many of the "incorrect" choices were statements in direct conflict with the purposes of the program. The significance of this misunderstanding is indicated by the program consultant's statement: "If teachers are to present drills properly, they should be able to . . . . state the program's overall objectives . . . ."

Changes Effected in the Program

Investigation by the evaluation staff has shown that action has already been taken consistent with the findings of the Cycle 2 evaluation. Beginning in February 1968, a consultant will spend a half day in each junior high school conducting appropriate inservice activities with pattern drills teachers.

Appendix E: Simplified Diagram of Pattern Drills Process

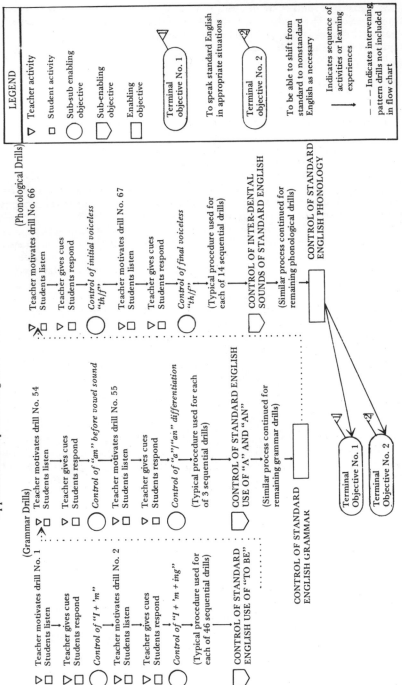

Appendix F: Cycle 3 Report

Summary of Preceding Report

The most recent evaluation report of the Standard Speech Development Program,* the Cycle 2 Report (see Appendix D), was distributed to staff members in February 1968. It was concerned with two major questions: (1) how often pattern drills were being taught and for what length of time at each session, and (2) whether teachers understood the program's objectives. Data collected in January 1968 showed pronounced discrepancies between the time recommended for teaching pattern drills (15 minutes each day) and time actually devoted to them in many classrooms (ranging from zero to five sessions a week of zero to ten minutes a session). The report also highlighted a confusion in teachers' minds about the valid objectives of the program. The inability of many teachers to distinguish between valid and inappropriate objectives cast considerable doubt on the program's successful implementation.

Scope of Present Report

The present document reports the impact of recent inservice training that attempted to change teachers' understanding of the time requirements and of the program's objectives. This inservice program was conducted after the issuance of the Cycle 2 Report. It was conducted in most of the participating schools, and included the majority of teachers in the program. According to the instructor, the training focused on the practical day-to-day operation of the program. In order to facilitate comparison, the same group of randomly selected teachers who were interviewed for the previous study in January were again polled, being asked to answer the same questions. In addition, these teachers were asked for an appraisal of the recent inservice training in terms of its value in enabling them to help students to realize the program's objectives.

Time Allocated to Drills

The serious discrepancy between guidelines and actual practice in the time allocated to the teaching of pattern drills has not been reduced since the preceding report. In fact, the discrepancy may have been accentuated by the inservice activity. In May 1967 the program's consultant recommended that pattern drills be taught for a minimum of 15 minutes every day in order to provide students with automatic control of standard speech. She reinforced this recommendation in a memorandum to the Office of Research in February 1968, by stating: "I recommend the use of the pattern drills materials for a minimum of 15 minutes five days a week . . . . The regular *daily* use of drills cannot be emphasized too strongly, since the immediate goal of developing a new set of language habits depends heavily on regular and repeated practice to establish automatic control."

Nevertheless, confronted with practical considerations as she perceived them, the inservice instructor advised teachers to schedule no more than three ten-minute pattern drills lessons a week. The following findings of the current

*formerly called Pattern Drills Program.

evaluation underline the conflict between expert opinion and classroom practice regarding time requirements:

1. Teachers do not see the need for daily presentation of the drills.

2. They fall somewhat short of realizing even the reduced frequency of presentation that they consider desirable.

3. They devote less time to teaching the drills in each succeeding grade.

4. Teachers are more likely to approach the recommended number of lessons per week than the recommended length per session.

5. The most common reasons teachers gave to explain the time discrepancy were: (a) too crowded a curriculum, and (b) lack of student interest.

Teachers' Understanding of Program Objectives

A slight improvement was noted in teachers' ability to identify the valid objectives of the program (69 percent appropriate responses versus 61 percent in the previous interviews). However, half of the teachers still saw two spurious objectives as valid: (1) to substitute formal acceptable words and phrases for overused slang expressions, and (2) to overcome noticeable speech impediments not requiring the services of a speech therapist. Further, one third of the teachers identified two other invalid objectives as authentic: (1) to spot errors in their friends' pronunciation and grammar, and (2) to increase their formal vocabulary. These findings indicate no substantial change in understanding of objectives as a result of the inservice training.

Teachers' Appraisal of Inservice Training

Over half the teachers credited the current inservice activity with helping them to lead their students to realize two crucial program objectives: (1) ability to reproduce the phonology and grammar of standard English, and (2) ability to use appropriate speech patterns automatically. However, the continued uncertainty of many teachers about program objectives is illustrated by the fact that almost one fourth also stated that the recent inservice training helped them to accomplish invalid objectives.

Problem Analysis

Several basic problems have characterized the Standard Speech Development Program since its inception. These have been further clarified by this cycle of evaluation.

1. Time Allocated to Drills. In May 1967 the program's consultant recommended that pattern drills be taught for a minimum of 15 minutes a day. However, the inservice instructor advised teachers to schedule no more than three five-to-ten minute pattern drills lessons each week. In practice, teachers are unable or unwilling to schedule pattern drills lessons as frequently as recommended. This problem could be ameliorated by:

(a) Realigning the components of the present course of study in English in participating schools to make a definite daily pattern drills lesson possible.

(b) Substituting the pattern drills program for large portions of the sections on grammar and speech in the present course of study. The three-track construction of the present English curriculum may make it feasible to effect this substitution for the lower-track classes with comparative ease.

(c) Modifying objectives by specifying a more limited, less rigorous set of expectations, that would in turn reduce the amount of time needed for the program.

2. Teachers' Understanding of Program Objectives. The data reflect that teachers still do not have a complete understanding of the program's objectives. The seriousness of this is emphasized by the consultant's statement that: "If teachers are to present drills properly they should be able to .... state the program's overall objectives . . . ."

3. Motivation of Students. Teachers need new techniques to improve the motivation of students. This need becomes increasingly urgent in the upper grades, to judge from the teachers' observations that the decreasing amount of time devoted to pattern drills in grades seven and eight is partly due to lack of student interest.

Both improved understanding of objectives and greater competence in motivating and presenting pattern drills may be accomplished by:

(a) Intensified inservice training before teachers begin to teach drills. This training should be designed to acquaint teachers with the philosophy of pattern drills as they relate to participating students in the Pittsburgh Public Schools.

(b) An ongoing inservice program during the school year, using demonstration, observation, and supervision tailored to specific classrooms and grade levels.

(c) Revision of existing materials to increase the relevance of the content for participating students. Attention should be given to writing new drills to attract the more mature students in the upper grades or to lowering the grade placement for the present program.

(d) Preparation of new materials on objectives and techniques for teacher reference.

A detailed report of the data and analysis can be found in the forthcoming annual report. Future evaluation will reexamine the aspects of the program considered here and will study the effect of pattern drills instruction on pupil performance as the instruments to measure achievement now being developed become available.

Appendix G: Preliminary Test*

Aural Discrimination Between Standard and Nonstandard English Sentences.

Narrator: You will hear a statement followed by two comparison statements. On your answer sheets circle the letter A or B identifying the statement that is most like the first in terms of language structure.

Example 1: I ain't got none.
Comparison A: I don't have any.
Comparison B: I ain't got none.

Now circle your answer. (five-second pause)
The correct answer is B. Do you see why?
If not raise your hand.
Here is another example.

*Prepared by Stuart Shafer, Office of Research, Pittsburgh Public Schools.

Example 2:   Dis is worser dan dat.
Comparison A: Dis is worser dan dat.
Comparison B: This is worse than that.

Now circle your answer. (five-second pause)
The correct answer is A. Do you see why?
If not raise your hand.
Now we will begin.

Number 1:   Jane look all right in dat dress.
              A: Jane looks all right in that dress.
              *B: Jane look all right in dat dress.

      2:     Jim's shirt don't look clean.
              A: Jim's shirt doesn't look clean.
              *B: Jim's shirt don't look clean.

      3:     The children rided on de bus.
              A: The children rode on the bus.
              *B: The children rided on de bus.

      4:     John an Susan haven' went ta church yet.
              A: John and Susan haven't gone to church yet.
              *B: John an Susan haven' went ta church yet.

      5:     At las, de TV man fix de set.
              *A: At las, de TV man fix de set.
              B: At last, the TV man fixed the set.

      6:     Mary may have come in for the interviews.
              A: Mary may have come in for de interviews.
              *B: Mary may have come in for the interviews.

      7:     I got no money.
              *A: I got no money.
              B: I don't have any money.

      8:     He looks like a policeman.
              A: He's look like a policeman.
              *B: He looks like a policeman.

      9:     It happen again. My car was broke down.
              *A: It happen again. My car was broke down.
              B: It happened again. My car broke down.

     10:     I waited until they got back, but June and Tom were late.
              *A: I waited until they got back, but June and Tom were
                      late.
              B: I wait until they got back, but June an Tom was late.

11:     I try to dance as best I could.
        *A: I try to dance as best I could.
        B: I try to dance as well as I can.

12:     The party was not fun. I don't think anything happened.
        *A: The party was not fun. I don't think anything happened.
        B: De party was no fun. I don' think nothin happen.

13:     Bob! It looks like the dogcatcher is coming out.
        A: Bob! It look like de dogcatcher's comin out.
        *B: Bob! It looks like the dogcatcher is coming out.

14:     He try to acts like de boss.
        *A: He try to acts like de boss.
        B: He tries to act like the boss.

15:     This is a nice car.
        *A: This is a nice car.
        B: Dis here's a nice car.

16:     Look—there are airplanes in the sky.
        A: Look—Der's airplanes in da sky.
        *B: Look—there are airplanes in the sky.

17:     After they win de ballgame they was so happy.
        A: After they won the ballgame they were so happy.
        *B: After they win de ballgame they were so happy.

18:     We were talking to some of the teachers.
        A: We was talkin to some of de teachers.
        *B: We were talking to some of the teachers.

19:     But maybe some of they are just sad.
        A: But maybe some of dem just sad.
        *B: But maybe some of them are just sad.

20:     That's just the name of the song.
        A: That jes de name of de song.
        *B: That's just the name of the song.

21:     She bout 16, I guess.
        A: She's about 16, I guess.
        *B: She bout 16, I guess.

22:     Are you gonna have a party on Saturday?
        A: Are you going to have a party on Saturday?
        *B: Are you gonna have a party on Saturday?

23:     I baby-sitted and made fifty cent.
        *A: I baby-sitted and made fifty cent.
        B: I baby-sat and made fifty cents.

24:     When I broked my leg it hurted alot.
        *A: When I broked my leg it hurted alot.
        B: When I broke my leg it hurt a lot.

25:     They were so happy we came to the basketball game.
        *A: They were so happy we came to the basketball game.
        B: They was so happy we come to de basketball game.

26:     There was three of us at de store.
        *A: There was three of us at de store.
        B: There were three of us at the store.

27:     I think they in classroom now.
        A: I think they're in the classroom now.
        *B: I think they in classroom now.

28:     She in 2nd grade, but I's in 4th.
        A: She is in 2nd grade, but I'm in 4th.
        *B: She in 2nd grade, but I's in 4th.

29:     They're waiting for the icecream man.
        *A: They're waiting for the icecream man.
        B: They waitin for de icecream man.

30:     After eatin too much, usually I be sick.
        *A: After eatin too much, usually I be sick.
        B: After eating too much, usually I am sick.

31:     I am hungry. I hope there is a candy machine.
        A: I is hungry. I hope there be a candy machine.
        *B: I am hungry. I hope there is a candy machine.

32:     If John don't want trouble, they be there.
        A: If John doesn't want trouble, they will be there.
        *B: If John don't want trouble, they be there.

33:     I like hotdogs cause dey taste good.
        A: I like hotdogs because they taste good.
        *B: I like hotdogs cause dey taste good.

34:     We will be traveling when it's summer.
        A: We be traveling when it's summer.
        *B: We will be traveling when it's summer.

35:     If I were you, I would have Jack pay for the scraped fender.
        A: If I's you, I be having Jack pay for the scraped fender.
        *B: If I were you, I would have Jack pay for the scraped
                fender.

36:     Some of the kids are riding in the Ford.
        A: Some of the kids be ridin in de Ford.
        *B: Some of the kids are riding in the Ford.

37:     Dat stove don't be electric.
     A: That stove isn't electric.
   *B: Dat stove don't be electric.

38:     What's the matter? Everytime I come looking for her, she isn't at home.
     A: What's da matter? Everytime I come lookin for her, she don't be at home.
   *B: What's the matter? Everytime I come looking for her, she isn't at home.

39:     No, I don't want any lunch. I'm not hungry now!
     A: No, I don' want no lunch. I don' be hungry now!
   *B: No, I don't want any lunch. I'm not hungry now!

40:     We are going to the zoo.
     A: We's goin to the zoo.
   *B: We are going to the zoo.

41:     My brudder be playin in de yard.
   *A: My brudder be playin in de yard.
     B: My brother is playing in the yard.

42:     Der's a fire in de kitchen!
   *A: Der's a fire in de kitchen!
     B: There's a fire in the kitchen!

43:     Ain't ya never on time?
   *A: Ain't ya never on time?
     B: Aren't you ever on time?

44:     Hey Tom, what are you doing there?
   *A: Hey Tom, what are you doing there?
     B: Hey Tom, what chew doin der?

45:     He isn't a mechanic. My car still doesn't run.
   *A: He isn't a mechanic. My car still doesn't run.
     B: He ain't no mechanic. My car still don't run.

46:     Sorry mister, I don't know where those stores are.
     A: Sorry mista, I don' know where dos stores is.
   *B: Sorry mister, I don't know where those stores are.

47:     No Jack, we aren't going to the grocery store.
   *A: No Jack, we aren't going to the grocery store.
     B: No Jack, we ain't goin' to de grocery store.

48:     We ain't never had such a good dance!
   *A: We ain't never had such a good dance!
     B: We have never had such a good dance!

49:     I da know. Maybe tha's what she done.
    A: I don't know. Maybe that's what she did.
   *B: I da know. Maybe tha's what she done.

50:     I've got to learn how to swim.
    A: I gotta learn ta swim.
   *B: I've got to learn how to swim.

51:     Ya' seen our ballfield?
   *A: Ya' seen our ballfield?
    B: Have you seen our ballfield?

52:     I did'n do it! I neva been der!
    A: I didn't do it. I've never been there!
   *B: I did'n do it! I neva been der!

53:     Teacha, I ain't got no pencil.
   *A: Teacha, I ain't got no pencil.
    B: Miss Smith, I don't have a pencil.

54:     We're going to talk about that movie.
    A: We gonna talk about dat movie.
   *B: We're going to talk about that movie.

55:     Hey Bill, what do you mean by that?
   *A: Hey Bill, what do you mean by that?
    B: Hey Bill, what ya mean by dat?

56:     All you're worrying about is the money.
   *A: All you're worrying about is the money.
    B: All you worrin' bout is de money.

57:     We ain't talkin', Miss. Ain't nobody said nothin'.
    A: We aren't talking, Miss Jones. Nobody said anything.
   *B: We ain't talkin', Miss. Ain't nobody said nothin'.

58:     When you late, you be in trouble.
   *A: When you late, you be in trouble.
    B: When you're late, you're in trouble.

59:     What da ya think? It look like an old Plymouth.
    A: What do you think? It looks like an old Plymouth.
   *B: What da ya think? It look like an old Plymouth.

60:     I don't like it. But ask Allen how he feels about it.
    A: I don' like it. But ast Allen how do he feel 'bout it.
   *B: I don't like it. But ask Allen how he feels about it.

61:     Pizza and spaghetti is alright, but Jane like hotdogs instead.
    A: Pizza and spaghetti are all right, but Jane likes hotdogs
       instead.

    *B: Pizza and spaghetti is alright, but Jane like hotdogs instead.

62:    You watch it! Your brain is going to break out of your head!
    A: You watch it! You' brain gonna bust out you' head!
    *B: You watch it! Your brain is going to break out of your head!

63:    I asked my mother if I could go, but she said no.
    *A: I asked my mother if I could go, but she said no.
    B: I ast my mother could I go, but she says no.

64:    We chase the dog out de house.
    *A: We chase the dog out de house.
    B: We chased the dog out of the house.

65:    You mean in school you be restless?
    A: Do you mean that in school you are restless?
    *B: You mean in school you be restless?

66:    This TV show is worse than that one.
    *A: This TV show is worse than that one.
    B: Dis TV show is worser dan dat one.

67:    What chew doin'? Kin I help?
    A: What are you doing? Can I help?
    *B: What chew doin'? Kin I help?

68:    All them football players is real good!
    A: All of those football players are good!
    *B: All them football players is real good!

69:    I ast my girl ta go to the dance.
    *A: I ast my girl ta go to the dance.
    B: I asked my girl to go to the dance.

70:    She's washing all of those dishes.
    *A: She's washing all of those dishes.
    B: She washin' all them dishes.

5

Critique of the Model

Remarks by Daniel Stufflebeam[1]

I think it is very difficult to react generally to the Discrepancy Model. Instead of attempting a comprehensive critique, I will list some specific impressions that I have developed from listening to the presentation.

My first reaction is that evaluation, as it is conceived in this model, is completely woven into the whole notion of educational change. In fact, I have the feeling that Mal and his people have developed a comprehensive strategy for educational change in addition to a strategy for evaluation.

As I thought about how I would write an evaluation design section for a proposal, using this model, I concluded that the evaluation material would not appear in any one section of the proposal. I think it would permeate the entire proposal.

That causes me to ask whether the model could be generalized to apply to situations outside of Pittsburgh. And I don't know the answer to that question. I suspect that the school people in this audience can answer it better than I can. To what extent would the administrators have to accept the assumptions that Mal is making in

See editor's note at beginning of chapter 3.—Ed.

terms of the program change strategy? To what extent would they be prone to accept these assumptions?

These are not criticisms; rather they are questions to be answered before we can safely judge the generalizability of the model.

Generally, I think that evaluation designs should encompass the delineation of the information to be collected, the means for collecting that information, and the means for helping decision makers to use that information. I think that this model has done an excellent job of covering these steps. And, further, I think that the usual overemphasis on the methodological steps of information collection, organization, and analysis is not here. I am glad to see that.

Also, I think that an evaluation model should deal with four classes of questions:

(1) What should the objectives be?

(2) What should the program design be for meeting those objectives?

(3) Is the program design being carried out effectively and efficiently?

(4) And was the program worth what we invested in it, considering the products achieved?

I think the model covers all of these questions, so in general I am pleased with what I have heard.

Let me speak to a few specific points that I have noted:

(1) The notion of staff involvement, I think, is one of the most important elements of this model. In the experience I have had in evaluation, I have noted that evaluation usually breaks down when staff members from the program at all levels are not involved in the evaluation, when they are not given feedback, when they do not know what the information will be used for, etc.

(2) Also implicit in the presentation here this morning is that evaluation has its own rules. It is not just a model for whitewashing problems in order to attract financial support. I think it is clear that this evaluation program will have teeth in it and that programs will indeed be phased out or continued on the basis of merit.

(3) The third strength is, I think, that traditional research design has been placed in its proper perspective. Many of us have criticized the use of experimental design for a long time, mainly because we thought it inappropriate to employ experimental design in the early stages of a program. At that point one usually didn't know what the treatment should be. If he did know, he wouldn't have many variations of it going on simultaneously. I am glad to see the notion of experimental design coming in later after a program has been stabi-

lized. It gives me new hope that evaluation can employ the tools of experimental design effectively.

(4) Another strength that I noted in my reading of the report was that of the policy for access to data. I don't think it was discussed in the presentation. The policies for access to data by all of the program participants according to the report are to be openly specified. If program personnel know where they stand when the evaluation begins, they also know what kind of information they will have access to. They know they will have access to the information that they provide and to the information that is collected about them and their performance in the program.

For all of those reasons, the Discrepancy Evaluation Model, I think offers a very promising approach to evaluation. Now let me briefly mention some of the problems. They are mainly questions that I don't think were answered.

(1) I like the idea of five stages, but I couldn't help wondering why they were included. I think that we need the rationale for those five stages. Maybe we need to investigate whether there might be alternative shortcuts that might apply to different kinds of programs.

(2) We couldn't have given much attention to it in this presentation, but I am very interested to know how the design criteria that we start with—the design criteria that form the basis for the whole program—are developed and applied. I guess I am a little bit worried that they get talked about in a panel discussion, that a few people then synthesize what happened, and that their synthesis becomes the set of design criteria.

I think that this is a very complex problem. It amounts to asking the question: What are the needs in our school system? What are the problems associated with meeting those needs? I would like to see more attention given to how those questions are answered by the model.

(3) The essence of the model seems to be convergence. I wonder if we are seeking this convergence prematurely. As a result, are we going to converge on the same old solutions to the same problems that we have had for years?

I think that is the major concern that I have about the model. It seems to me that we ought to exploit the alternatives that might exist and, indeed, the evaluators ought to get the program people to seek other alternatives. I doubt that bringing in a consultant from a university is a very strong strategy for doing that.

(4) We noted in passing that the purpose of this model is to serve the information requirements for decisionmaking, but we heard very

little about how the team would project the decisionmaking requirements. It seems to me that they started out with a set of assumptions about what those requirements would be and then they followed them systematically through the five stages. I think we have to talk more about the interaction of the various levels of decisionmaking and projection of new information requirements throughout the program.

(5) The last major criticism I have is that the model seems to exclude the continuous monitoring of the total school program. I think that it was built out of a response to Federal money, so I can understand why that has happened. It does seem to me however, that we are talking about variables that ought to be monitored systematically in the total school system so that we can identify needs to be served and problems to be solved.

Those are my comments. I think that the Discrepancy Model holds great promise. In fact, this is the best effort I have seen to develop a comprehensive model of evaluation in relation to the change process in schools.

Remarks by Egon G. Guba[2]

I must first echo Dan's remarks that this is a very impressive effort, the most impressive one that I have seen anywhere. The program that our university worked on is not as well researched as this one.

This is impressive for a number of reasons. It is obviously the most comprehensive model we have, and it seems to have attended to all of the details one could ordinarily think of. It is operational. On the basis of the evaluation that we heard about in the presentation at least one program has been thrown out because this model was used. That's about as nitty gritty as you can get.

It is obviously reality oriented. They don't start out with pretty balloons. You heard them say here that the kind of program plan contained in a proposal obviously is not the thing to start out with when one is talking about design. A lot of people miss that point and go out chasing balloons.

It is a model that is unconstrained by many of the faulty assumptions typically made by evaluators that some of us are particularly concerned about. So I am pleased to hear Dan remark that the model puts "experimental design" into proper perspective, which, I think is very relevant.

Aside from these generally laudatory comments there are two or three major observations that I would like to make about the characteristics of this model. One that I am very impressed with is the symbiotic relationship between program and evaluation.

As one reads the documents that the staff prepared and sent to the consultants before the meeting, the terms, "assessment" and "improvement," occur over and over again relative to each other. Evaluation is simultaneously seen as a way of assessing a program and as a way of improving it. We have just seen that demonstrated operationally here under the five stages of the model.

The various kinds of staff roles that we have heard described—roles that interface evaluation staff with the actual program personnel at all levels—indicate the interdependent nature of assessment and improvement in the model. The kinds of things that happen in the design panel meetings, the struggle for staff agreement about standards for evaluation and after it was made, to devise some concurrence, some involvement of staff at even the lowest level of personnel, suggest a kind of interfacing that is not typical of what we usually think of when we think about evaluation.

Dan made the point that there is a lot of change agent work in this model. The evaluator is as much a change agent as he is an assessor, or, at least, as much an improvisor as he is an assessor.

We have heard talk about links with decision makers—that the information being provided under this model by evaluators was used by decision makers, who apparently are people other than the evaluators themselves. That, again, implies some kind of very close professional relationship. Indeed, that may be the relationship that makes an evaluation a profession in its truest sense: the legal counselor or the attorney-like role that one might play in relation to a decision maker.

So, the characteristics of this type of evaluation are quite different from those we have heard defined before. Now I would like to return to another one of Dan's points. That is, that the rationale for the model's stages on which all of this activity is predicated is rather unclear, even though it is obviously partly a change rationale.

These stages seem to be the steps one would go through with or without an evaluation in trying to make changes in a program. However, one obviously would also use this same process to make an evaluation, without regard to changing a program and hence I am never quite clear of the basic principles we are operating on here.

Moreover, the five stages seem to deal with different levels of discourse. The first four of the five stages, "Design, Installation, Process, and Product," obviously relate to a designed program. It is designed then put into operation and then processed. The processes of implementation have to be tested to see whether they are relevant to the outcome.

Those are all things that relate to the design and installation of specific programs. Obviously one can carry on many of these programs and evaluations simultaneously. We could have 15 programs in operation and be going through all of these steps simultaneously in each of the 15 programs.

Then, we come to the fifth stage, which seems to me to be a different kind of criterion stage—"Cost". Here we are at a different level of discourse, because obviously we are comparing at least two programs that are designed to have the same output. When one begins to think that way, it is perfectly clear that cost is only one of a number of ways in which one can begin to compare programs. A whole set of new criteria or standards can be generated when one compares programs with one another.

Now, I suppose that since Mal says he hasn't yet gotten to that stage in any of his programs and doesn't anticipate doing so for several years, this poses a highly uninteresting question at this point. But someday we must examine how this stage is different from the others and what criteria beyond cost should be employed. This past summer I did identify some 20-odd criteria, in addition to cost, that one might wish to compare in programs that were purportedly designed to use the same output. For example, there is the whole question of negative side effects. Namely, of similar benefits but quite different side effects, like penicillin or streptomycin on a test, for example. Another criterion is the political viability of alternative programs. Given an educational problem, many alternative programs may be designed, as I found working with migrant children this summer in Texas. One of the program solutions was to pass a law requiring parents to keep their kids in school even though they were migrants. But that wouldn't have any political viability. The Texas Legislature would never do that. So, other program alternatives must be considered.

Third, there's the matter of social viability. This can be terribly important if, for example, you are working with Negro youngsters, and you have some kind of program that requires segregating them. However educationally sound your reason might be for wanting to segregate them in order to apply the treatment, it is perfectly clear that that is not a socially viable solution these days.

Another criterion for choosing between programs that comes directly to mind particularly in view of our experience with foundation-sponsored improvement programs in the past, is the whole notion of recidivism. How fast does a program backslide once you take out the props that were there when it was being developed? I suspect that a good many millions of dollars have been wasted over the past years because of this tendency. Sooner or later, after the angel takes the money away, the program collapses. Can we choose between programs with this consideration in mind?

That gives you the kind of flavor of other criteria that might be applied, and that I think would be as important as a cost criterion. The whole question of which criteria and how to apply them to programs with comparable benefits I leave unanswered.

Another point I would like to make has to do with how this model relates to the whole question of evaluation. It has to do partly with how one defines evaluation and partly how one structures a strategy for change.

This is a discrepancy model, the title reminds us, and generally speaking, the object of the game is to devise an operational equation such that goals "G" minus output "O" is equal to zero. That is the ideal situation, and to the extent they don't equal zero, there is an increment of difference. The game is played by discovering why that increment exists so that somehow it may be eliminated or ameliorated in some way.

Now, that seems to imply, and I think the presentation that we have heard confirms, that there is a procedure for specifying what is actually going on compared with what is supposed to be going on so that we can, in fact, make essential comparisons. That also seems to be the implication of one or more common definitions of evaluation that we are all familiar with; that is to say, evaluation has something to do with determining discrepancies between performance and objectives. That definition is quite common in the field, and again, it seems to imply that we sort of know what the objectives are ahead of time. Yet, we all know that in this day and age there is a great deal of uneasiness about this whole notion of objectives. This is partly a conceptual problem (I will return to this point in a moment) and it is partly an operational problem.

We know it is very difficult to get people to write objectives, and having them written down, the tendency is to put them in the back drawer of the file and forget about them. One has to assume that either people are terribly lazy or ignorant about the utility of objectives or there is something intrinsically wrong about the function of objectives in the real world of the practitioner. What is wrong?

Well, what is wrong, I think, is the notion that there is some kind of an ideal model out there which one can specify in great detail in advance and use as a consistent standard. Now, in fact, we know that even in this program this is not the case. If that were the case, if one possessed an ideal model, why didn't it occur in the proposal? What Mal's people say is, "Forget about the proposal. Don't go looking for the ideal there." Well, why didn't it occur in the proposal, to start with?

One might argue that the object of the proposal, obviously, is to get money. Proposals are usually written under great stress and strain. So that is why it does not appear in the proposal. Then I would ask why didn't the staff go into a corner and make one up? Or why didn't they get consultants from outside the system to make up an ideal model?

Instead, what they did was to go to the program staff and say, "What do you think you are doing?" Then, they went to the field and watched to find out what they were doing, and then, by process of elimination, as I pointed out, they finally arrived at something they were willing to accept as a design.

There were a few problems: For example, when they found that the pipe wasn't long enough to reach the water because somebody has guessed wrong where the level was. So, they just changed the design. In other words, when the world doesn't fit the ideal, they just change the ideal.

So, it is a kind of incremental process by which one arrives at a design of a program. Now, I would like to suggest that the strategy that actually underlies this evaluation model is fundamentally different from the one that has been implied here, that of the projection of an ideal as a basis for a series of comparisons at points in the future.

Rather we have here a kind of an incremental strategy in which objectives are not, in effect, the differences between where you are and where you would like to be, or the objectives are not statements of where you would like to be, but the objectives are statements of what seems to be. In essence, objectives are connecting steps to get you from where you are to someplace that appears on its face as a desirable next place to be.

So, for example, let us say you were interested in new federal policies to affect our present social security and retirement plans. If we ask whether the present plan is working or not, we don't compare that social security program to some ideal of what a social security program is like. In fact, nobody really knows what this is, and it has never been defined. Rather, we look for the preservation of the system, and we look for present problems in the system.

So somebody says, "You know, the cost of living index has gone up ten percent in the last five years. But we haven't done anything about increasing social security payments, and those retired folks are feeling the pinch in this inflation, and they are starving to death."

So somebody says, "Oh, is that what the problem is? Why don't we give them an additional increment of ten percent? Why don't we give them a 15-percent increment, and that will take care of that and for the next couple of years, we wouldn't have to worry about that."

That is the way an objective is defined, by some kind of consideration of what was wrong.

Or somebody says, "You know, what's the matter with growing old in this country? We give people social security but that's not enough to live on. It doesn't take into account all of the effects of medical disasters. People are subject to disease and illness. They may fall down and break bones and be in the hospital for six months. They have no way of dealing with these medical expenses."

So someone says, "Is that the problem? Why don't we have a Medicare program? That ought to take care of it."

Thus is another objective born. It is an increment that emerges from a process of evaluation. It comes partly from finding out whether the last little step you took did take care of the problem that you were trying to respond to, and partly whether another little step can be taken to improve on the situation still further.

Now, I would like to point out that that is a philosophy or a concept essentially different both from what they purport to be doing under their model and from traditional practice, where evaluation proceeds on the basis of defined objectives. One of the big problems in evaluation right now is that working from defined objectives is not a reasonable way to work because that is not the way people intuitively work. In fact, it's not a possible way to work.

Having said that, however, or having espoused, in a sense, a position of incrementalism, I have to take the next step, too, and say that there are times when change by increment isn't good enough. There are times when there is marching in the streets and there are teacher strikes. There are times in the universities when the SDS comes in and lays down some nonnegotiable demands on your desk. In cases like that incrementalism isn't good enough. There are huge red flags that come up in your life once in a while, and huge green ones too.

All of a sudden, ESEA provides a million dollars now for viable programs. If we move by increment we may fail to get our share or if we do get our share we may waste the money. In other words, incremental strategies may fail at times of extreme stress or trauma. I don't think that is any criticism. I simply want to point out that Mal's staff has a particular arena in which they operated, and they devised an increment strategy, which is obviously not always appropriate. It is not relevant to the other kind of situation, and we need to work on that one too.

Remarks by Walter J. Foley[3]

I think that if you assume that Egon's comments are reasonably accurate, most of what we do in evaluation is make adjustments or add increments. I think you have to start with knowing where you are rather than just start with what you have. Let me elaborate: You have to start with a kind of information system that defines where you are—the present status—and perhaps this should be the first step in building any evaluation strategy, rather than by starting with a discrepancy between what the program says and a standard, I think that someone ought to put down some information as to where we are, overall in the system.

The first note I have jotted down is "Product Specifications." What I have in mind here is that probably we should gather information and set up some minimum specifications for any program that exists in terms of what the product of the program is supposed to be. As a starting point, I would like to propose that this minimum should specify just what is necessary to enter into the next stage of the program. For example, the most realistic third grade reading level product specification would be one that states what the teacher will accept for entrance into the fourth grade. That is a great place to start.

Second, I think that Mal said evaluation is the monitoring of a system for decisionmaking. The examination of output or product on only those criteria specified in the design standard ignores the fact that if we limit ourselves to a single focus of discrepancy we lose a great deal of information related to the impact of side effects inherent in any program.

The consideration of things that might accidentally occur when we really were not expecting them in a program, can be fruitful. Even though we focus on a discrepancy between what a program purports to do and what it really does, some other effects that are very essential for program replication are overlooked.

Another question deals with a definition of adequate information across programs. Perhaps the teacher who is running a particular program might get all the information she needs to successfully run that program under this model. But the decision maker stationed in a central office might be getting no information across projects for decisions at a school system level. The person who has to make decisions based on cost of the programs needs program-related information.

Another consideration of mine is that the model doesn't take into consideration the relationship of those programs to everything else that is going on in the school.

To move on, I think, the idea of group consensus posited as a key for program success is an excellent idea, but it is also a very limited one. It leaves off all that could be said about innovation and technological change. Getting group consensus may not permit us to consider the effectiveness of teaching machines or the evaluation of computers in an institution or the evaluation of paraprofessionals and other "extra people" changes that are effecting the process of education in a school.

I think that the discrepancy model did not address itself to the multiple audiences of the programs evaluated. An evaluation model should have something to say to all the different audiences of a public program. Perhaps in terms of the community, the legislature, and the school people, to name a few of these audiences, the model should have been addressed to them in terms of relating the program to their specific needs. A program can be effective as far as the profession is concerned and ineffective as far as the community is concerned. The New York City Higher Horizons program evaluation is a good example of that kind of discrepancy. Another problem is related to the levels of evaluation. You can evaluate a program at a paraprogram level, and forget that you should be evaluating a program in the context of the changing role of education at the various levels of decisionmaking.

The national strategies for education are changing and perhaps a program that is very effective for an older established strategy is not effective for a newer one. Information for decisionmaking—that is, in fact, what evaluation is—should address itself to the many different audiences that represent different levels of decisionmaking in the educational system.

As it stands, the model assumes that the structures and goals that exist in the particular program are, in fact, those that exist for decisionmaking across programs at the local level and across state levels and at the Federal level. I don't think that is necessarily a valid assumption. We must gather data about both the macrolevel and the microlevel of educational systems.

The thing that I think is very interesting here is the idea of the evaluation of a program. You have set up a completely different kind of evaluation for a program than for a pupil. Tracking a pupil through his particular changes is quite different from tracking a program through its changes. This is an interesting idea. Technology has advanced to the point where we can track pupils and look at pupil change over a period of time. As a result, the program is often viewed as a side effect to pupil change, rather than having the focus on the program with the pupil change as a side effect.

Perhaps we should be tracking pupils in relation to a program rather than averaging their scores at the program level. Also, we should consider other areas of evaluation than change in pupil behavior. I expect that if this is a change model, we should be monitoring the changes in staff; soft ware, including the textbooks and whatever else is used in the classroom; hardware; and management system that went into governing this program as it has evolved. If we are going to say that evaluation is part of the change process, then these are facets of the change process that should be the focus of evaluation.

Remarks by William B. Gephart[4]

There are two points that I would call to your attention. First, the design criteria, as described in this model and as described in the materials that we have had the opportunity to study, are exceedingly important. The model seems to be based on something that is going on. If, as Dan said, we operate strictly on that basis, we close out alternatives that are not in that system when we start with the evaluative effort. That has been hit on enough times, so I won't belabor it any further.

The second point is one that has been touched on by two or three other people on this panel, but I don't think quite explicitly enough. That point is the need for continued systematic study of the decisionmaking process.

As I followed these five stages sequentially through the report and had the opportunity to study them, I began to get the feeling that we have moved away from the actual decision to a variety of things that need to be done to produce "p" minus "o" or "o" minus "p." In doing them we are going to get "reality" minus what our "objective" is. And, we feed that information to the decision maker. He adjusts the system to make that difference smaller.

This predicates evaluation on a very rational basis. It means that the decision maker, if the work is going to proceed to reach that zero discrepancy, operates on a very rational basis in his decisionmaking. We know that we don't do that. Evidence of this knowledge is displayed in the criteria that are stated in the design criteria section of the model.

Two problems seem apparent: (1) What criteria shall we employ in our rational information processing before making a decision, and (2) what are the irrational elements of our decisionmaking process. In the establishment of the outside effect at Stages 1 and 2, the decision maker can call up quite different criteria information on which the decision may be based. Where did we get them? How were they used? What contribution did they make?

Many of us in the audience have experienced instances in which either we or somebody for whom we were working has made a decision on the basis of criteria that were not stated in the design criteria. These criteria seem unrelated to discrepancies that might have been pointed out.

I think we have to be aware of how our decisions are made, and I think an evaluation model, to be effective, has to continually call our attention to this need. A positive proposal based on this criticism is that a model for evaluation ought to have components that include the study of the way decisions are made.

As an evaluation specialist, I have to serve or assist the decision maker. The assistance has a complex base. Decisions about a program are made all the way from the initiator down to the implementor, in fact, down to the child who decides whether to use the set of instructions that have been provided. If we are not aware of that process as we make decisions, we can run into the trap of readily providing information that is totally irrelevant to the decision maker and the decision setting. Thus, as a part of a model for evaluation, I would urge the inclusion of a component in which we study the manner in which decisions are made in the institution in which we are working and the manner in which the decisions might be made.

As my closing comment, I have one question of Mal: How do we evaluate the evaluation process?

Chairman Provus: I am an administrator too—one of the irrational variety. Therefore, I am not going to attempt to answer that right now.

Remarks by John I. Goodlad[5]

Let me talk a little bit about what I think are the contributions of the model.

(1) There is no doubt in my mind that an evaluation of this kind, leading to a more precise definition of the program to be implemented, is absolutely essential. Certainly, it goes a long way toward correcting the problems arising from the use of traditional research that have been mentioned earlier. Too often an evaluator has gone to see whether or not differences exist between the outcomes of experimental and control programs only to discover that there are no differences between the actual, operating programs. In order to be able to correct that problem, it is necessary to have a very clearly defined program, which I think is a step forward.

However, in regard to that, I find myself questioning the process used to identify a program. Dan Stufflebeam implied that the use of a panel to establish identity of the program is rather weak, and I agree with him. I realize that you still have to use a process that involves the people implementing the program, and you have to start where these people are and arrive at a definition in operational terms rather than in abstractions. But are these people the only source of a program definition?

One of the concerns researchers have in regard to identifying and specifying a program is to make some estimate of the potential power of that program. That is, if implemented, does the program offer some potential power in relation to all of the other factors that might be contributing to the learning process as a whole? And I think it is here that I begin to question this evaluation model because it sounds as though some pretty hard research data should be introduced to establish the potential value of a program, and I don't see that being done. In fact, shouldn't hard research data get into this evaluation system all along the way? Of course, some of us who hark back to the days of action research asked the same questions then.

Nonetheless, the notion of having a program with ingredients that are definable and clear enough so that we can see the component parts and tell which one is out of whack is very important. It is one that has been much neglected in the more traditional research designs for change.

(2) Very often programs that have been recommended to produce educational change, fall short because of the prerequisites to their operations. We have seen this in the curriculum reform movement of

the last dozen years. For example, enormous amounts of money have been spent on defining a curriculum innovation, but the program has been blunted on the classroom door because of the failure of teachers to use the materials as intended. Teachers have long used deductive methods of instruction, and consequently a program that assumed the inductive use of materials was perhaps doomed to failure.

So, when installing new programs, it is essential to specify the learning process and to determine its compatibility with the program we are trying to put across. This seems to me to be another tremendous asset of this model.

(3) We have overlooked the value of feedback to the strengthening of process itself. The subsequent reexamination of both the program and the process on the basis of feedback seems so obviously essential that one wonders why we have completely neglected it in the past. We had the researcher or the evaluator over here, and we had the implementer of the program over there. But we lacked systematic process for getting the information about a program back into the system, so that the people in the field could respond to that information and, in turn, their responses could be monitored.

Well, so much for the contributions of the model that I think are major, and when all put together, give us a model of considerable power.

Now, I want to raise one question that I don't think anyone else has touched on. I would be very interested in some of the case study reports from those using the model in order to examine the problem of "conflicts of social system." A teacher lives inevitably in a milieu—a social system where there are very strong directives with respect to the kind of activity in which the teacher should engage. There are various kinds of rewards the teacher gets for engaging in these activities, and so forth.

If a new social system exists or is created, conflicts are almost inevitable. I think the evaluation model described here creates a new social system, one of the evaluator and teacher and principal in a new kind of team. But this system is not as powerful in some ways as the old social system of which the teacher is a daily part. It seems to me that the new social system is going to be subverted because the rewards of conforming to that system simply are not great enough. In other words, is it more important that you respond to certain pressures from the principle, the community, or the parent, and so on, than to respond to the reward of having feedback data on which to operate?

It seems to me that the teacher, the implementer of the program,

the   person on the firing line, may live in a social system, very
different from that of the evaluator. Certain statements have been
made here to the effect that the evaluator is divorcing himself, to
some degree, from his traditional research community. Nonetheless, I
think there is built into the evaluator's background an orientation to
the research community; he wants its support and recognition. In
fact, I think this meeting testifies to that fact, to some degree.
Consequently, as one seeks to be "respectable in a research community" and "to be an accepted teacher in the community," there are
conflicts. As a matter of fact, I would like to propose that it would
be very interesting to conduct a research study on Bill Gephart's
question, "How do we evaluate evaluation?" to really identify some
of the problems that are involved in bringing what I think are two
differently motivated groups of people together and observing them
attempt to work together.

As I read the model report, I was struck by its enormous reliance
on interpersonal relationships, staff agreements, the designation of
roles, consistency of role performance, and so on. Complex human
dynamics are involved here. Questions about which social system
individuals belong to are going to arise and frustrate roles taken
under the model. Consequently, the model may be sabotaged at
many points along the way. Perhaps in some quiet session, Mal will
tell us something about this problem, because I am sure he faced it.

Finally, I would like to interject a different perspective on a point
I think everyone has mentioned. There seems to be a basic assumption that the teacher or program implementer in the field must stay
close to a clearly defined program. If he does not stay with that
program consistently, then one cannot have any idea whether the
program was a good one or not. The program is subject to subversion
at this level of consistency.

Related to this is the matter of multiple programs. If you have 150
programs, instead of the one program that was intended and supposed to remain consistent, do you have 150 pieces of garbage (I use
the word that was used earlier), or do you really have 150 programs
that are defensible in their own right?

I would like to comment on this question because I could define
three distinctly different team teaching programs in one school all of
which I could justify on relevant criteria:

(1) A team teaching program in early childhood education designed to extend the range of association of youngsters beyond one
teacher and one group so that youngsters have a wider range of peer
group association;

(2) A team teaching process designed to put in the mix highly specialized personnel in the teaching of reading at a lower elementary level; and

(3) A team teaching program designed to bring into the mix specialists in math, science, and so on, in another level.

The comment that I would make, to put it rather bluntly, is: I would seriously question attempting to use a program of team teaching for all ages, all levels, all schools in an identical fashion. In fact, I am so troubled about this that I question the assumption itself, and I wonder whether this is what has been meant by consistency. I think there must be some other meaning here that I haven't caught.

As I look at it, if I were to get a description of a simple program, a simple process, a simple criterion, and a simple product, it seems to me that feedback would clearly tell me what is happening to this program, what is wrong with it, and what might need to be done. It seems to me that it is relatively easy for teachers to conform to program specifications, including content and process.

However, it is also true while you are working to improve the operations of a program, that the program may be impotent. It may be operationally successful, but it is not going to do anything. Thus, for example, you are introducing phonics in the teaching of reading and there are so many factors that are more powerful than that particular approach to reading in the total constellation of things that you throw out phonics or throw in something else, and you can keep refining the process continuously, but the impact of that particular program is going to remain nil. I think that is where research comes in. We must have some way of anticipating the impact of various innovations or changes.

Now, let us look at a still more complex kind of program. Let's say, keeping reading again, that I increase my understanding and I am no longer trying to achieve the objective of having youngsters learning phonetic analysis. I now want youngsters to read. I have broader objectives and also more detailed subobjectives. In addition, I ask the question. Are there really reading specialists who are able to do the job? So, I use a team teaching model, because I want to be sure to use specialists. But then, I have to broaden my perspective. What about the pupil mix? To answer this question, am I using sociological research findings, such as the Coleman Report? Am I using the kind of findings that Herb Thelen has come up with in regard to learning style?

Now you can see I have vastly compounded the program. And

phonics, by itself, obviously isn't going to have phonetic effect and I
know this on the basis of research investigation and information. It
seems to me the need for research data on the cumulative effect of a
program's components is essential. If there are about six major
factors operating, you may put in an enormous amount of effort to
influence one, but its ceiling of influence may be only 20 percent.

The more you move toward program complexity, the more you
are counting on the flexibility of teachers while in effect, the
evaluation design called for in the model requires conformity on the
part of the teacher. What you obviously want is fluidity on the part
of the teacher as you move toward more complex definitions. Therefore, it may be more important that teachers be able to define
objectives and determine the various alternatives for achieving them.
Then it is assured that a teacher's behavior is sufficiently well
regulated to ensure that the objective is achieved. I hope we may get
to look at some more complex programs in order to assess the extent
to which the model can encompass them.

Remarks by Ralph W. Tyler[6]

In many respects, I am reminded of the Englishman who discovered, after he had been a writer for some years, that all these years he
had been writing prose. I encountered problems in evaluation in the
Eight Year Study in the 1930s, in the Cooperative Study of General
Education in the early 1940s, and in the New York Activity Schools
Study in the mid-1940s that would have been made clearer and more
explicit had this discrepancy model been available.

For example, when the evaluation staff came into the Eight Year
Study after plans had carefully been laid, we found, as Mal and his
group found here, that most of the schools did not have a design. So
they did not know what they were trying to do in the improvement
of secondary education, and there was a considerable period of
interaction with the evaluation staff before they could move forward.

The same was true of the New York Activity Schools Study. When
we examined what the supposed activity schools were, we found we
could identify 61 characteristics that were supposed to be in operation. We visited all of the classrooms in the 18 schools and we found
that perhaps a third of the classrooms used most of the 61 characteristics. But at the other extreme, we had activity programs in classrooms that had fewer of those characteristics than the average
number we found in the control schools. Again we had the same

problem of having to clarify just what the design was and of moving on through other essential activities, such as interaction between evaluators and the program planners.

The value of this model is that it helps to identify areas of concern. In a certain sense, the stages of the model are somewhat empty categories to be filled in through the use of particular criteria. We have heard illustrations that these same kinds of categories can be used whether you are looking at a program whose purpose is specific, such as trying to develop in youngsters a more accepted language pattern, or much broader, such as trying to get youngsters to participate in a social studies program in a way that is meaningful to them.

The same kinds of questions are raised about both of these programs and hence the categories of the model appear generalizable. On the other hand, the kinds of criteria used might be very different in order to be relevent to each of the programs.

In the first case, I think most of us realize that children who do not now practice a conventional language pattern must come to see the value of trying to develop another pattern if they are eventually to benefit from the program. It is rather useless to talk about how much practice will be carried on, because we have a great deal of evidence to show that if one practices something that he is not interested in and doesn't really attend to, it has very little lasting effect. So, when you talk about a specific thing you often find it imbedded in a larger thing. Practice is imbedded in interest. A reading skill program is not so different from a social attitudes program. And these categories of the model are of the same sort. One leads to another and is subsumed by it.

Now, if children are being coerced into changing their language patterns, then a program that drills them from morning to night is doomed to failure. This seems to me to illustrate what John Goodlad would call a relatively silly program because essential conditions as determined by research aren't there to begin with. We found this same kind of program in the Eight Year Study. The question is what to do about it.

I assume that what to do about it is what this model provides through a series of questions that are raised. They are questions based on what we already know enough about to be reasonably sure that important considerations are at issue.

And so we begin by determining where we are. Whether we are talking about a specific exercise with a specific purpose or a much more general program, we can then specify the general questions that are relevant. The kinds of categories found in the model are used to generate meaningful questions. These questions help program people find criteria against which they can test what is significant or unimportant in a program.

Now, John says that his experience leads him to define three different kinds of team teaching. This grows out of the employment of criteria that leads to experiences with something more than minimally defined team teaching. Correspondingly, when I was working in the Palo Alto area with some of the schools using PSSC, we found that some of the most important questions were:

(1) What teachers thought the objectives of particular lessons were;

(2) How important they thought those objectives were compared to other possible objectives;

(3) What the kids thought they were trying to learn in a given lesson; and

(4) Whether there were more important ways of determining what the program was than by an examination of its formal or external structure.

If the kid thought he was trying to learn to inquire, then, he reacted in quite a different fashion than if he thought he was trying to memorize all the junk that was in a particular textbook.

So this is the kind of thing that you learn. In many cases you start with whatever exists from your previous knowledge and research in an area, but as you begin to look at the specifications of a program and then its operation, new learning occurs and new kinds of questions come to mind that help break down the different kinds of areas or sets that previously existed in our minds. These questions help to establish new priorities and activities.

I share the point that Walter Foley made about a greater variety of audience for evaluation, but I think if we use any particular model to try to cover everything, we are overloading it. We would be no more justified than if we asked a person who is trying to do cancer research whether he has considered the effect of his findings on tobacco manufacturers. That question is appropriate when you have a total national program of prevention. But we would like to know whether tobacco makes a difference before we invest a lot of energy in fighting the tobacco manufacturers.

I think that we ought to recognize that this is a model for the kind of evaluation that pertains when programs have either been installed or are being considered for installation. But there are lots of other purposes for evaluation, and they will require other kinds of models.

I do share the view that was pointed out by two or three of the commentators that it is very helpful to know where you are before you begin. In the Eight Year Study, we found that we had to examine an existing secondary school program and find serious deficiencies in it before the staff would be willing to work hard at developing a new program. Otherwise whenever there was any difficulty in the new program they would say, "Why the hell do we spend so much energy on it? Why don't we go back to the other program that was so easy and successful?"

You have to have what, in my younger days, administrators used to call "conviction of sin." The effort required to effect reform must be based on some pretty basic data that force teachers to admit to some failures. They must say, "Gosh, we didn't accomplish these objectives after all in this mathematics program. We didn't get the student to do this." Then they cannot escape their responsibility as so many of us inevitably try to do. Therefore I believe it is important, before going very far with a new program that requires effort to actualize it, that teachers and all concerned have information about the inadequacies of the previous one.

In the matter of costs, I am glad that Mr. Guba pointed out the many kinds of costs that have to be considered. We found in earlier studies that a very important kind of cost was the continuing maintenance cost of just getting people ready for new programs. If you don't have a ready supply of teachers, every time a new teacher comes in to a program there is considerable preparation cost that has to be considered.

On the other side, we found that most teachers after five or six years of teaching in the same program feel a great deal of boredom. So there is a need for inservice programs to help teachers change themselves and their ongoing program just as there is a need to indoctrinate teachers into a new program in the first place. Another great value of inservice programs is their carryover effect. If they were working, for example, on a mathematics program, efforts to try something new led to greater excitement about the science program.

So when you are looking at costs relative to outcomes, you must include in outcomes the extent to which both pupils and teachers become self-directed, self-motivated, or self-educated. Balanced against these outcomes must be a consideration of such costs as fatigue, stress, boredom, and dissipation of human energy.

Now, I would like to argue a little with my friend Egon. How do we go about stating objectives or setting goals when we sense the need for something better than we are doing? In answering this question, I am greatly aided by studies made by sociologists. These indicate that in any kind of institutionalized effort, the first generation of professionals is dedicated to trying to work out programs that will serve clients.

The best educational illustration, I think, is in the clearly documented American history of the land grant college. There were the great pressures then, much like the pressures of today from lower income groups. The children of agricultural and mechanical workers wanted to get into college but were generally denied college admission by the Ivy League colleges on the ground that they didn't know Latin or Greek and hence couldn't do college work. The matter was decided in Washington by the passing of the Moore Act and the establishment of land grant colleges, with which many of us have been connected.

Suddenly the faculty in these schools were confronted with problems. They had generally been drawn from the Eastern schools and they asked, "How are we going to educate students from such a limited background? What do these students mean when they talk about the irrelevance of our curriculum and about things that are more important to them?" If you read the efforts of Michigan State, for example, you will find all the things they tried to do to make botany meaningful to people like that and the kinds of courses they introduced. You will discover that they developed a lot of new objectives in new programs when they were faced with that new clientele.

But then, after 15 or 20 years, at least pretty soon, the new professors came in and began to worship the existing program; then they began to select those students who could get along in that program and to ignore a new group of students who were not adequately prepared for the defined program. When one worships a program one doesn't stop to ask about its original objectives. Instead, these teachers say, "Well, they ought to be able to take Chem. I. So and so are able to handle it. They ought to be able to take Physics I and Math II" and so on.

There is a need to ask oneself again and again, "What are we about? And is my role and is this program appropriate? But do not scoff at teachers because they do not continually ask themselves what they are about. Most of us fail to do this. The trick is to get that dialogue started and to keep it going. It has been my experience, and I think this checks out with a good deal of the writings of modern philosophers, that we do not have served up to us from heaven a perfect definition of Utopia. We do not know the ultimate end. Instead we participate in a continuing dialogue in which we look at past experience and begin to clarify better goals. I think that is the kind of thing that is outlined in this model. It is a way of getting better goals, and often it is also a way of achieving a big quantum jump, not just little changes. I don't think that quantum jumps usually just come in dreams. I think quantum jumps often come from such continuing dialogue as has been described here.

But it may be that you and I have different views about this kind of issue. I think that in a continuing dialogue about objectives, you look back at the accumulated data or experience and you begin to ask, "Well, where is this grant taking me and is it really worth getting there?" It's a very important dialogue essential to the improved quality of educational programs, and again, I think the rationale of the model provides an opportunity for that.

And I think the terminology is something that we perhaps don't want to use, although I will say that some cost effectiveness in the system is needed and it is needed more rapidly than provided for in the model. I think that administrators must have within one year or so some sort of rough data about whether to make a "Go" or "No go" decision on their projects, and I hope that as Stage 5 is refined in the Pittsburgh model, some attention will be given to that.

And, finally, one last thing that impressed me. As a proposal reader—I don't read novels much any more; I just read proposals, and some of them are novels—I would like the recognition that proposals are methods of obtaining funds and are not grand schemes that someone found on stone tablets on a high mountain. It might be that with the use of a model like this one, with a built-in assessment notion, we might at least reduce the size of the proposals that we get. We could, for instance, have proposal writers tell us in the initial application, not how grand their project will be, but how they plan to develop it systematically so it will get better.

Remarks by Donald Carroll[7]

I have been asked to comment at the practitioner level. A general practitioner is a user of a variety of models, as he works with school boards, school district administrators, state education agencies, the state board of education, and legislative bodies at both the state and the national level.

I didn't know in 1961 when I participated as a team leader in the Pittsburgh Team Teaching Project that it would return to haunt me as much as it has today. That is another part of my background that may influence how carefully you listen to some of the things that I say.

These decisionmaking groups that we deal with—and I have heard it restated here—generally hold evaluation in low regard. They are the kind of activist people who feel that they can't wait for the results of an experiment or quasi-experimental studies to give them any kind of direction. They need to know "now" and they want to be sure they know where they are going.

I am reminded of an experience about a week ago in which I was called in to see the Speaker of our House of Representatives. He was considering proposing legislation to redo special education in Pennsylvania, and I suggested to him that perhaps rather than redoing it, we might want to look at what is going on, since there must be something good there. His retort was, "I am tired of all that philosophy. What we want to do is write legislation." So we quickly got to the political reality of where we stood.

There is a need on the part of these people, and I think this can't be underestimated, to correct things at midterm, so to speak, if they are not going well. One of the strengths of this evaluation model, and this has been said by several people, is that it does provide for midcourse correction, so that when we educational navigators, find that we are a degree or two off course, we can correct our course and be more likely to arrive at our intended destination.

I feel that the model, as described, is generally exportable. I go to a lot of meetings, and I am not overly attentive to one problem rather than another. Instead, I try to maintain a balanced view of education through the state. How applicable is the model? As I listen here and try to think of the 800 separate projects that have come into Pennsylvania, each spending about 350 million dollars, I really find it hard to name any project where this model could not make some type of contribution. So when the question of exportablility comes up, I really think that this model can be used rather extensively. And I suggest to Mal that we get together and try to work out, at least in Pennsylvania, how we might export this to other areas in the state.

I am, however, concerned about the program design stage of the model and this idea of achieving consensus on a design. People can hold very strong feelings about curriculum and I think this is one place where we are at times guided by gut level feelings. I wonder if we can achieve the consensus called for in the early stage of a design. From some of my experiences, it might be that that is where the project both begins and ends, and, I assume from Leonard Glassner's presentation on the speech development project, that one way to facilitate evaluation by consensus is to reduce the number of teachers involved in the design meeting.

So, I think this technique might be a problem. I see a logistics problem posed by the model. Not an insurmountable one, but one we all have to face up to. I have a feeling that bringing teachers and project administrators together in order to go through the elaborate discussion necessary under this model might be a monumental task. Let us remember that a lack of central evaluation staff of any kind in most of our school systems is par for the course.

The attitude of decision makers is also a major problem. If, in handling the Title 1 program of ESEA, there is one thing that impressed me, it was the attitude of the superintendent, that he really does feel he knows what those kids need. In fact, in one of the proposals we received, the justification for the proposal was simply, "I have been a superintendent in this county for 25 years. I know what they need." I am afraid that we have a lot of attitude change to work on here, although I am sure it has been improved in the past few years.

Stage 5, the cost benefit stage of this program, was not discussed much. I think we should say something about it. I would caution you on the use of the term, "cost-benefit analysis" in its very narrow sense. I know what it means in terms of the broad sense of making decisions. I also know how it is being applied.

Pennsylvania is placing its entire state government next year on something called PPBS, and I am working on analyzing and developing the scheme for basic education. We are then going to be developing a budgeting system for the school districts, and cost-benefit analysis is one of the tools we are going to use. When I deal with our Office of Administration and our business counterpart, they talk about cost benefits, and they mean cost reduction. This is the name of the game.

Remarks by Richard A. Dershimer[8]

If one of your purposes of this meeting, Mal, was to obtain the blessing of a representative cross-section of the research community, I think you have it. Let me add my voice to the consensus here that you have a model that is very usable and valuable. I have been trying to figure out this morning while reading your document how I could use aspects of it in my own operation, and I guess that is the best compliment you can pay anyone.

There are some internal problems, most of which have been mentioned. However, I think that the case study you used was very unfortunate. We know how to do what that program was trying to do better than that, and I am bothered that in the course of applying your model no one said that. I suspect one of the reasons may be that while the model uses the internal resources of your school system generally quite well, I wonder if they are able to spend the time in looking at the literature and interacting with people outside of your immediate institution, in testing the new ideas.

I realize that you were handed a proposal, you didn't generate it. And by the way, I have never had adequately explained to me why you enter at that stage, why you are not involved in the very beginning of the project planning. So the problem that two or three people talked about of identifying the major goals, I think, is still a critical one, not adequately handled in your model. I suspect it may be outside the model completely, but it is in some of the antecedent conditions that you still have to look at.

I want to raise another question. You made the statement that teachers need to internalize the program from the beginning. I think there is evidence to show that almost all teachers are capable of wearing new roles in projects. Some can teach in what is for them an atypical manner for at least a limited period of time. In other words, even though they are not internalizing certain behavior, you can still examine the effects of that behavior. The only evidence I can cite offhand is the study in Pennsylvania where Dr. Sid Archer randomly assigned teachers to five different conditions, in I think 70 schools, and found the teachers performed remarkably close to the assigned, prescribed behavior. Being paid for doing it helped.

Also, after having read the document I am still not sure who the evaluator is, where he comes from, and what his position is in the system. I would like to have you talk about that. I think you glossed over the question of how you get compatibility between the program goals and the entire systems goals, and I would like to have you talk about that, too.

I also don't think you are giving yourself enough credit here in your oral presentation for a very valuable part of the model. You've highlighted much better in your other document that at each critical point you can decide whether to continue or to close out the program. This is a very valuable contribution.

And that leads to my final comment, which is: You emphasize how you can close out things and get rid of programs. Maybe it is because you concentrate on the discrepancy between what is and what is not desired that you are always in a kind of negative position. You should try to discern how performance can exceed the original expectation as well as fall beneath it.

Footnotes

1. Director, Evaluation Center, Ohio State University, Columbus, Ohio.

2. Director, National Institute for the Study of Educational Change, Bloomington, Indiana.

3. Director, Iowa Educational Information Center, University of Iowa, Iowa City.

4. Director of Research Services, Phi Delta Kappa, Bloomington, Indiana.

5. Dean, Graduate School Of Education, University of California , at Los Angeles.

6. Director Emeritus, Center for Advanced Study in the Behavioral Sciences.

7. Assistant Commissioner of Education, Department of Public Instruction, Pennsylvania.

8. Executive Officer, American Educational Research Association, Washington, D.C.

6

Discussion from the Floor

The material presented here is a reasonably faithful representation of the substance and mood of open discussion of the model, within the constraints of the reporter's accuracy and the author's editorial parsimony. Redundancy and vagueness have been removed and re-writing has been done only where it did not appear that the speaker's original intent would be distorted. When application of this criterion was in doubt, material was simply deleted.

Chairman Provus: There are seated in our audience a number of people who could easily have been on this panel, and one of the great advantages of having this kind of talent in the room is that we now are in a position to tap a larger resource. So if you are willing to accept a bit of structure, I would just like to invite you to interact freely.

Mr. Ralph Walker (Wichita, Kansas): I would like you to go into a little greater detail on how this model provides for handling what might be considered the interaction problem. For example, some federally funded programs have such a variety of objectives that they have a variety of programs within them. How will this model provide for the interactions of these programs?

Mr. Gordon Welty: We have run into this frequently. And as you

See editor's note at beginning of chapter 3.—Ed.

may recall, when I was talking about the design criteria, I suggested that what we do is look into the process and see to what extent there are subprograms. The Opportunity School in Pittsburgh is an experimental program for juvenile delinquents. In our design work we have found that subprograms within the process section include a remedial reading program and a counseling program, among others. Each of these programs is being pulled out and systematically developed. The Opportunity School design also includes an inservice training program within the process section.

Moving from the problem of micro to macroanalysis, we are confronted by the system problem. To what extent can we generalize from this program to the whole system, the whole school system, of which this program is just one component? This presents a great deal more difficulty than the microanalysis approach, largely because of the problems of budgeting in the public schools. The fact that they use accounting budgets rather than functional budgets makes systems analysis an impossibility.

When the school administrator talks about his budget, he is not talking about an economic instrument. He is talking about a list of items, such as ten boxes of chalk and 20 erasers. The economist would call this a commodity bundle. The school administrator is *not* talking about any kind of functional relationship. This makes it virtually impossible to move to the general system level in most public school systems.

We have been trying to go both down and up in our analysis of school system programs and their subparts, and to deal with the problem of the interface of projects. It is a very complex problem, needless to say. I would say we are only beginning to cope with it.

Mr. W. James Popham (UCLA): I would like to ask one of the people whose job it was to introduce the model to users in your system a question.

The thing I have been concerned about over the last few years is that if you look at evaluation models and structural models in a continuum from the simple to the esoteric, you find that the esoteric is more conceptually satisfying, but it may be promulgationally less effective.

In other words, I have always been pleased with Professor Tyler's model, because although it is fairly simple and it's just got a few empty boxes, I find that I can transmit that empty box model to people and they can tolerate it. This model certainly lends itself to esoteric overlays and transparencies, but when you have to give it to a new user, can they tolerate this much?

Chairman Provus: Seated in our audience is another evaluator who is working on a specific program under the model. And, Dave, I think you are facing the problem right now of communicating with program staff. Would you be willing to react to that without any preparation?

Mr. David M. McCahon: In evaluating the Instructional Leadership program in Pittsburgh and attempting to work with the model and trying to present the concept of the model to the staff people, I have talked to them only generally about the five stages of the model.

Actually, I have been working in just the first two stages rather than all five, and going into some depth—starting with people where they are and going into whatever depth of explanation they could tolerate. But some people will accept just the idea of finding what the program should do and trying to draw a map of that and trying to draw a map of what is going on in the program and just comparing those. There are times when that is as deep as you can go. I don't think that I would ever go to the depth that it has been gone into here today. So I think we have been able to communicate about the model in such a way that the program staff can share in our work.

Mr. Vince Clift (Ohio State): From the experience we have had, you have got to come in at a simple level and not hit them with the sophistication. I mean, you can use simplicity as an entree to get to the sophistication, the things you want to get to. Where there is a group of educators who don't know how to present evaluation to the people, then we have to have other kinds of specialists who can compensate for this shortcoming.

Mr. Desmond Cook: As I heard the presentation this morning, it kind of reminded me of Eric Berne's book *Games People Play.* I am sure some of you have read this book. It is one of those famous games that is played: A wife asks her husband if he loves her. And while he is saying, "Yes, I love you," all the time he is thinking, "but you're a bitch." I heard this in a general kind of way about the model being presented. It's a good one, but I think there are things wrong with it, and I think Mal recognizes it.

Generally, I am supportive of it as a model. But I think both the model and the programs within it to which the model is being applied are basically being conceived as systems implicitly, if not explicitly. And this isn't too well stated, at least, in what you have brought out this morning.

I think when you get into systems, you get into system design. When you are talking about the program or the model itself, you get into the systems engineering and all the other elements of it. And this relates to one of the comments made this morning: You've got to start where you are and move from there.

Well, anybody who is designing a system automatically starts from where he is. You wouldn't think of designing a system if you are not concerned with a problem. Just so you don't start it *de novo* completely.

Another point has already been mentioned by a couple of the reactors—that discrepancies are not always negative, which is implied here. There are very positive ones and the manager also has to be concerned with them. I would cite you a case. The success of Apollo 7 permitted them to move right on to Apollo 8 in the lunar orbit, which they had not planned to do.

To my mind, the model basically is derived from management control theory. The more I study and work with management control theory, the more I am beginning to be convinced that this is the basis for evaluation itself. I don't want to see that kind of theory being thrown out as being bad in some kind of way. I think it is a fundamental part of any evaluation. And with regard to Bill Gephart's question about: How do you evaluate the evaluation model? I am going to make a suggestion that we could use the discrepancy model itself as a way of evaluating the evaluation model.

I do agree with Ralph Tyler's comments that what we are trying to do in the evaluation process is to increase rationality a little bit more than now exists. We can't make irrational people rational: We can increase their rationality. I think the model has a great deal of generalizability. I don't think that exportability is a real problem.

Mr. Harry Silberman: I wonder how you determine when your operational system is sufficiently stable to compare against your standard. What criteria do you use, for example, in pursuing the Sullivan Program, in ascertaining the turbulence? Has it settled down enough so that now you can compare it with the design of the program as envisioned by your staff?

Chairman Provus: Under the model, we need not wait for a program to stabilize before comparing it with a standard—at least not in stages 2 and 3. In fact, under Stage 2 we would capitalize on feedback describing instability as the basis for improving and ultimately stabilizing the program.

Mr. Gordon Welty: Basically, if you view the problem in the conceptual framework of the calculus of variations, you have a problem when as change continues to decrease you are approaching stability. The problem of program stabilization is a variant of the problem of finding a variational minimum with subsidiary constraints. So you are continually providing feedback and you are at the same time observing change on the part of the managers. And as the change diminishes, the program is reaching some stable value.

Mr. Silberman: Did you collect base line data rates on your students and wait until that became actually stable?

Mr. Welty: No. We were comparing the amount of material that actually depicted black people or black context with the amount of material that **could** have depicted black people with black contexts.

Mr. Silberman: So you did not use a student's performance criteria, then?

Mr. Welty: Not at all. This was not a performance measure. It was an evaluation of the media as such.

Chairman Provus: I think there is another point here. We would not want to use student base rate data as a criterion for making the kind of decision you are asking us about. We would reserve that for a Stage 3 decision.

What we want to know, and the difficult problem you are asking us about, is: How do we know when we are close enough to our standard to feel fairly secure about using performance as a new standard in the next stage of the model? This is where, at the present time, Braybrooke and Lindblom's notion of incrementalism is very useful.[1] We, by successive approximation, see ourselves coming closer and closer to what we have defined as the standard. There is at least some kind of intuitive process going on that leads us to believe that we are getting closer than we were. But there is another factor here, and that is, that depending on the particular structural components you are looking at at any given time, you may be able to set certain kinds of criterion levels.

In Stage 2, for instance, the existence of instructional material is an all-or-nothing kind of thing. Either it is present or it is not. Once it is present, you can then assume its existence as part of the program and then you can proceed to use it, as a basis for raising the kinds of questions that characterize Stage 3. That is, do kids reach instructional objectives using these materials?

Mr. Malcolm Richland (State of California): Implicit in your presentation was the implication that all of the project proposals that had been submitted did not relate to actual operation of the project at some later date, and, therefore, you had to start back in and identify the objectives, and what have you. Is it not possible in your design stage to enter the system sooner so that you get involved at the project development stage rather than after the project has been funded? Wouldn't the same principles apply, but enter the system earlier?

Chairman Provus: Yes, they will. The Opportunity School Program that Gordon Welty mentioned is an example of a program that we entered in the design stage. But what we have to fear most is that the program design will become a function of our knowledge and value, and we may rob the program staff not only of their initiative but of their standard, which is essential to their interpreting and acting on the feedback we give them.

We see the advantage of entering program planning deliberations early, but this must be at the invitation of program management. When we are invited, then we believe we can make substantial contributions to the adequacy of a program design—not by providing superior knowledge, but by asking the right questions.

Mr. Sam McClelland (New York Public Schools): I think for a large school system, program evaluation has to be approached on a pilot basis at the beginning, because, otherwise, it seems to be absolutely beyond the capacities of the research organization.

Now, in Dr. Tyler's day, their single program was a premier evaluation system. There was nothing like it in the school system. It had the attention, the approval, and the devotion of everyone. Today, in New York City, there are 35 ESEA Title 1 projects and many Title 3 projects, and New York State has an Urban Education Fund of $46 million. There are other titles. We can't do it all. Half of it—no—two thirds of it is contracted to outside agencies.

So I would say that the large school system has to try to work with staff in implementation, taking advantage of the systems approach, and I think this has proven to be a valuable setup. But we cannot for the forseeable future get into the business of doing this on all programs.

It is going to take a long time to establish the kind of position in the school system where all 30 assistant superintendents will turn to the Research Bureau and you will have the staff to make up all of these teams that are necessary. Of course, in New York we have the additional problem of decentralization.

Mr. Brinkwater: Going back to an earlier statement when one of the panelists was saying that the model is more than an evaluation model, that it offers itself as a change model, that notion is not quite accurate.

If you try to develop a change model from the evaluator's point of view, or a disseminator's point of view, or a developer's point of view, or a researcher's point of view, you may not do justice to any of these perspectives, and this ought to serve as a warning. It may be easy for us to ask an evaluator to come in to do program development work at the design stage, for example. But your evaluation model would not be fully adequate to such a demand. That is too much to expect of it.

Others on the educational change scene, I think, would have to assume major responsibility for design. When you try to expand the function of the evaluator to include design, you do a disservice to, or slight, all the other things to be done.

The phase called design could more accurately be called description. What is done in the Discrepancy Evaluation Model is to describe accurately what is going on and call for convergence, so there can be a description of a single program. As a method of obtaining description, the strategy seems adequate and sophisticated. As a way of getting the design done—of developing, creating, engineering, and originating a new program or alternative new programs—the model probably is inadequate. We shouldn't expect it to be adequate. It wasn't made by developers or by designers. It did not maximize the conditions for designing and developing the program. It does a brilliant job in the evaluation phase and permits linkage to the development that should precede the dissemination installation that ought to follow.

Chairman Provus: There are many things our model is not intended to do: It does not accommodate divergent thinking that leads to a variety of alternative program strategies; it was not intended to select from among alternative programs eligible for installation, and it cannot guide or solve the kind of R & D problems that come up in the course of evaluation and program development work.

Mr. Charles Nix (State Department of Education, Texas): I think what Dr. Brinkwater says is very true. It seems to me, too, that what you find in an overwhelming number of programs is that their design has not been done adequately, and when the evaluator starts to look at the program and tries to get into it for evaluation purposes, he immediately gets his back up to the wall, because he cannot discern just what the program is supposed to do. As I interpret what you just said, it is not that your model presumes to take this over but that it is necessary to do that because in an overwhelming number of cases, it has not been done adequately.

But it seems to me it is more than description. In the experiences that we have had, it is a matter of going back in and having people not just clarify what they thought, but perhaps do some original thinking on the goals they didn't set in the first place.

A voice: I would like to argue with Mr. Nix a little bit on this. It may be that at the present time your design phase is not yet fully expanded to include the problem of alternatives. But I think it can be, and if you are concerned with program improvements, you are certainly going to have to give consideration to alternatives.

Eventually, you will be able to settle on the best program before you apply it through all of the stages of that program's development. The model might also be applied to other alternatives generated in the design phase. If the systems designer is only interested in describing one particular program alternative then he is not a very good systems designer.

Mr. Brinkwater: Quite so, but it would be unfair to ask the evaluators, given their training, background, and view, to be general purpose system designers.

A voice: Pardon me. The point of my argument is that they ought to have that training.

Mr. Brinkwater: That's too much to ask. When they call for stability in the program, for convergence, not 138 programs but one, there is the evaluator's viewpoint at work. He has to have a clear knowledge of what it is. It must be stable. There has to be a singleness in whatever is called for in a program. These constraints are naturally imposed on the evaluator. That is the way he ought to behave, and that way doesn't generate alternative designs. The conditions that they would set and call for are unhealthy for originating alternative designs, because the tools they bring to bear don't include the ingenuity and divergence in originating multiple ways to get at the objective. And it is not reasonable to ask them either to supply it or, I think, to design the system to contain it.

Now, if you want to stretch evaluators out, then they have to look at the techniques of modifying teaching behavior that follow the reporting of the discrepancy. Because then you must intervene in this system and change the behavior to reduce the discrepancy.

Having reported the discrepancy, the evaluators are coming toward the end of what their skills let them do. Other skills come into play to invent and apply the techniques of teaching behavior, for example. So I wouldn't stretch them out too far myself—into the prior development or design work that has preceded their evaluation work—nor pull them too far over to the installation or implementation of programs that are under way.

Mr. Frank Nelson (Kansas City): Esther Kresh was describing Step 3 in some detail, going into task analysis and coming up with interim products. I am wondering who specified those. And the reason I am raising this question is because I want to know whether these are goals that you set, or goals that the people in the system set.

Miss Esther Kresh: It is not the job of the evaluator to set any of the objectives in the program. If the program staff is going to talk about a reading program, then it's fine to say that they are trying to improve reading achievement. As a terminal goal, this is great, but what does it mean to say this? What are the behaviors that define reading achievement? The evaluators have to work with them to get more precise definitions, but it ultimately is the program staff that has to give them to you.

Mr. Nelson: Who writes it? Do you write it and get them to agree with it?

Miss Kresh: No. You may end up stating it in behavioral terms for them, but they are the ones who give you the statement. You may rewrite what they have said. But it's their statement, not yours. The evaluator performs an editorial function.

Mr. Ray Sweigert (California State Department of Education): I don't think it is a question as much of where the evaluator enters the system as of where the evaluation begins. It bothers me somewhat, since, as I understand it, the model implies that the evaluation begins after funding has occurred and the program is under way.

I think I understand your reasons for entering at this point, and I think they are good reasons. It seems to me there is another kind of discrepancy that is very important that might be looked at. This is the discrepancy between the contract itself, or the proposal as contracted, and the program as you describe it through site visitation. It seems to be that whereas there may be very good reasons for discrepancies, these reasons should be specified. This is part of the ongoing design work. And where the discrepancies between the proposal as funded and the ongoing program cannot be justified, then this is very important in determining the quality of the program.

You know, in most projects where you find these departures from contract proposals, you find that these discrepancies are basic. Many of the discrepancies will be fortuitous and will be the result of a breakdown in whatever system is in operation. And that, I think, is a very important part of the evaluation.

Another point along this same line is that there is an implication in the statement that proposals are written to get funds, which we all know is true, and that these proposals then have little relation to what is going on afterwards. It seems to me that this implies that the rationale for funding is basically irrational or that there is no rationale for funding, and this may be true to a large extent. But I think this is something that people who are involved in the funding of proposals should be aware of and pay more attention to.

The system has to start at the level of development and at the level of proposal review and funding. And when the proposal is funded, there is an inherent implication that the design of the program as presented in the proposal does provide a system that will lead to the realization or achievement of certain objectives. And that, it seems to me, is the starting point for evaluation.

Chairman Provus: I think the relationship between proposal and program is essentially a relationship between expectancy and experience.

Mr. Ralph Tyler: It is more like the difference between a proposal for marriage and what goes on after marrigage. They can both be intentional, but I hope, as you say, experience only determines what is possible.

Mr. Richard Dershimer: To follow up on this point, I raise the question of when the evaluator—whatever the evaluator is—gets into the business of this design. If he is going to have to come back and goad people to redesign or clarify their design anyway, why shouldn't he do this in the preproposal stage and come in and fill some function there?

Maybe it is not the evaluator's function to do that; maybe it is some sort of general manager's function to tie in what the evaluator does and what the designer is doing. But it seems to me that it is probably less costly in terms of manpower and effort to do this before the proposal is ever written.

I think it also begins to get away from this other proposition that this gentleman was talking about—that a proposal is regarded as some kind of ruse to get money. We even use the term, "boiler-plate," or "boiler-plate plans," and that sort of thing, that are really designed to go ahead and get the money staked out. When the money is obtained, then we actually do what we originally had in mind to do in developing it.

I guess if the evaluation people are going to spend time doing this, they should do it before the program has gone into operation instead of having to come back in a remedial sense and make corrections.

Mr. Tyler: You are certainly quite right, if you are unaffected by all the other factors associated with ESEA. When the proposal is finally approved and the funds are made available, there is the expectation that the operation will materialize soon and there is a pressure that is hard to anticipate.

You also have the problem that in the school systems the people who teach and who operate have to be a very important part of the design, because you cannot easily impose a design on others. You've got the problem of how much effort they will put into it without some reassurance that they are going to get money, or have some hope for it. So if you expect them to have a very perfect design before there is any payment, in my long experience with groups, I don't think you can get many teachers willing to invest that much. You've got to have some sort of feedback in one way or another, and what usually happens is you get some assurance that there is going to be some money and you can start and keep on going further.

So I think you have to consider those reality factors when you recognize that you don't have a complete design when you really have to start operating, and that is why a lot of this effort is necessary. I don't really see how you are going to avoid it, because of the peculiar conditions of education involving the planning, and so on, on the part of the people who operate it. It is somewhat different from planning and designing a material object. Don't you think that is true?

Mr. Dershimer: Yes, sir, I do. It is no doubt very true, in particular for projects that have not had some kind of ongoing operation before.

Mr. Tyler: Along with doing that, when they start this modification and all this kind of procedure that is outlined, there seem to me to be better and better ways of designing.

A voice: It occurs to me that in the program funded by Title 1, ESEA, for instance, which is in operation now for the third or fourth year, that there hasn't been this kind of use of resources from the previous year to do this kind of detailing for next year's operation.

Mr. Tyler: Have you seen the annual report for the National Advisory Council on the Education of Disabled and Disadvantaged Children? Under the law, the council, of which I am a member, has to report annually to the Congress. And the best estimate we can get from a number of contractors going into the field and sampling is that perhaps 25 percent of the Title 1 projects really are accomplishing something.

Now, I don't know whether you would say this is awfully wasteful for three or four years. When you consider that for hundreds of years no school system has really reached the most disadvantaged, this is encouraging.

I don't know why it is, but wherever you can get into this kind of planning and begin to improve it, I think good things begin to happen.

Mr. Egon Guba: I have never been involved in any evaluation in which you couldn't say "Gee whiz, if they had only called me last week or last month." And I sometimes get the feeling that we treasure that because it seems to be a convenient rationalization. If things don't go well you say, "They called me in so late, what could I do?"

The fact is, however, that the evaluator never gets involved in a project in the beginning unless you want to assume that the idea for the project comes from the evaluator himself. I suppose it sometimes does, but typically, somebody has thought about it or worked at it and asked some other people about it and evolved some ideas and materials.

What is more important, it seems to me, is not to fret about the stage in which you were called in, but to have some mechanics for responding to what you might have done if you had been called in earlier. And it seems to me one of the great virtues of this model is that it provides the mechanics for catching up and refining and redoing some of the things that should have been done if only you had been notified earlier to give them the advice. I think the realities are that we ought to develop the mechanics rather than castigate people, because this is just fruitless.

Dr. William Gephart: I wanted to say something quite similar to that. I don't believe it is a question of: Should he be involved or should he not be involved? No one seems to be questioning that. How the evaluation specialist is involved is the more important question. If he moves into a situation in which he is structuring the instructional program, the area in which he does not have the expertise, then, he is violating his role and he ought not to be involved on that basis. But if he is in that preliminary planning on the basis of structuring what is needed for the evaluation, then, he is performing a more legitimate role. So the question is: How can we contribute to the decisionmaking process without being so presumptuous as to structure education as we think it ought to be? Typically, we don't have that big a vision. We need to stick to our role as evaluation specialists and not move in as curriculum experts.

A voice: Just as an offshoot of that, I would say that I do not think that when the evaluator comes in, is so important if the persons doing the design realize fairly early that they are going to be subjected to certain questions and that there are some standards injected into the procedures that they will have to meet.

Mr. Louis Rubin: Mal, could I ask you, or some of your staff, to speculate about the utility of the model and refer to some points, I think, that have been made with considerable insight.

It is a most impressive model. Would you bet it might be possible to simplify it to such a point that it might be used in Los Angeles as well as in Pittsburgh?

Secondly, is it conceivable that you might alter the first two stages so that it would be possible to generate some alternatives, and particularly, to tie it into some of the large-scale payoffs that John Goodlad referred to?

And the third point is one that interested me mightily. In our own operation, we find that the evaluation data has very little significance for the teacher. Most teachers, understandably, are happier with their methodology than they are with data. Is there a way, then, to build a feedback movement that would get to the scene of the action?

Chairman Provus: The third question is easy. The answer is "Yes," and our model does that. We do feed back this information to all practitioners, including teachers.

Now, it is true that when large numbers of teachers are involved in a program we often draw a sample of teachers to insure the involvement of program staff in our design work and for these teachers our feedback is meaningful. Generally speaking, we create an appetite for feedbacks so that it is used when provided.

Mr. Rubin: I heard that, but what happens to the feedback?

Chairman Provus: The program manager is responsible for determining whether anything of consequence comes of the feedback. Remember, there are two alternatives: The staff can modify its behavior, or the program can be redesigned. That is not our responsibility, but that of the program staff. It is our responsibility to see that the program manager is aware of his management role.

On the first question we have some pretty strong hunches. Given the variety of programs we have handled in Pittsburgh and the similarity of conditions between Pittsburgh and other large cities' evaluations problems we believe the model is generalizable.

Now, Esther Kresh has some thoughts on the second question.

Miss Esther Kresh: I think the point you are referring to, Dr. Rubin, is basic. We keep hearing about these alternatives, but I think when you start talking about alternatives, you are asking a completely different question.

We are working with a different problem. In one case, you are faced with the problem of determining whether a program is implemented as the design intends. So you are interested in the type of Stage 1 and Stage 2 activities that are represented in the model.

Now, when you get into the problem of providing for alternatives, you are asking a different kind of question, so that actually you need a new Stage 1 and Stage 2, which are going to give you a different kind of information. I don't think this can be encompassed in one set of Stage 1 and Stage 2 specifications. You might need two sets there.

I think there is a possible way to get around the problem of examining alternatives, but that is a different kind of problem altogether. The model, I think, handles the first problem very well. The program staff decides to implement a particular design, and when this is done, the model handles it very well. It doesn't handle the problem of generating alternatives. That is true.

Mr. Rubin: Well, I guess I was happier before I got your answer.

First, it seems to me, without too much manipulation, you might be able to find some self-correcting mechanisms that could be applied to each of the stages that would give you greater payoff rather than going through the entire process without any flexibility. One of the things that has concerned me is coming to the end of Stage 2 where you have stabilized the program without any real information about possible alternatives or simply whether or not the program is working. I think you are wasting a lot of time and a lot of effort if the program becomes stabilized on *a priori* assumptions that may not work. My second concern is: In your evaluation feedback, once you get your data and you go back only as far as the program manager, then, you are stopping short of the horse's mouth. I think that you have to get back to the teacher whose behavior you are assessing in order to do any real good. Could that be done?

Miss Kresh: I think Mal said earlier that this information is given to all levels of program staff, including teachers. Does that answer your question?

Chairman Provus: Egon Guba has asked whether it might be interesting if he shared with you some of the problems he faced in his R & D regional laboratory lately in trying to come up with program innovations.

Mr. Guba: I just wanted to give you a little case study of what we did in the regional laboratory in Texas where I went this summer. It was good to find out what the real world was like. I took two months off this summer and went to work in the regional laboratory in relation to a new program that they were just getting under way on the problems of migrant youngsters in school.

In these migrant groups, you know, there are many Spanish-American youngsters, in this case, the children of migrant agricultural workers. These families leave in April or May on migrant work tours, and the kids go out of school, and they don't come back until late October or early November, so the kids are late coming back to school.

Some money became available through Congress to try to cope with some of those problems, and the laboratory was offered the money on the condition that they come up with some reasonable kind of program.

Now, what do you do in this case? This is a little bit further back than these people were in relation to the case studies of various examples they provided, but it does open up the question of alternatives. And, obviously, there are at least two sets of alternatives.

One is: What is the nature of the problem that we are going to try to confront?

There are, obviously, lots of problems that these children have. They are almost all Spanish-Americans, for example, so they speak Spanish when they get together. They don't speak English. They come from a different socio-cultural class. They have different kinds of class characteristics. They are mainly retarded in school, because of the previous history. They are mobile, and their mobility causes discontinuity in this program and their contact with teachers. They are very poor, and so on.

There are at least eight or ten major kinds of problems, so one of the questions you have to ask yourself in dealing with this alternative is: Which one of these problems are we going to respond to? Some of the problems are essentially educational; others are not. Others are more political in nature, or whatever.

So that is one set of alternatives you have to cope with: You have to identify the problems and try to decide which of those are acceptable and reasonable for you to try to deal with, depending on who you are and what kind of resources you have, and so on.

In the second set of alternatives given, suppose you have selected, Problem X. What can you do about it? There are always a variety of things you can do. If you have chosen to deal with the mobility question per se, you try to do something about that.

There is a big class of alternatives. You could, for example, try to get a law passed that would tie the kids down in school; or you could try to build a mobile classroom and follow them around; or you could try to make individual material, things they could carry with them. You have got to somehow identify some of those alternatives and decide which of those you are going to pursue.

Well, to try to resolve that question, just operationally—and I don't want to take too much time in this; it just seems to be an important issue—we held two conferences. One was a so-called actors conference, to which we invited subgroups of people who actually were involved with the problem: the kids themselves, their parents, their teachers, their school administrators, their counselors, the welfare workers in the towns, the employment agency people and business people that related to them, the priests, the physicians, and a whole series of such people whom we simply called actors.

And for another conference, we invited in a group of people who presumably had some professional leverage on their problems, the anthropologists, the sociologists, labor economists, and so on.

In each case, we asked these people to tell us what they thought the problems were. In order to begin to get together a jump on the second step of the solution, we also said, "In the case of each problem, tell us some things that you think we might do."

As a result of that, we were able to come up with a big matrix, the rows being defined by problems and the columns being defined by solutions. And as you might expect, some solutions might deal with several problems at once, so you might get some feeling of the power of solutions or the tractability of the problems that can help people think of ways to deal with the problem. In some cases, this is very difficult when you look at the number of X's that you have. In itself, you have some idea of how tractable the solutions are or the problems are or how powerful various solutions are. Having done that, that gave us an idea in the sense of rating what we might do, and so we were able to narrow down by this kind of process to, say, three alternatives that on their face, on the basis of this, looked pretty good.

We then went to what we called an advocate team strategy. We actually divided them into three teams and gave each team one of the problems and some subsets of solutions and said, "You now go out. Here are all of our data banks and all the information we have about these kids. Anything else you think you need, we will provide. Go out and make the best possible case that you can to the laboratory as to why they ought to attack that particular problem. And make the best possible case you can for some system that they ought to follow in attacking that problem."

That, in essence, now is coming back to the laboratory, and they will have three advocate cases laid before them as a basis for making their decisions.

Now, that is one way. That is, obviously, one of the many ways, but it seems to have worked fairly well and does give you a pretty good grasp of what the problems are and what the solutions are. As a matter of fact, you get some idea of how those things act in priority, some idea of tractability, some idea of power of solution, and some idea of the kind of cases that can be made when an advocate team really puts its mind to just that one thing and doesn't try to deal with all of them at once.

Chairman Provus: Thank you. I would like to comment on that. I think what Egon has just gone through is a rather imaginative strategy for problem solving. It is our position that evaluation is not synonymous with problem solving but that problem solving requires evaluation.

A voice: I hate to beat a dead horse, but since most of your ESEA programs require that in the submission of an application you indicate how you evaluate, I think it is so important that the evaluation people be involved early.

Chairman Provus: Right.

A voice: And since the proposal requires this, I see no reason why there shouldn't be built into any evaluation scheme or model the ability to enter at that point if for no other reason that to design at that point what the evaluation is going to be before the proposal is submitted. Otherwise, I see no point in requiring that there be an evaluation design included in the proposal.

Chairman Provus: I think every proposal should have an evaluation section that posits design criteria and explains as operationally as possible a procedure for verifying that the design criteria are satisfied, that the program is installed, that the process is then analyzed and, finally, that the project is assessed.

That is all. It can be spelled out more or less, and that is what should be in every proposal. One can go on infinitely into detail. But this is a levels problem. As Ralph Tyler was suggesting, you don't want all that detail in a proposal. You could be hung by it. It will be a noose around your neck. You are going to have to find out how detailed to be as you actually get into your project.

Mr. Malcolm Richland: Now that the discrepancy evaluation model is a reality, and you might call it an act of intervention or maybe imposition on the school district, I wondered if you might just speak about some of the outcomes or some of the generalized outcomes that you have observed by virtue of this thing being a reality in the school district.

Chairman Provus: Half of our ESEA programs were cut last year. We cut from 24 to 12, and I think we are going to cut back to six this year. That is one massive consequence I can think of. I can talk about how we have sensitized school administrators to their management responsibilities, and on and on about the interpersonal effects, but that is not very tangible.

Mr. Sam McClelland: If the design is reacted on by the evaluators and the program managers, must you not also get the community into it, for legal, if not for other reasons? And how do you deal with a situation where the community says "We don't want after school study centers to put teachers on the gravy train, we want paraprofessional jobs given to the people in our district"?

Chairman Provus: I think you are confronting us with, again, the value conflict problem at the macrolevel. Conflicts between staff and community will be revealed and will have to be reconciled under the model, if program staff includes the community in program planning. Obviously, they fail to do so at their own risk.

A voice: There is another concern I have about the model. I think I heard it described today, and you seemed to have talked there very adequately of how you can relate some kind of strategy to some kind of output within the short term. Particularly, for long-range projects, however, planning might last over a period of three to five years. The plan would need to be reviewed and reconstituted periodically.

Do you have any provision in the model for testing the relevance of the objectives that you had already set, or does your model assume that the objectives are fixed?

Chairman Provus: No, no. Objectives change as a function of design work. Objectives are always changing until you reach Stage 4. That is where you can assume that the program has stabilized. The design is adequate; the performance relative to that design is adequate. At Stage 4 we can look at the product in great detail. We are then perfectly comfortable about shooting for a specific target.

Mr. John Goodlad: In this last hour of discussion, I have been impressed with the fact that the persons who are working with the model have given precise "Yes" and "No" answers about what the model will and won't do—more precise, I think, than in some of the earlier documents.

Just as an aside, you might say this is often true with the creators. The danger occurs in the second and third and fourth levels, until you begin to do all kinds of things that you wish you never had done. But it would be helpful, I think, if you talked more in describing the model, of inclusion-exclusion criteria with respect to what the model is designed to do and not do, so that you won't begin to get people reading into it all kinds of things that you rejected.

Some of the answers you have given might well be used as a discussion of the model itself.

Now, specifically, I am less interested in trying to get you to revise

Stages 1 and 2 than I am in understanding more about the flexibility you have in Stages 1 and 2, because it seems to me a lot of the questions that have arisen here are hitting on that point.

Let's for a moment get rid of the whole business of evaluating specific funded projects, because presumably, in due course of time, this model will be applicable to all kinds of things that are going on in the system design, and many kinds of people will be coming to you and saying, "Look, we want to do this, that, and the other," rather than, "We are already doing this, that, and the other."

Now, tell me a little more about how your model does two things:

(1) How the educational viability of what people want to do or are already doing is checked within your initial steps? I thought I heard that you brought in an expert in the business. Dan Stufflebeam commented on that, and I think that would have been very powerful.

(2) What experience you have had, or what you would do with the situation where, on the basis of whatever that sort of quality control at that point was, you decided, "Well, we ought not do this anyway, not right now"?

Let me take a specific example: We go around and around the clock with respect to homogeneous groupings. All right. These teachers, or this particular school wants to develop homogeneous patterns or groupings of some kind. So you raise questions on the basis of your model. Then, you discover that what they are really talking about is achievement groupings, not ability groupings, and you begin to refine it, and so on.

Now, what provision do you make for bringing in evidence about what we know about that sort of technique, in the first place? And what do you do if the teacher says, "Look, I don't care about youngsters' achievement any more. I simply can't handle individual differences, and it would make my life simpler."

Mr. Gordon Welty: The problem of consultants is, I think, the major problem that I run into in my work. You know that you can always find another expert of just as great eminence who is going to hold just the opposite position.

Mr. John Goodlad: This is why I picked this problem. Here is a very genuine desire on the part of some program coordinator, principal, or what-not. They suddenly discover grouping as an answer to reading. This goes on periodically. They rediscover grouping and they want to do it. They think it's a good idea.

Now, one of the things that strikes me as I look at your letterhead is: You are a research office. Consequently, presumably, you are doing more than developing an evaluative design.

The question here is: I don't want to step out of evaluative design and I am wondering whether within the evaluative design you take care of the double-barrelled problem of reviewing what we really know apart from what the teacher wants to do and answering the problem of what they want to do, or whether that simply isn't inside your model but is the responsibility of some other branch of the research office.

That would help me to know whether I want to tinker around with Steps 1 and 2 or not.

Mr. Ralph Tyler: I don't know whether this is relevant, but drawing again on my experience of some years ago, there is the matter here of what has to happen before evaluation. That is, there are some basic philosophic or psychological principles that we have found school systems must accept before you can begin answering evaluation questions.

For example, there are many large city systems in the United States that really accept the basic principle that the job of the school is in some way to separate out, to provide differential ways of assigning people to different groups. Some students are going to go to college, others are going elsewhere. And the basic evaluation question is: "How well are we separating them so that they get where they're supposed to go?" The whole notion of criteria for evaluation grows out of the basic question: "What is this school for?"

It is very tempting in a large, complex city to think of education as a system for separating sheep from goats. Then, the system doesn't do too much teaching. It mostly separates according to existing social strata in our society.

On the other hand, we found some high schools that we were working with, in which the notion was: "The role of the school is in some way to break through social stratification, to keep providing opportunities, to keep actualizing initiative on the part of the kid." You begin to raise questions about existing programs, and pretty soon you find, very different answers about what the evaluation design should be—not because people didn't have answers to questions, but because they had very different ideas, which they felt were reinforced by the community and by the school board, about what the nature of the school is: To educate, not just to operate.

Throughout society for thousands of years, these two issues have always come up, and I think these are the kinds of things that we have to go into before we do an evaluation.

Chairman Provus: That is a very interesting point. I would like to respond to it.

We have come to the conclusion that, although it would be logical and proper under our model, we cannot identify the ultimate values of the system, nor can we expect anyone to rank those values in order for us to deal with them in a consistent, systematic way.

It seems to me it is an assumption of the Tyler rationale that values be identified and the way one does that is to apply the philosophy screen that Tyler included in his rationale. But it is our experience that this simply isn't possible. Instead, we have found it necessary to determine only the values underlying a given program— planned or operating.

Different programs serve different values. That is, a whole set of discrete, rather independent values exist in any large system. We start with what is and deal with these values only as they relate to a given program. We don't ever try to proceed as some economists suggest and interrelate all the values in a system.

We take a program that is, let's say, half formed in the minds of the program staff, and when we get to that part of our program definition that asks about giving up a resource for a benefit, that is, using an input to get an output, we don't ask, "Why are you willing to pay the input price?"; we ask "Do you think the input will buy the output?" The first question is a value question, which we believe is beyond the discretion of the evaluator. The second question is a theory or state of knowledge question. And it is at that point that a program staff either exhibits a defensible rationale or not; either they have some theory underlying their program or they don't. The reason we call in a consultant is to certify the viability of the theory. We don't really even care whether there are conflicting theories in a school system. We only care that there is a defensible theory for a given program.

Now, the result is that we are forcing up like mushrooms, independent of one another, little programs and the supporting theories from which they emerge. There may, indeed, be a day of reckoning for all this. Someday all of these programs may grow big enough to compete with one another. Such competition may be painful but good. We suspect that is the nature of the real world anyway, and that when the day comes that some of these programs must be lopped off, there will at least be a pragmatic basis for the decision. By that time, new needs, new values, and new theories may have arisen to spawn new programs. And so the cycle goes on.

Miss Esther Kresh: I think one of the things I keep hearing here is an assumption that the evaluator has more power than he actually has. At least, I think in Pittsburgh the program staff views the evaluator as someone who collects and analyzes data, not as someone who can perform the role of consultant in the development process.

Mr. Ralph Tyler: I think the evaluator's power lies in the relevance and the clarity of the question he asks. He's got to ask again and again, "How rational is it? Does it fit with your own notion? Have you thought this thing through in that sense?"

There is a certain sense in which I agree with Mal that those of us who worked on evaluation in the Eight Year Study had an advantage in being outside the school systems with which we worked. We could talk with the Superintendent of the Los Angeles Schools, asking him, "Do you really think that is an appropriate philosophy for the Los Angeles Schools?" As outsiders we could ask the question and discuss it without the possible embarrassment that would have entered in had we been within the school system.

Some of the most difficult problems are solved by rationales—and this is true of the rationale that I developed for evaluation in our Eight Year Study and the rationale that we sometimes use for curriculum development—that are really empty boxes. They remind you of areas that must be looked at.

Of course one still has the problems of "What do you ask about?" and "How skillfully is this done?" and "What sort of evidence can be obtained?" But my experience again is much more optimistic than one of our speakers. I believe that when we engage in this question and answer process that the decisions we arrive at are remarkably sound. The trouble is we often overlook this process. When the teacher asks if he really wants the outcomes of a certain program he is weighing alternatives essential to a sound decision. His decision is not an all-or-none thing. It is equivocal, balanced, and not based on irrefutable research evidence.

I think we are both rational and irrational, and the addition of empirical evidence and intellectual ambiguity to other kinds of impulses are the basis for making decisions. The continuing dialogue in the continuing examination of data in relation to questions about where we want to go, how we want to do it, whether this fits in with other knowledge we have, and how it relates to new data about the changing society and the changing nature of education, is a way of providing continuous development for sound program improvement.

What I am saying is that if our purpose as educators is to provide very generalizable knowledge about, for example, the role of motivation in learning, then this particular evaluation model is not efficient. But if our purpose is to reveal alternatives (here are the kinds of things we can do, here are some ways to reach these disadvantaged children, and here are some ways to get a program into operation) then, we must try and err; we must find out what "works" for us and internalize it. For this purpose, I think this kind of rationale is a great improvement over what we usually do.

No doubt, it will be modified in the years ahead, but it reminds us that instead of looking at some unorganized statement that we have about a program—some statement served up by "authorities" or researchers on a silver platter—we must begin to analyze and define much more specifically what we actually have and what we have learned from having it that will help us do a better job. This, it seems to me, will permit us both to get additional knowledge and also to get programs in operation that will succeed in improving education in this country.

Mr. Egon Guba: I want to go on record that I don't think we have been playing the game of "Yes, I love you, but you are a bitch." It seems to me that it has been a spirited discussion this morning and this afternoon. The discussion was possible only because the people of Pittsburgh have done a really splendid job. I certainly want to go on record as reiterating what I said earlier that I think this is the best job that I have ever seen anywhere.

Footnotes

1. David Braybrooke and Charles Lindblom, *A Strategy of Decision* (New York: Free Press, 1963), pp. 84-86.

7

Response to the Critique:
A Broader Rationale

Objections to the Model

The purpose of the critique of the Discrepancy Evaluation Model was to permit a professional airing of its strengths and weaknesses. Those of us who presented the model were particularly interested in stimulating a discussion between practitioners and theoreticians. Where both agreed, we were ready to give heavy weight to their conclusions. Where they disagreed, we would give careful thought to reconciling these differences through a clearer description of the model, its purposes, and the nature of the problems to which it was addressed. In either event, clear directions for revision of the model would be in order.

An inspection of chapters 4 and 5 suggests that most of the objections raised can be grouped in three major areas: (1) assumptions of the model, (2) operation of the model, and (3) benefits of the model. In each area there were some points of agreement by both theoreticians and practitioners.

Under the category *assumptions of the model*, there was considerable agreement, or at least no serious disagreement, among conference participants that:

(1) The model and its stages were without adequate rationale.

(2) A needs assessment or context evaluation is an essential first stage found lacking in the model.

(3) New program ideas from all sources should be considered by a staff before it initiates a new program, and the evaluation of these ideas is an essential early phase of any evaluation.

(4) The model may constrict or limit the creative, adaptive responsiveness of a program staff because of its imposition of behavioral standards.

(5) One can never adequately anticipate the design of a program in sufficient detail to permit its use as a standard. Yet, this appears to be an assumption of the model.

(6) There is no clear way to validate the criteria a decision maker must use to choose between alternatives available under the model.

(7) The model requires a close working relationship between evaluator, program manager, and teachers. Yet, given the dynamics of most school systems, conflicts in interests, affiliations, and values appear inevitable when the model is applied.

(8) Decision makers are not always rational, yet the model assumes such behavior.

(9) The model is not capable of evaluating rapid, large-scale changes.

(10) The audience for evaluation under the model is not clear. Can the model really serve the information needs of all parties interested in public education—students, teachers, parents, program managers, superintendents, board members, state legislators, federal staffers, and congressmen?

Under the category *operation of the model*, conference participants seemed to agree that there was more need to ask:

(11) Exactly what kind of information is collected at each stage?

(12) How is this information used by the decision maker?

(13) How can research findings contribute to program development under this model?

(14) How feasible is staff consensus?

(15) What data collection, processing, and analysis capacity is required to operate the model?

(16) How are evaluators recruited, trained, and supported in the system?

Under the category *benefits of the model*: we were asked:

(17) Can the model evaluate more than one program at a time? Can it evaluate the efficiency and quality of relationships between programs and foster the strengthening of these relationships?

(18) Can the model monitor the effects of an entire school system?

(19) Can it compare programs on use of resources other than money, such as scarce personnel, and outcomes other than academic achievement, such as political values?

(20) Does the model provide for serendipity?

Some of these questions are outside the scope of the model, but are all related to its use by any practitioner. For every one of these questions a specific answer has been formulated in this chapter. The basis for answering these questions was found in a more thorough examination of the conceptual structure underlying the model. That structure is provided here and rests on the nature of problem-solving in institutional settings—more specifically, on an analysis of (a) decisionmaking, (b) criteria, and (c) field conditions as defined in systems terminology. This frame of reference provides the larger rationale for the model, which was called for at the symposium but not presented there.

The Search for New Constructs

Interest in evaluation derives from a desire to provide the "best possible" educational programs and from a skepticism about present programs. We evaluate on the assumption that a problem exists, that a solution can be found, and that evaluation will aid in the solution process. It is this understanding of evaluation as part of the problem-solving process that constitutes the only adequate rationale for an evaluation system that supports decisionmaking. Therefore it is necessary to examine the problem-solving process more fully and to study the basis on which one chooses between alternatives.

Problem solving and decisionmaking can be equated if one defines the latter as a choice between alternatives to serve some purpose. That is, decisionmaking occurs when two or more objects are distinguished from each other for some purpose. When objects are distinguished from each other without purpose, discrimination rather than decisionmaking occurs. This is the same basis on which problem-solving activity may be distinguished from other forms of human work and activity: the making of a choice to serve some purpose. Hence, we equate problem solving with decisionmaking. A large and convenient body of literature on problem solving and decisionmaking is thereby opened to us.

Much of this literature is based on the study of individuals. Care must therefore be exercised in applying this literature to the focus of our own interest: institutional decisionmaking. However, just as there is literature of perception,[1] exploration,[2] and insight that applies to individuals and the basis for personal choice, so there is a

body of literature that deals with the social and institutional framework within which the individual acts to solve problems and with the
interaction effect of individual and environment.[3] Finally, there is a
somewhat more recent body of literature dealing with how any
institution is subject to constraining and complex field boundaries
and how these boundaries may be analyzed and rationally controlled.[4]

On consideration, the major weaknesses of the Discrepancy Evaluation Model, as revealed by the Los Angeles symposium,
seem to stem from our failure to understand the limits on institutional behavior set by field conditions, the intricacies of the decisionmaking process, and the origin and use of criteria in that process.
Questions raised at the symposium concerning the validity of the
model's stages, the depth of staff understanding of criteria, the
extent to which we can anticipate the stability of staff expectation as
a standard, the method of determining the kind of information needed
at each stage of the model, the need or lack of need for a data base,
the feasibility of achieving design consensus, and desirable characteristics of the evaluator himself, will be answered on the basis of our
ability to describe the process that brings criteria into existence and
ensures their relevance.

Questions concerning the possibility of the model stifling teacher
creativity and program flexibility, the inadequacy of initial program
designs, the lack of an adequate research base in the early phases of a
program, the irrationality of decision makers, conflicts of social
system and reward system, and the failure of the model to report
positive as well as negative discrepancy, will be answered depending
on our ability to understand the convoluted (two steps forward, one
step backward) process of human decisionmaking.

Finally, questions concerning the desirability of "needs" study or
context evaluation before Stage 1, the proper audience for an evaluation, the relationships of simultaneous programs and a program's
goals to larger school system goals, and the basis for assigning
resources (all of which pertain to the multiple levels of operation and
span of control within the system in which an evaluation occurs) will
be answered by means of our ability to analyze the boundary
conditions of systems and subsystems to which the model is applied.

The Decisionmaking Process

The evaluation model is a problem-solving model. It is predicated
on four basic steps in the solution of any problem: (1) identify,
(2) compare, (3) choose, and (4) act in accordance with choice. Each

of these steps in turn reveals the existence of a new problem and requires the creation of a system to solve that problem through identification, comparison, choice, and action. For each step, one or more sets of steps may be generated, leading not to solution but to more problems.

The model's stages assume that problems will arise at many points in the development of an educational program (which is a solution to a problem) and that these same four steps are repeated at least once at each stage and may be repeated many times in a given stage. The role of evaluation in the problem-solving process is to limit the number of problem-solving steps required for solution by facilitating a rational compromise between the decision maker's values and the real world he is trying to control. The scientific method provides us with research canons that systematically mitigate between hunch and reality by testing (comparing or evoking) definitions and choices. Our task is to understand the relationship between problem solving, evaluation, and research activity.

Man's nature is the starting point for understanding problem solving, as attested to by men like John Dewey, William James, and Kurt Goldstein. Studies of man reveal an organism whose major preoccupation is with the creation and solution of problems. Whether we call man researcher, evaluator, manipulator, or clown, he is consumed with and continuously engaged in the process of solving problems. The general process has been defined by countless persons in verbal, artistic, and analytic forms. All of these definitions include the somewhat expanded list of steps:

(1) Sensing a problem,

(2) Defining the major elements of the problem,

(3) Reorganizing the elements,

(4) Devising alternative courses of action to solve the problems,

(5) Choosing between alternatives,

(6) Acting in accordance with choice, and

(7) Reappraising the original problem and/or formulating new problems.[5]

Each of these steps in turn contains a set of design, choice, and action alternatives. Rational human activity is predicated on this same sequence of behavior: Man, as rational problem solver, can be found imbedded in a nested, continuous chain of these processes. Just as an isotope can be used to track the flow of some agent through a plant, so a man could theoretically be tracked through a complex flow of processes to his position at any given point in time in a complex decisionmaking web of problems. Someday a psychoanalytic computer may do this for us.

Even quiescent man must constantly monitor the world to sense problems. So he, too, is engaged in at least the first step of the decisionmaking process. And in carrying out that step, he must, again, go through the nested processes of design, choose, and act.

We cannot overemphasize that each of the four stages of the decisionmaking process contains in turn a design, choice, and action component, because the critical question for man as a problem-solver in any step of the process is, "On what basis do I choose?"

In the decisionmaking process, we first choose some information from an infinity of phenomena, then we choose some alternatives, and then we choose between alternatives. The basis for choosing information and alternatives derives from the same standard or criterion used to choose between alternatives that arise at each step in the problem-solving process. To arrive at the ultimate basis for choice in regard to these alternatives one must be able to solve the "criterion problem."

To estimate the value of anything, it is necessary to establish one or more standards against which the thing is compared. In agronomy, an egg is grade A or B, more or less valuable, depending on how it compares with the standard for grade A egg or grade B egg. These standards exist as idealized, immutable models in the Department of Agriculture. In education, standards as ideal models are more difficult to come by, but they constitute the same essential basis for all evaluation. To define these ideal models is to solve the criterion problem in education.

We must now decide in our society what we shall use as standards in education, and the nature of the ideal models from which they derive. The models of social value we carry around in our hearts and heads must now be explicated, whether they originate in fairy tales or television tubes. Ideal models come from personal experience, written knowledge, expectation, socialization, culture, authority, tyranny, or fear.

Today, those who are being evaluated demand that they determine the values that give rise to the standard against which they will be compared. The democratization of our institutions seems to mean that people will make decisions for themselves and that, as decision makers, they alone will determine the standards against which they are to be compared.

All standards regardless of how derived, are descriptions of an idealized representation of what a thing or process "should be." All are criteria for choice, depending on the level of analysis one uses when applying them. All criteria derive from value and knowledge, and value gives them their utility. We will use the term *criterion model* to designate that "ideal" view of the world or some minute aspect of the world that man employs to understand, explore, or shape his "real" world. Criterion models, then, are the explication of our values, usually unquestioned. They can also be the result of self-conscious tests of assumptions, consequences, and costs. They should always be based on dream as well as reality to make our dreams more likely to come true through research, evaluation, and any other human problem-solving activity.

Considerable misconception about evaluation has resulted from our failure to make clear distinctions between research and evaluation processes. They play complementary parts in a single decision-making process, but they are not to be equated. Rather, research is defined as an activity that creates criterion models, and evaluation is defined as an activity that uses criterion models.

Now, obviously, what is a scientist's discovery today is his cookbook recipe tomorrow. We create criterion models in order to use them, hence we are all in the research business of creating criterion models and the evaluation business of using them. The researcher is an evaluator and the evaluator is a researcher. But, as problem-solving functions, these operations are distinguishable.

How are these distinctions made operative from the perspective of an enlightened manager or school administrator? The decision maker lives in a network of problems that he attempts to solve by making decisions. The problem-solving process begins with an awareness of a discrepancy between what "should be" and "what is," between a standard (S) and performance (P). To correct the discrepancy between S and P, either S or P may be changed. The decision maker will generally try to change P. To change P requires a new performance or correction method for which there must be a new standard (S_2), against which the new performance or correction method (P_2) may be compared. If the decision maker's efforts to change P are frustrated, or if he has been careful to question the assumptions of his original standard (the fit between his dream and reality), then he will address himself to changing S. To change S, the decision-maker will either execute a structural analysis of S, or he will summarily reject and replace it, in which case a new standard must be found or created (S_a). Usually S will be analyzed before being rejected. Analysis consists of explication and elaboration of the type propounded by Gagne and Silvern.[6] So, more specific referents of the type S_1, S_2, and S_3 are teased out to make available more specific performance data P_1, P_2, and P_3. Generally, when these subcomparisons are made, one or more discrepancies are found. To correct these discrepancies involves the same process as in S-P comparisions. That is, an S_2 correction method will be needed. Again it must be found or created.

Notice in all of this that the decision-making process at the most general level consists of S-P comparision, analysis of standards, execution of change in performance, and the discovery of new standards. These four basic operations—compare, analyze, act or manipulate, and define or discover—are, of course, the same four problem-solving steps we studied earlier in somewhat different sequence and form. Discovery is "definition," which now appears last rather than first, but which will establish the same basis for comparison as previously. Similarly, "manipulation" is "action," which gives rise to discovery or new definition, and "analyze" is discrimination with purpose, *i.e.*, choice. At the microlevel, anyone involved in making a decision has a criterion model with which some bit of phenomena is compared, the reason for discrepancy is determined by analysis, which leads to a criterion model for remedial action that in turn leads to new definitions of either the original phenomena or the original criterion model. At the macrolevel, responsibility for these steps is divided between members of the organization who seek to rationalize decisions.

Generally, the comparison function is evaluation; the manipulation function is management; the discovery function is research; and the analysis function is essential to and part of all three. In the Discrepancy Evaluation Model, we have defined the evaluator's role responsibilities to include the comparison and analysis functions. Discovery and analysis of standards are the province of the researcher, and management is concerned with analysis and manipulation. Note that analysis is a necessary tool used by all. Unless the functions of comparison, manipulation, and discovery share the function of analysis, they are not likely to produce solutions, and their operation will be inefficient. Notice also that to execute any of these steps, all decisionmaking steps will have to be negotiated within that step. Whether the work of these nested steps is again subdivided between evaluating, research, and management within an organization and assigned by function, is a question that must be resolved in any real situation. Obviously, team experience and personal satisfaction from team rather than individual problem solving is a factor here. At the lowest level of microanalysis, however, the individual must have control over all four steps. At all higher levels of analysis the individual need only be aware of the place of his work in the total problem-solving system.

Until we understand that evaluation depends on helping to explicate a standard and its underlying values, comparing phenomena with
that standard, and assessing the difference, we will labor under a
variety of misconceptions about the place of research and evaluation
in problem solving. For example, we may forget that measurement is
for the purpose of precise description and comparison, that inferential statistics helps us determine the meaningfulness of observed
differences and that both measurement and statistics are aids to the
comparison step in the decisionmaking process. If we remember that
this step occurs and recurs in the nested decision-making network, it
is foolish to talk of experimental design or measurement techniques
as though they were modes of evaluation in competition with other
modes of evaluation. Obviously, experimental design is a way of
determining the meaningfulness of a comparison, and the principles
of good design may be employed many ways, at many times, in the
process of solving a problem.

But for the problem solver in the public schools, political questions are usually more important that psychometric ones. In public
schools, as in most other institutions, models and standards derive
from the decision maker's willingness to analyze his values, and the
evaluator and the researcher work to serve those values. That is not
to say, however, that they cannot or should not question the values.
Indeed, neither evaluator nor researcher can perform his respective
functions unless these values have been explicated, analyzed, and even
challenged to ensure the decision maker's confidence in their defensi-
bility. However, in the process of institutional problem solving, a
metavalue must be relatively constant and acceptable to all participants while they are in "the process."

Criteria

The term *criteria* has long been equated with precise measurement
in the field of evaluation. Traditionally, one formulates goals, analyzes them into performance objectives, and then establishes levels of
performance or standards, which are called criteria. The profession
has been so preoccupied with measurement problems that the more
basic meaning of criteria in evaluation methodology has been overlooked: Criteria are the basis on which choice is made. It is indeed
true that to choose between students on some performance task,
criteria in the form of some point on a scale of values may be needed.
However, it is also true that to choose the task requires criteria, as
does a choice between needs, programs, and their clients. These
choices require criteria in a broader sense of the word then is used by

measurement people. It requires an awareness of one's basis for choice in any decisionmaking situation.

The decision maker seeks to bring "what is" into accordance with "what should be." A problem or reason for making a decision originally comes into the awareness of the decision maker on the basis of this same discrepancy. The task of the rational decision maker is to submit his belief about what should be and the real world of what is to objective analysis so that he can decide on a course of action that will make them congruent with each other. It is the evaluator's task to facilitate the administrator's need for the analysis and action required to solve a problem. The evaluator does this by providing relevant information, by guiding the decision maker through the steps of the decisionmaking process (helping him collect and interpret the information he needs), and by sensitizing him to decisions required by the process as they arise.

But first the occasion for choice must be identified. The interaction of the decision maker's knowledge with his values—what we might call his "frame of reference"—both makes him aware that a problem has arisen and forms the basis for the solution of his problem.

The fully explicated frame of reference, with the decision procedures it delineates, is what we call the criterion model and what we posit here as the solution to the criterion problem. A model, in this sense, is an idealized representation of the real world—the platonic essence of what should be. Analytic man monitors the real world and uses his model of what should be as a standard with which he can compare what actually is, so that when a discrepancy between his real world and his ideal world occurs, he knows about it. Once he knows about it he has identified a need for change: in other words, a problem. Problems imply desired solutions. Solutions are effected through decision activity, and that activity requires generating alternatives and choosing between them.

Given a problem, a model is both implied and must be made explicit before any problem can be defined or solved. Model is used in the sense of a blueprint or a "miniature drawn according to scale of something to be built or already in existence."[7] As an idealized construct of reality, a model is superior to reality and represents a rational standard for the measurement of reality. Therefore, a model represents a standard in the sense that a model of a grade A Jonathan apple exists in the Department of Agriculture or a cube of steel exists in the Bureau of Standards.

The derivation of a criterion model in the applied social sciences is obviously a matter of considerable import. Models are derived from knowledge criteria, value criteria, and prudential criteria.

Knowledge Criteria

Neither a problem nor a question can be formulated by man without reference to a body of knowledge. Man's heritage of organized information about the world in which he lives constitutes one essential form of reference for selecting a model and identifying information in the real world relative to its use. For example, knowledge criteria for identifying a suitable model for dealing with the question "Should I build a home?" has to do with the mass of accumulated knowledge and technical information available on home building. The problem of selecting from among this knowledge and of identifying criteria to do so is a second order problem to be dealt with only peripherally in this book.

Value Criteria

Quite apart from the knowledge that gives rise to a question and is essential to its answer are the attitudes of men toward the importance of the question and the relative value of its alternative answers. There can be no value without knowledge, but there can be no knowledge used as a model or standard unless that knowledge has the value of serving some purpose. The selection of a model as a standard requires that the web of value or affect associated with particular knowledge be thoroughly explored in any given situation and that estimates be made of public and private opinions, power structure vectors, and the mores of a given community, as the basis for the selection of a model. How these forces are weighed prudentially is a second order problem to be dealt with later.

Prudence Criteria

Once a model has been selected based on value and knowledge criteria, it may require modification because of conflict between the value consequences of its application and other values of the decision maker. Although a problem is defined by one or more values, other values may exist in a large web of value that are not entirely unified or consistent. When the probable consequence of a choice jeopardizes any part of the value web, prudence is required and probability estimates are needed to establish the level of risk involved in exercising prudential criteria.

Second Order Problems

Let us review all of the major steps in the decisionmaking process. Given dissonance that leads to a problem, these steps are:

(1) Derive model from (a) knowledge criteria, (b) value criteria, and (c) prudential criteria;

(2) Derive reality from (a) relevant information, (b) knowledge of data handling capacity of system, and (c) data actually generated;

(3) Produce discrepancy information;

(4) Choose between alternative categories of action; and

(5) Use resulting states of "what is" and "what should be" to generate a new "what should be" standard (recycle).

Such a model is obviously incomplete for at least two reasons. First, it is oversimplified and conceals a host of intervening events in the decisionmaking process. Each of the nine major steps described above represents a point where problems may arise and enabling decisions may be required. That is, each of these steps (we call them second order steps here) may be the occasion for decisionmaking within the decisionmaking process. These subloops require their own criteria and models used as standards and hence are nested replicas of the model. The importance of these second order steps or loops cannot be overlooked in the analysis of decisionmaking because, although the process steps are the same, their content will vary with the nature of a problem, the process step at which a second order problem arises, and the level of decisionmaking analysis ultimately required. (Third to nth level problems and loops are possible though constrained by practical considerations.)

Secondly, the model fails to illustrate the basis on which a choice is made between categories of action alternatives. Given discrepancy information as a result of congruence testing, the administrator uses some set of criteria to choose between changing reality, changing the model, or making no change. Further, if he chooses to change reality, he must have available a means of generating change alternatives and choosing among them. These shortcomings in the model can again be traced to its level of generalization.

The first shortcoming can be dealt with through an examination of innumerable steps that go beyond the scope of this book. The second shortcoming, that of no clear basis for action, derives from the analytical nature of the model. Another model, one dealing with action, must be used if the administrator is to act as well as understand. The analysis model is a replica of what can be done. The action model is a replica of what is done.

The action model might be seen as a mirror image of the analysis model with a comparable point in the model of action for each major point in the model of analysis. Taken together, these dimensions comprise an analysis-action model. Each step in the analysis model is followed by the comparable step in the action model. In the course of dealing with any problem there will be continuous movement back and forth across these dimensions.

The description of decisionmaking at the level of second order steps can now be recognized as a complex network based on relatively simple constructs. At each stage of every level, questions can be raised, about what can be done and what is done, and each decision will require its own criteria. The steps that provide criteria at a first order level themselves require second order or higher level criteria as well.

If the operation of these models is ever to be thoroughly understood, there appears to be no alternative but that someday someone must study the second order decisionmaking loops at each step in the action and analysis dimensions. Since these loops themselves contain action and analysis dimensions, we are confronted with a topology of three dimensions, two of which contain three dimensions within them that in turn mirror the same topological configuration to infinity.

It is not within the scope of this book to attempt such a detailed description but rather to establish the framework in which the description will some day be carried out. Like a convoluted mirror house that reflects the patterned complexity of man's mind, the topology, and the steps and levels of criteria it implies, may indeed represent the basis on which human decisions are made. If so, it establishes the prime assumptions of evaluation—formal or informal—whether for individuals or institutions.

Technical Criteria

Once a criterion model has been defined by the decision maker it gives rise to management operations that attempt to shape the world in the image of the model. The evaluation of these operations and their products depends on the same criterion model. The model is used both to identify relevant performance data and as the basis for determining the adequacy of performance. Adequacy is determined by predicating that performance is isomorphic with the criterion model and that observed differences between observed performance and expected performance are indices of inadequacy. The comparison of expected values with performance values obviously involves sampling and measurement of errors which give rise to the need for inferential statistics. As soon as the need for inferential statistics is recognized, a whole new set of decision criteria are imposed by the generalizable knowledge, value, and prudential wisdom of statisticians, experimental design experts, and psychometricians.

Criteria for choosing methods of sound measurement and comparison in order to avoid unwarranted conclusions always apply to an evaluation. But a recognition of their proper place and the commonsense form they may take is as important as a knowledge of their subtleties. Even when complex, statistical assumptions and methods of analysis are always an adjunct to, not the essence of, conclusions about discrepancy information.

Criteria for Decisionmaking under the Model

To employ criteria under the Discrepancy Evaluation Model, one must take into account the program development stage one is in and the nature of the operation or product that is being evaluated.

At each stage of the evaluation model it is necessary to decide whether a program should be continued or terminated. This determination is based on (1) the value of its products or outcomes, (2) the success of its developmental operations or process achievements, (3) the availability of relevant data, and (4) the technical adequacy of the collection and interpretation of this data.

The determination of whether a program has been successfully installed is based in part on decisions made during the design phase of the program, in part on judgment of what information about a program is relevant, and in part on a knowledge of how to collect and interpret this data. A decision about whether a program has been adequately designed is based in part on "need" or problem during a planning phase or program development and in part on knowledge of design specification and what activities are needed to achieve these specifications.

The Systems Concept

We have seen how evaluation serves problem solving or decisionmaking and is in turn dependent on the generation of criteria that define standards and identify performance data to be compared with standards.

As a practical matter, decisionmaking usually seeks to control one or more aspects of the real world. We are concerned here with decisionmaking as an institutional activity that has a defined span of control and limited resources. All educational programs are defined to affect a target group using limited goods and services. Therefore, the manager of a program is by definition a decisionmaker subject to conditions that limit his purpose and his selection of a criterion model. The study of these limiting conditions is essential to an understanding of how any real program develops, how decisions are made, how criteria are generated, and how evaluation operates. Program conditions are defined by a set of nested, permeable boundaries, which in turn define a system. The system concept occupies an important place in the rationale for the Discrepancy Evaluation Model.

Within any large or complex operation, suboperations can be identified through analysis so that a chain of related events can be so described as to show the flow of inputs to outputs for any suboperation. For example, in sending a letter to a friend, the sender must (1) locate his friend's address, (2) find paper, envelope, and pen, (3) write the letter, (4) fold and seal the letter, (5) stamp it, (6) write the mailing and return address on the letter, and (7) deposit it in the mailbox at the street corner.

An analysis of the resources required to effect each step (Figure 1) shows that some resources are derived from the previous step and some from elsewhere.

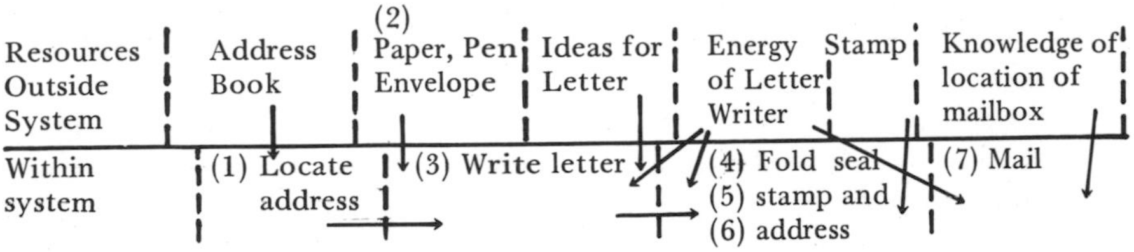

Figure 1

On the basis of the origin of resources alone it is possible to define a system. However, the span of control of resources available to an operator or manager is obviously pertinent to what he will produce and how he will produce it. Further, the identification of his products or goals is obviously the reason the operation and the need to define a system of inputs and outputs exist in the first place. Clearly, a number of conditions from outside the system help to define it. Therefore, to facilitate the understanding of an operation we divide it into logical parts or suboperations and define their conditions to establish a span of control of each operation, the goal of the operation, and the resources of the operation.

If thousands of letters were written each day it is likely that at least some of the suboperations described in Figure 1 would be "systematized" by establishing a limited goal and resources for the conduct of each basic event in the letter-sending chain. So, for example, one person might have the goal of producing names and addresses, using as input an address book, human energy, some form of mechanism such as a typewriter, and paper. The product—a typed address list—meets the goal conditions of the system within the limits of the available resource. The manager's span of control is clearly circumscribed; his system is defined. But clearly his system is also part of a larger system—the one for which his product serves as an input. The larger system may be composed of many smaller systems and may in turn exist to satisfy one or more still larger systems.

The definition of the ultimate purpose of the largest system served by all other systems raises the criterion problem, which, if resolved, defines the boundaries within which all lower order systems will operate. The resources available to the sum of all subsystems will then be known as will their ultimate purpose. However, the particular allocation of any part of the total resource and the specific outputs it will produce, as well as the purpose these outputs will serve in the overall system, are not determined by goal setting. Instead, new subgoals must be chosen based on criteria that take into account purpose, a knowledge of production techniques, and an estimate of the value consequences of choice (prudence).

It is therefore obvious that in any practical situation, a clear knowledge of an organization's goals is essential to an efficient partitioning of functions and authority into subsystems responsible for essential interim events or outputs. Logical analysis is also necessary to the identification of these functional subsystems, as is an awareness of subsystem values, technology, and prudential considerations. However, at both macro and microlevel, goals, values, and consequences can only be partially defined. They are in a constant state of emergence through the incremental experience of the decision maker. The more we know of them, the more precise our work can be. When they are totally defined only routine operations remain.

The concept of "system" can help us understand conditions affecting problem solving, program development and evaluation at any level of control within an organization. The manager of any large organization, such as a school system, will attempt to determine the goals of the system before subsystem program goals are established, program operations are defined, and school system resources are allocated. To do this, he must ask what ends are best for the school system. The criteria needed to provide and test an answer to this question are derived from knowledge of what a community needs to survive, and the social, political, and economic values of the community served by the system.

Value criteria are the first consideration. If new money has just been given to a district, its use will reflect a consciously perceived or vaguely felt discrepancy between expected educational attainment and actual attainment. In some cases formal assessment will be needed to identify the discrepancy between what should be and what is. This discrepancy represents the educational needs of the community and establishes the purpose or goal of the educational activity, program, or programs to be mounted to meet the community's educational purposes.

But the school system already serves other educational purposes than the resolution of the particular needs identified through assessment. The relationship of the purpose of a new program to the larger system's purposes should be understood if conflicts in purpose and function are not to occur.

The school system can be defined as meeting the community's needs for the education of all its members (output) through the conversion (processing) of community and national resources (input). The school system can be so divided into subunits that one or more input-process-output subunits that use the larger system's resources and contribute to its outputs may be identified. For instance, if a school program is to produce students who can read at grade level, required resources will include teachers, students, books, and processes that control interactions of these resources in order to yield expected output. However, the preparation of an input like the selection of a reading textbook may require identification of the subsystem that uses teachers at a more specific level as resource, a library index card as additional input, a decision by the teacher as process, and the selection of a particular book as output, all of which contribute to the creation of a resource, a particular input to the larger system.

Interrelated subsystems may be found in any part of a system. Inputs to a subsystem will be from the outputs of other subsystems and from the higher order systems. The input to the higher order system is defined to include inputs to all subsystems. Subsystem inputs may come from a system at the same level, a higher level, or the same level of organization. Each of these levels of systems in turn include their own subsystems.

Some inputs must always come from outside the system. These inputs suggest the existence of systems that are not defined as higher or lower order parts of the basic system and are therefore outside the system. The definition of a boundary that circumscribes some systems and excludes other systems is an essential and inevitable convenience for studying and controlling any activity or operation whether it be a conversation, the production of the world's food supply, or the conduct of a school reading program.

Subsystems are primarily designed to provide outputs that are ultimately used as inputs to a higher order system. (Outputs of systems will also furnish input to other subsystems and to inputs of systems outside the higher order system.) Hence, in the main, higher order systems control the inputs and outputs of lower order systems.

When a school system or state conducts a needs assessment study, it is usually trying to define the inputs and outputs of the higher level system served by all subsystems. Given no desire for change in a higher level output, the need study at a lower level becomes a matter of defining inputs that are better than existing inputs at this level. The use of the word *better* in the last sentence immediately suggests the need for criteria to select possible inputs.

If the outputs of a higher order system are to be changed, then they must be changed before outputs at a lower level can be defined. As with subsystem outputs, higher level outputs may be changed to serve the input or output needs of a still higher level system. It can be seen that this is a continuous process. As long as outputs at a higher or ultimate level are undefined, outputs at a lower level must remain undefined. Once outputs at the highest level are defined, a choice can be made of the "best" inputs at that level, and outputs at the next lower level can be made to optimize higher level input. Optimization is the logical end of "good" systems management. But logic is insufficient.

Obviously, the ultimate end of nested systems at various levels is a value matter. It is predicated on the goal that is most worth attaining or for which all activity is ordered. The ultimate purpose is of the same stuff as ultimate criteria. Ultimate criteria take on the characteristics of an Aristotelian First Cause. Somehow there is a sequence that comes full circle; the beginning is also the end. From beginning to end, from smallest to largest, these dynamic movements are somehow frozen in a fixed, absolute system, which encompasses them and represents the limits of our knowledge.

What is important from a management point of view is to recognize that a change in any input, output, or process is likely to effect the input and output of some other part of the total system. Perspective is everything in managing change. If the decision maker sees the immediate utility of a substitution of one input for another but overlooks the consequence of this choice on the output of a lower order subsystem or the input of the same order system, considerable damage may be done to the larger system. Decisions within a given area of authority must therefore be constrained to prevent damage to the system. Therefore, managers are generally given a span of operations control defined by the resources they must use and the product they must produce. This systems boundary ensures that the conditions under which they operate are compatible with those of the larger system and all other subsystems.

In the area of conversion of resources or the processing of inputs to outputs, managers may generally exercise great latitude of discretion. Thus, process is in the hands of a program manager and staff, while input and output conditions are defined by the larger system (macrosystem) of which they are a part. However, the ultimate consequence of optimization is a static system in which management can play no role at its given level of authority for changing the metavalues of the system.

Any process is implicitly composed of microsystems of input, process, and output. For example, the actual process of writing involves hand and eye movements coordinated by thought to produce strings of words, each of which can be viewed as a function of a subsystem. Logical analysis can identify these subsystems in great detail and management can assign responsibility for their operation to the span of control of an existing management authority or to new authority. In any event, the discovery or creation of subsystems through logical analysis is often necessary to the mastery and control of an operation and the attainment of the larger system's goals.

It is this same method of logical analysis, task analysis, or work breakdown that has proven most successful in the creation of new learning sequences (operations) to facilitate student mastery of learning. To the extent systems are subject to rigorous control, they use minimal inputs to produce only anticipated outputs. To achieve this control, efficient managers of systems usually define the input and output conditions of all systems within their span of authority. The boundary of a basic system is defined to exclude and include certain categories of resources and to indicate the relationship of the system to all other systems in terms of the flow of input and output.

Therefore systems analysis defines the sequence of flow on input-output operations at various levels of activity within a macrosystem with reasonably final, though undoubtedly and inevitably permeable boundaries. (Truly closed systems exist only in laboratories and toys.)

The Discrepancy Evaluation Model facilitates the analysis of program performance through input, process, and output functions; systems flow or sequence over defined intervals of time; and managerial levels of activity required to furnish outputs to some larger system in order to serve higher order purposes. Moreover, it facilitates institutional change by permitting decisions to be made on criteria other than suboptimization and by permitting goals and values to be changed or at least influenced at any management level.

A definition of program expectation should take these components, sequence, and levels into account. Similarly they must be understood by the decision maker at those points in problem-solving activity when criteria are being formulated and applied. To the extent one can conceptualize a problem in relation to tangential problems—a system in relation to other systems, as well as its subsystems—one has a sufficiently commanding perspective to be close to omniscient. On the other hand, when one examines a problem without knowledge of its larger framework and smaller parts, one's plans and actions will be tentative and more human.

The evaluator who seeks to be a watchdog for the adequacy of standards must be as constantly on the alert for the levels problem as he is for the criterion problem. Although there can be no absolute and ultimate criteria, there can be conscious knowledge of the basis for using criteria, and although one cannot be totally aware of the intricacy of systems, one can be vigilant to the inevitable and contingent relationships of systems.

A frequent dilemma in institutional decisionmaking or curriculum development arises when an intervention or change in one part of a system is made without reference to higher order and lower order systems impinging on the system being changed. Large organizations in industry often avoid this dilemma by establishing firm subsystem boundaries and mechanisms for ensuring that managers adhere to the conditions established by these boundaries. However, less formal organizations or individuals are not so constrained, and decisions that pass for constructive change on one day in one sphere of activity, over time and from a different vantage point, turn out to be counterproductive. Innumerable school innovations appear to belong in this category. When these errors occur, because of ignorance of relationships between systems at various levels, a levels problem exists. Solution of a levels problem depends first on an awareness of the nature of the problem and then on an analysis of subsystems and boundary definitions, and finally on the somewhat arbitrary but firm assignment of subsystem operations authority to one management sphere of control or another.

Review of Objections to the Model

On the basis of the preceding discussion, it should now be possible to respond to each of the major questions raised at the AERA symposium. To facilitate this response we shall review the objections raised at the beginning of this chapter.

(1) The model and the stages are without an adequate rationale.

The rationale for the model is based firmly on the nature of human and institutional problem solving and the functions of comparison and feedback in the problem-solving process. Because programs are developed in response to institutional needs, their planning, installation, and control are natural and cyclical phases of the problem-solving process that require evaluation activity. The first three stages of the model ensure the natural progress of a program through the basic problem-solving activity of definition of criterion model, installation, and control through comparison of operation with standard derived from criterion model. Within each of these three stages of the model, the same problem-solving steps are required to further explicate criteria, install or take action, and control or correct action through comparison. The three major structural dimensions of any program—input, process, and output—so define the system's boundary for a program and its subsystems that program development or problem solving may be subjected to more precise analysis and control.

The fourth stage of the model assumes that the institutional problem has been solved but asks whether the solution (program) is generalizable. And the optional fifth stage of the model asks whether other generalizable solutions are available at less cost for the same or greater benefits. The first three stages contribute to the creation of a new and successful program by giving emphasis to the shaping of values that define new program designs just as values contribute to the shaping of a criterion model. The fourth and fifth stages provide a basis for choosing between programs aimed at solving an educational problem: The fourth stage is required to satisfy the knowledge criterion, and the fifth stage is required to satisfy the prudence or estimate of consequence criterion. The prime criterion, value, continues to operate at all stages of program development and is lodged in the private or public consciousness of the decision maker, depending on his rationality and openness.

The last two stages of the model close the circle on program development as institutional problem solving by returning the decision maker to the problem situation context in which he began. As with all problem solving, the original problem will be redefined or solved and a host of new questions will have been raised.

(2)   A needs assessment stage should be added to the model.

The model does not ignore the context in which program development occurs. Indeed, since the model sees program development as problem solving, it constantly forces the program staff to test their assumptions and constructs against reality. However, the model argues against a formal test of the conditions that give rise to the need for a program. A formal assessment is both artificial and doomed to the error of serious omission because of the limited experience of the staff making the study. The staff, as any problem solver knows, starts where it is. It does not yet know what criteria to employ in selecting information from the context. It cannot establish criteria on theroretical or introspective grounds. Rather, it must gradually immerse itself in the nest of problem-solving loops that facilitate the careful construction of a tentative, operating, experimental program subject to constant revision through Stages 2 and 3 of the model. Through this process the staff acquires the knowledge and insight necessary to understand what is important in the context and what is not, what must be accepted, what may be controlled, and what can probably be ignored. The ultimate justification for a context evaluation imbedded in program development rather than antecedent to it is therefore dependent on its efficiency.

(3)   New program ideas from all sources should be considered by a staff before it initiates a new program.

This objection is compatible with the model but goes beyond its assumptions. The model posits nothing about the origin of a program design. A program design may have been carefully chosen from many, or it may have been tossed together at a dinner speech. The only condition of the model is that the ideas in a given program be carefully examined and reconstructed if necessary as a function of Stage 1 design work. The history of a program design is less important that its present form and substance, just as in client-centered therapy the genesis of emotional disorder is less important than the adequacy of present behavior and self-concept. The model does assume that program design is often inadequate, because of poor planning, but when this is not the case, an evaluation can simply move through its design-testing phase rapidly and less expensively than otherwise.

(4) The model can constrict or limit the creative, adaptive responsiveness of a program staff because of its imposition of behavioral standards.

Unfortunately, this objection can be well founded under program conditions foreign to the philosophy of the Discrepancy Evaluation Model. If management uses discrepancy information to force conformity, if standards of behavior are not really formulated by teachers or staff, and if the interpretation of discrepancy information is in the hands of managers rather than practitioners, then an anxiety syndrome can certainly surround the use of the model resulting in constricted behavior on the part of staff. However, where feedback has utility for practitioners without stigma, only the pain of self-awareness and the balm of self-acceptance accompanies the use of the model. The role of a facilitating administration should be obvious here. Support and understanding are the effective mode, not fault-finding and deprecation. Once teachers and administration come to recognize the value of discrepancy information, the staff should experience the greater sense of freedom that is required to change standards and experiment with one's own behavior. Thus, the model can have the stimulating effect of increasing personal creativity and program innovation as was observed in the Chicago Creativity Project.

(5) One can never adequately anticipate the design of a program in sufficient detail to permit its use as a standard. Yet, this appears to be an assumption of the model.

Design is emergent and takes on the detail necessary to later stages of evaluation. The staff or some decision maker always has an initial notion, though perhaps a vague notion of how resources are to be exchanged for benefits, and it is this notion that is the initiating seed of the program design. Whether this seed can produce a full-blown project design capable of meeting criteria of design adequacy and operational feasibility is a pragmatic question the first three stages of the model are intended to answer. Given the nature of criteria, the performance observed under the model is never more precise than the standard that defines it. As the design of a program emerges and the standards of performance become increasingly specific, it is ever more possible to study all of the nuances of a program operation under the design available at any given moment in time. Hence, the variable level of specificity of a design is its greatest assurance of functional value to the program staff.

(6) There is no clear way to validate the criteria decision makers must use to choose between alternatives available under the model.

The answer to this objection remains shrouded in the shadows that edge our analysis of the problem-solving process and decisionmaking criteria. We can only suggest tentative answers to criterion problems. There are three major categories of decisions under the Discrepancy Evaluation Model. The first applies to all decisions that advance the design and development of a program. The second includes the decisions that advance the comparison of standard and performance at each stage of the model as well as decisions to recycle an evaluation stage or go on to the next stage (at least in regard to some component of the design). The third category applies to the staff or management of a program receiving feedback information, that is, whether to continue or expand a program or not, and if so, at what level of support. The first category of decisions requires the application of the general critieria leading to the formulation of a criterion model—prudence, knowledge, and value. The adequacy of these criteria in a given problem situation seems to depend on our knowledge of their completeness relative to available resources and the degree of change required for a solution. The second category of decisions depends on the application of design adequacy criteria in Stage 1, the measurement and interpretation of discrepancy between installation frequency and standards in Stage 2, and the measurement and interpretation of discrepancy between operative performance and standards in Stage 3 as defined under the model. The third set of decisions depends on the emphasis staff and management give to prudential evidence, such as political cost and social considerations, as well as the ability of staff and management to compare the assumptions of the criterion model underlying its standards with actual conditions in the field that the program must be either compatiable with or able to control.

(7) The model requires a close working relationship between evaluator, program manager, and teachers. Yet, given the dynamics of most school systems, conflicts in interests, affiliations, and values appear inevitable when the model is applied.

The rationale of the model does not provide an answer to this objection. The philosophy of the model suggests that a more desirable social system than presently exists in most schools would be both satisfying to teachers and functional to problem solving. Further, the new social system implied by the model would make staff far less dependent on authority for status and other rewards. However, in its present form, the model appears incompatible with an administration that attempts to maintain the traditional social structure of a school system.

(8) Decision makers are not always rational, yet the model assumes such behavior.

Decisionmaking is functional, problem-solving behavior. The model increases the rationality of decision makers by clarifying alternatives and making clear the basis on which decisions are made. Decisionmaking always serves value, and value is neither rational or irrational; it is "arational."

(9) The model is not capable of evaluating rapid, large-scale changes.

To the extent program development and decision criteria are incremental, and evolve from experience, the model will be effective. However, where programs are revolutionary, in that they are without an experiential base, the model is inappropriate. When there is no knowledge of how to convert inputs to outputs, or when this information is completely imposed in an axiomatic and authoritarian manner, there is no value in feedback and only externally imposed standards of output are worth measuring. Of course, if the goals of such a program are not realized, a more rational, contemplative approach to change may prove prudent and necessary, in which case use of the Discrepancy Evaluation Model would again be justified.

(10) The audience for discrepancy information is not clear. Can the model really serve the information needs of all parties interested in public education?

Under the model, discrepancy information has functional utility only for those who are in a position to change or influence performance. When an educational institution and its client population are analyzed to determine operating sphere of influence or scope of authority, it should be possible to define the membership of subsystems that have responsibility for various kinds of performance required under the model. For example, board members may be responsible for making certain kinds of resources available, administrators may be responsible for providing such preconditions to program operations as facilities, skilled staff, and supportive interpersonal climate; and teachers may be responsible for creating certain kinds of student-teacher interactions. Clearly, students may be given a defined area of responsibility, such as ensuring the establishment, development, and maintenance of many aspects of program performance. Parents, too, may have a defined area of program responsibility.

However, the problem of defining the audience of discrepancy information arises when one identifies the value origin of the program standard and the interest that value reference groups have in discrepancy information. Under the model, only the staff (which includes administrators and practitioners) has the power to define program standards. Now, clearly, most decision makers include the values of public school constituents in their criteria for selecting and modeling program standards. It is the inclusion of this broad public base in standards formulation that poses questions about the proper audience for discrepancy information. The answer to these questions is a matter of public policy and philosophy. An expression of one point of view on this subject is deferred until the last chapter in this book.

(11) Exactly what kind of information is collected at each stage of the model?

The major categories of information called for under the model are the input, process, and output specifications of the design (Stage 1), the input and process performance of the program (Stage 2), the process and output performance of the program (Stage 3), the empirically verified generalizable relationships between the program's inputs and outputs (Stage 4) and the comparability of input-output relationships for several programs serving similar purposes (Stage 5, optional). In addition, summary information is occasionally collected across stages. Finally, an infinite amount of detailed information may be collected to define or test any performance of any particular specification contained in the major design categories. This information is defined and limited by the criterion model and design criteria discussed previously. There is no limit to the variations of information that can be collected under the model. Only categories of information are uniform.

(12) How is this information used by the decision maker?

It isn't. It is used by the evaluator to generate discrepancy information, which has previously defined utility for the decision maker.

(13) How can research findings contribute to program development under this model?

Every time the model casts doubt on program standard, it confronts decision makers with a problem to which there is no readily apparent answer. The wise decision maker turns for solutions to a research and development laboratory or to a research and development unit in the school system if it is available. The model excludes the use of evaluation staff from the creation or selection of new models of excellence because their participation robs the program staff of its proper problem-solving initiative and responsibility and also serves to disqualify the evaluator from rendering an objective description of discrepancy (*i.e.*, from making a disinterested evaluation).

(14) How feasible is staff consensus?

There appears to be nothing in the rationale of the model to provide an answer to this question. Consensus is a desirable condition, but it does not appear to be a prerequisite of the model. For example, it should be possible to define a different set of standards for each group of members who are able to reach consensus about the sphere of operations for which they have responsibility. The provision of these value alternatives within a system, as long as they are compatible with the overall purpose of the system, suggests some philosophically appealing program alternatives when the model is used. The model need not force consensus. Rather, it can be used to identify staff groups holding common values.

(15) What data collection, processing, and analysis capacity is required to employ the model?

By implication, considerable capacity is required. Although some evaluations under the model are going to be largely a matter of commonsense activity, others will call for considerable technical sophistication, particularly at Stages 3 and 4. The strength of the model, however, is that it does not automatically prescribe the use of experimental design and intricate measurement for all projects being evaluated. The model can also help to clarify the specialized competencies to be purchased by an evaluation unit for short periods of time in order to execute a particular phase or stage of an evaluation.

(16) How are evaluators recruited, trained, and supported in the system?

With training assistance available from outside the system, it should be possible to recruit and train evaluators from within the school system. An extensive answer to this question is contained in a wide variety of supplementary information prepared by the author and his associates.[8]

(17-18) Can the model monitor the effects of an entire school system? Can it evaluate more than one program at a time?

Chapters 10 and 11 are devoted to questions of this sort.

(19-20) Can the model compare programs on use of resources other than money? Does the model provide for serendipity?

The model ultimately provides a massive record of the original contributions, change in intentions over time, and actual conse-

quences of all programs to which it is applied. Because the design
criteria of the model apply uniform and comparable categories of
information to programs, it becomes possible to compare the history
of development of programs, their expected and unexpected outcomes, and the various costs at which these outcomes have been
achieved. Under design criteria, the model defines costs only as goods
and services distributed over the variable resources of staff, student,
administration, media, and facility at varying amounts of time and
money. The generality of these resource categories is both their
strength and their weakness in that they leave to each evaluator the
design of relevant subcategories of information, while at the same
time making the evaluation or programs comparable. The model
encourages the recording and assessment of unexpected program outcomes and a cost-benefit analysis at Stage 5, which defines benefit in
the broadest of terms and costs as a wide variety of resources.

Footnotes

1. Karl Dunker, *On Problem Solving* (Evanston, Illinois: The American
Psychological Association, 1945); Abraham S. Luchins, *Mechanization in Problem Solving: The Effect of Einstellung* (Evanston, Illinois: The American
Psychological Association, 1942): Max Wertheimer, *Productive Thinking*, rev.
ed. Michael Wertheimer (New York: Harper and Brothers, 1959).

2. Good examples of this are found in Karl Mannheim's *Sociology of Knowledge*, ed. Palu Kecskemeti (New York: Oxford University Press, 1952) and Carl
Becker's *Heavenly City* (New Haven: Yale University Press, 1932).

3. Gardner Murphy, "The Relationships of Culture and Personality," in
Culture and Personality, eds. S. S. Sargent & Marian W. Smith (New York: The
Viking Fund, 1949), pp. 13-27. Talcott Parsons, *The Social System* (Glencoe,
Illinois: The Free Press, 1951).

4. David I. Cleland, and William R. King, *Systems Analysis and Project
Management* (New York: McGraw-Hill, 1968).

5. See David Russell's *Children's Thinking* (Boston, Ginn, 1956) for a number of such lists of steps.

6. Robert M. Gagne, *Factors in Acquiring Knowledge of a Mathematical Task*
(Princeton, New Jersey: Princeton University, 1962); Leonard C. Silvern, *Ad-
ministrative Factors Guide to Basic Analysis* (Los Angeles: Education and
Training Consultants, 1965).

7. *Harcourt Brace and World Standard College Dictionary*, tech. ed. (New
York: 1963).

8. Available in mimeographed form from The Evaluation Research Center,
University of Virginia.

8

The Revised Model

Introduction

This chapter sets forth the Discrepancy Evaluation Model in its current form on the basis of the AERA critique and intervening experience.[1] The model will no doubt continue to change form and find better means of expression in future years.

Program Evaluation Defined

Program evaluation is the process of (1) defining program standards; (2) determining whether a discrepancy exists between some aspect of program performance and the standards governing that aspect of the program; and (3) using discrepancy information either to change performance or to change program standards. Program management is responsible for the conduct of educational programs and for employing problem-solving techniques once discrepancies between performance and standards have been identified. These techniques have been widely discussed elsewhere and will be referred to here only to indicate their relation to evaluation and management activity.

Under the Discrepancy Evaluation Model, the evaluation of a

program already staffed and under way contains four major developmental stages and three major content categories.

Stages	Content		
	Input	Process	Output
1. Design	Design Adequacy		
2. Installation	Installation Fidelity		
3. Process	Process Adjustment		
4. Product	Product Assessment		
5. Program Comparison	Cost-Benefit Analysis		

Figure 1

Stages 1 through 4 evaluate single programs. As shown in Figure 1, however, there is a fifth, optional stage to facilitate the comparison of two or more programs. The essential work of program evaluation at each stage is shown in the boxes cutting across content categories. The process of evaluation consists of moving through stages and content categories in such a way as to facilitate a comparison between program performance and standards while at the same time identifying standards to be used for future comparisons. This process of comparison at stages is illustrated by the flow chart in Figure 2.

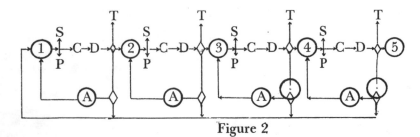

Figure 2

Here S is standard, P is program performance, C is compare, D is discrepancy information, A is change in program performance or standards, and T is terminate. Stage 5 represents the cost-benefit option available to the evaluator only after the first four stages have been negotiated. Notice that the use of discrepancy information always leads to a decision to either (1) go on to the next stage, (2) recycle the stage after there has been a change in the program's standards or operations, (3) recycle to the first stage, or (4) terminate the project. From a program manager's point of view, discrepancy information permits him to pinpoint a shortcoming in the program for one of two purposes: to change the operation of the program, or to change the specifications under which the program operates. A superintendent of schools or board of education will be as concerned with the movement of a project through its evaluation stages as with discrepancy information at any given stage. Usually, the longer it takes to get to the second, third, and fourth stages, the greater the cost if the project fails. The faster a project moves into advanced stages, the less the risk of failure.

At each stage of the model, performance information is obtained and compared with a standard that serves as the criterion for judging the adequacy of that performance.

At Stage 1, a description of the program's design is obtained as "performance" information. This performance is compared with the design criteria postulated as a standard. (See chapter 3 for a discussion of design criteria.) Discrepancy between performance and standard is reported to those responsible for the management of the program. At Stage 2 the standard for judging performance is the program design arrived at in Stage 1. Program performance information consists of field observations of the program's installation. Discrepancy information may be used by the program manager to redefine the program or change installation procedures. At Stage 3 performance information is collected on a program's interim products. The standard used is the part of the program design that describes the relationship between program processes and interim products. Discrepancy information is used either to redefine process and relationship of process to interim product or to improve control of the process being used in the field. As Stage 4 the standard is the part of the program design that refers to terminal objectives. Program performance information consists of criterion measures used to estimate the terminal effects of the project. At this point in time, if decision makers have more than one project with similar outcomes available to them for analysis, they may elect to do a cost-benefit analysis to determine program efficiency.

Assumptions

The manner in which an evaluation based on the Discrepancy Model can be conducted is perhaps more important to practitioners than the assumptions of the model and its theoretical adequacy. As is usually the case, however, a discussion of methodology discloses new theoretical issues to be further considered and resolved. Such a discussion, when based on experience, also constitutes the essential test of sound theory. Therefore an essential purpose of this chapter is to illuminate the distinctions and procedures needed to activate the model.

Some assumptions must be posited and further discussion of the evaluation process is necessary if we are to proceed with a clear description of evaluation methodology. The following assumptions are given:

(1) It is necessary to evaluate ongoing school programs to make sound decisions about whether to improve, terminate, or maintain them.

(2) There is administrative support for program change initiated by program staff rather than by authority superordinate to staff. The initiative action takes the form of setting standards and interpreting discrepancy information.

(3) There is administrative support for a distinction between program and evaluation staff personnel and functions. Program staff is defined as the persons responsible for planning, organizing, and conducting the work of a project.

(4) A nondirective, objective evaluation staff can assist in the definition of standards according to structural criteria, identify and collect performance information relative to standards, and estimate the significance of the observed differences between standard and performance.

(5) Problem-solving activity required by program staff to improve school programs, is dependent on reliable discrepancy information provided by evaluation staff.

(6) Problem-solving activity will be successful only if program staff is involved in and committed to the change process.

(7) A state of tension can be fostered in program staff that will result in problem-solving activity.

(8) Problem-solving success requires pertinent information from evaluation staff and sound decisions from program staff.

(9) If an evaluation staff is to have the support of the program staff it seeks to evaluate, it must provide visible assistance in a form acceptable to program staff. The only assurance of acceptability is that program purposes be defined by the program staff and the methods of change be determined by them as well. (For further discussion of staff relationships see the section "The Evaluation Staff" later in this chapter.)

Evaluation for Problem Solving

To distinguish between the functions of evaluation staff and program staff it is necessary to look at the entire web of questions and answers that constitute the problem-solving situation we call program evaluation. Figure 3 depicts the flow of questions raised in

Figure 3

Stage 1.

Step 1. Is the Program Defined?

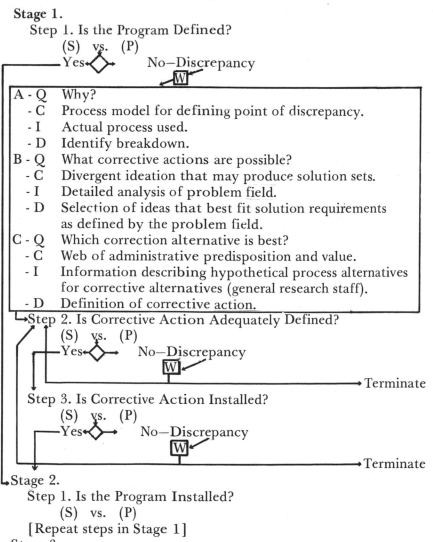

A - Q   Why?
  - C   Process model for defining point of discrepancy.
  - I   Actual process used.
  - D   Identify breakdown.
B - Q   What corrective actions are possible?
  - C   Divergent ideation that may produce solution sets.
  - I   Detailed analysis of problem field.
  - D   Selection of ideas that best fit solution requirements as defined by the problem field.
C - Q   Which correction alternative is best?
  - C   Web of administrative predisposition and value.
  - I   Information describing hypothetical process alternatives for corrective alternatives (general research staff).
  - D   Definition of corrective action.

Step 2. Is Corrective Action Adequately Defined?

Step 3. Is Corrective Action Installed?

Stage 2.

Step 1. Is the Program Installed?
        (S) vs. (P)
[Repeat steps in Stage 1]

Stage 3.

Step 1. Are the Enabling Objectives Being Met?

Stage 4.

Step 1. Are the Terminal Products Achieved?

Stage 5. Cost-Benefit Analysis

the course of an evaluation and also makes clear how these questions are often nested one within another. The answer to these questions is as much contained in the criterion models used to answer them as in the information used to obtain an answer.[2] For our purposes, it is only necessary to see that every question (A) implies criteria (C), new information (I), and a decision (D) and that in answering a question different functions are involved. It is a tenet of our model that these functions should be carried out by different people with different responsibilities. The formulation of the question is the job of the evaluator. The criterion belongs to the program manager; the collection of information is a function of both evaluation and program staff activity. The decision alternatives are outlined by the evaluator while the choice between alternatives belongs to the project director. More about this later.

Figure 3 shows that there are three major steps in Stage 1. Each step is derived from a question. These steps represent a sequence of probelm-solving efforts that may be needed to define an ongoing program. The same steps are used in Stage 2 to determine whether the program has been installed as defined. Where either a definition or installation is not obtained, further identification of some new criterion model for definition or installation becomes necessary. If after considerable problem-solving effort the program still is not defined and installed, the principle of diminishing returns dictates program termination.

Block W in Figure 3 shows the essential problem-solving sequence used to identify a corrective alternative whenever discrepancy information exists about definition (Stage 1), installation (Stage 2), process (Stage 3), or product (Stage 4). A series of questions is raised: A. Why is there a discrepancy? B. What corrective actions are possible? C. Which corrective action is best? To answer these questions, three elements are necessary: (1) criteria for identifying relevant information and knowing how to interpret it based on some standard for the point of discrepancy being investigated, (2) new information about actual performance or practice, and (3) a decision based on a comparison of information with standard. (As the reader may remember, these elements are also used to answer the primary question of each step.)

Let us see how block W might be applied to the study of one of the program components in the design criteria, for example, the input variable of student entry behavior. Suppose that the program description fails to provide any information about student entry behavior. Question A in block W asks, "Why does this discrepancy exist?" The criterion for this question is the ideal way to arrive at a description of student entry behavior. For example, the staff might study the behavior of students for whom the program is intended before their enrollment in the program. The staff could then isolate performance variables that on their face appear relevant to criterion performance. The staff should find ways to measure at least some of these variables in pretreatment subjects and then describe how the information will be routinely obtained as part of the program. Such a criterion model for defining any component so that it is congruent with the program design criteria constitutes the essential criterion for answering question A. The information required to answer question A is a description of the process that was actually used in order to arrive at a definition of student entry level. On investigation it may be determined that someone merely told someone else to "describe students to be enrolled in the program" and in fact this description took the form of age and grade-level means. A comparison of the criterion model with actual practice makes likely a clear-cut decision about the cause of the discrepancy.

The "Why" question A has been answered. The B question, "What corrective actions are possible?" is now pertinent. Continuing with our example, questions B asks, "How many ways are there of obtaining a definition of student entry behavior?" The criteria for this question consist of a variety of ways of generating this type of information under various situational constraints. For example, if no one in the school system has a knowledge of tests and measurements, consultants may be employed. If there are no students in the system who have not already been enrolled in the program, students in other systems may be identified and studied or the behavior of students now in the program may be extrapolated to their level before the program. The information needed to answer question B is a collection of all information about the system that may be relevant in satisfying the possible ideal courses of action. A comparison of this information with the criteria permits the identification of courses of action compatible with existing conditions and constraints of the school system.

Question C of block W raises the final question in the problem solving sequence: "Given a number of alternative courses of action which is best?" The criteria for this question are located in the judgmental web of the decision maker. These criteria are rarely explicit though through introspection they can be made so. Such values as system homeostasis, societal norms, professional standards, the importance of interest groups, and personal expectations are all

involved. The decision maker obtains estimates of the possible consequences of each alternative and compares these consequences with
his criterion of value. He can thereby make a decision about which
alternative is best, *i.e.*, optimally satisfies his value web.

It should be noted that the use of block W inevitably raises
questions demanding further refinement of criteria. The criterion
problem consists of unraveling the values implicit in descriptions of
standards, and criterion models needed to identify relevant information for problem solving. Generally some absolute assumption is
ultimately accepted as the basis for an operational criterion, and it is
generally not safe for the evaluator to transgress this microcosmic
point.

Further inspection of Figure 3 shows that the problem-solving
block can be used to resolve discrepancies arising under each of the
steps for each stage of evaluation. Discrepancies may occur at any of
the points where a comparison is made between the program taxonomy and the program definition. It may be helpful to look at
examples of questions from Stages 2 and 3.

Stage 2.

Step 1: (Q) Has the program been installed?
         (C) Compare program definition with installation infor-
             mation for congruance.
         (I) Information about installation obtained from field
             observations.
         (D) Decide if program is congruant with standards for
             Stage 2.

Block W
    A - (Q) If program is not congruant, why has the program not
            been installed?
        (C) Model of program installation procedure.
        (I) Description of actual installation procedure used.
        (D) Decide where procedural breakdown exists.
    B - (Q) What should be done to install the program?
        (C) Alternative installation strategies of a general nature.
        (I) Information about operational constraints on alterna-
           tive strategies.
        (D) Select possible specific strategies.
    C - (Q) Which strategy is best?
        (C) Value priorities of the decision maker.

        (I) Estimates of the actual value consequences of each workable strategy.

        (D) Selection of the strategy that optimizes values.

Stage 3.

Step 1: (Q) Is the program achieving its enabling objectives?

        (C) Model of relationship of student-teacher interactions to enabling objectives.

        (I) Discrepancy information based on actual program performance of students.

        (D) Yes/No.

Block W

    A -(Q) If not, why not?

        (C) Model of curriculum analysis procedure.

        (I) Actual analysis of learning events and their sequence.

        (D) Description of breakdown points.

    B - (Q) What corrective alternatives appear possible under the model?

        (C) Corrective alternatives possible within the problem field.

        (I) Detailed analysis of actual constraints in the problem field.

        (D) Choose alternatives that meet field requirements.

    C - (Q) What corrective alternative appears best?

        (C) Model of value web.

        (I) Information describing value consequences of alternatives.

        (D) Choose alternative with best value configuration fit.

Step 2: (Q) Is the "corrective action" adequately defined?

        (C) Model of "corrective action" definition adequacy criteria.

        (I) Information describing existing "corrective action" definition.

        (D) Determine if corrective action is adequate in terms of the model.

Block W

    A -(Q) If not, why not?

        (C) Detailed description or analysis of corrective action definition model (also reanalyze previous models).

        (I) Identify definition process actually used.

        (D) Describe points at which the definition process has broken down.

B - (Q) What corrective alternatives appear possible under the
model?
(C) Corrective alternatives.
(I) Detailed description analysis of problem field based
on problem-solving model.
(D) Choose alternatives that satisfy field demands.
C - (Q) What corrective alternative appears best?
(C) Model of value web.
(I) Information describing value consequences of correc-
tive alternatives.
(D) Choose alternative with best value configuration fit.
Step 3: (Q) Is the corrective action installed?
(C) Model of corrective action derived from definition of
corrective action.
(I) Information describing actual field conditions.
(D) Determine if congruence exists.
Block W
A - (Q) If discrepancy, then why? (If not, why not?)
(C) Restate and reanalyze all previous models in Stage 3.
(I) Describe actual processes used in the field.
(D) Identify breakdown points.

The similarity of the questions raised in an evaluation at any stage
should now be apparent. The content of the answers, however, vary
across the components in the program design and across stages of
development.

The use of a computer comes to mind as an aid in charting one's
decisionmaking course through an evaluation composed of this maze
of steps. A computer could be used to control the sequence of
questions, to store criteria generated by previous decision makers
who face similar evaluation questions, to store information descriptive of a particular school system or educational program that might
be "called up" by criteria, and, finally, to identify for the decision
maker the alternatives available to him. In fact, except for the need
of a human solution to the criterion problem, machines appear capable
of going through all necessary decisionmaking functions. It should be
remembered, however, that criteria depend on value assumptions,
and in our society values are pluralistic. Only if a single value system
becomes universal will man be dispensable.

Having described in some detail the steps involved in the evaluation of an ongoing program, let us now turn to a consideration of
who takes these steps and how they are implemented.

The Evaluation Staff

A few years ago when school systems first tried to decide how they should organize to satisy the evaluation requirements of ESEA, there was a rather spirited discussion in the literature about whether evaluation should be the responsibility of an internal unit of the school system or an external organization. The importance of objectivity and credibility were emphasized at that time. It was said that if a school system subcontracted with a university or a nonprofit agency, an evaluation would be free from charges of self-interest and partiality. Now with hindsight it seems safe to say that this strategy has not worked. On the other hand, from somewhat random information coming from throughout the country, it appears that although the internal evaluation units of school systems are producing highly reliable results, they are of little real meaning or value to the administrators to whom they report.

Obviously what is needed is a better understanding of how evaluation can serve management as well as the dictates of its own research heart. Whether an evaluation unit is internal or external is perhaps less important than a clear definition of agreement on purposes by all parties concerned, and an adequate staff selected and trained to do the necessary job. Further, since an evaluation unit, like a program unit, derives its reason for existence from the school district parent organization, it is obviously subject to the same organizational constraints as the program unit. Even when the evaluation unit is an outside contractor, it exists within the web of expectations and relationships laid down by the school system. Therefore, interdependence between program and evaluation staff and mutual dependence on the parent structure is generally an evaluation fact of life.

Figure 4 makes clear how evaluation serves as the handmaiden of administration in the management of program development through sound decisionmaking. Evaluator and administrator are interdependent.

Figure 4

Evaluation Staff Activity	Program Staff Activity
Identify decision points in the entire evaluation process	
Establish and maintain an apparatus whereby staff may formulate standards	Identify standards

(Figure 4 cont'd)

Find ways in which to reformulate standards if necessary

Insure the adequacy of standards through the application of explicit criteria

Find ways to resolve differences in standards used by the program staff

Communicate statement of standards to staff

Identify information needed to compare performance with standards

Identify information available or attainable in order to compare performance with standards

Design a method of obtaining program performance information

Provide information descriptive of program performance

Report standard vs. performance discrepancy

Choose between action alternatives in regard to discrepancy

Identify decision points in the problem-solving process

Identify kind of information needed to identify cause of program performance deficiency

Locate information about cause of program performance deficiency

Identify decision points in choosing criteria to be used for selecting "possible" and "best" corrective alternatives

Detail criteria used to identify cause of discrepancy

Identify available corrective alternatives

Identify information needed to generate alternatives

Locate and synthesize information as requested

Identify criteria underlying choice of best alternative

Choose "best" alternative for corrective action

The evaluator tells the program manager what decision must be made, and the manager makes these decisions on the basis of information identified by the evaluator. The choice between available decision alternatives as well as the selection of criteria underlying the generation of alternatives is the administrator's responsibility.

The evaluation staff acts as the watchdog of program standards. It ensures that standards can be used for assessing program performance. It applies to standards the criteria of clarity, internal consistency, comprehensiveness, and compatibility at each stage of program performance. When standards are not stated clearly, the evaluation unit restates them on its own initiative and then obtains confirmation of the restatement's validity from program staff. Only program staff, however, may reformulate program standards to improve their internal consistency, comprehensiveness, or compatibility. Generally, they will not do so unless specific contradictions or omissions in the standard are pointed out to them by evaluation staff.

The evaluation staff is also responsible for ensuring that the "standard vs. performance" comparison is actually made and that any resultant discrepancy information is reported to program staff. To facilitate this comparison the evaluation staff stands ready to identify necessary information, collect it, and analyze it for report purposes.

The problem-solving loop block W is in the province of the program staff. The evaluator's job is to track the administrator through the problem-solving process, remind him of his methodological alternatives and choice points, and collect and analyze information as needed, although this acitivity could be carried out equally well by a school system research and development unit if this is available to the program manager.

Skills unique to the evaluator member of the team permit him to achieve a close working relationship with the program director and to accomplish productive small group work with the program staff. Measurement, sampling, report writing, statistical analysis, and other technical functions are generally provided by other specialists on the evaluation team.

Evaluation, then is a team effort, preferably a task-oriented team of the type suggested by Miles.[3] Generally in a large school system, it will consist of the following team members:

(1) Several nondirective evaluation specialists skilled in small group process work and ethnological techniques each of whom has responsibility for project evaluation management but all of whom may team up to facilitate group work.

(2) One or more psychometrists familiar with a wide range of group cognitive and affective instruments and capable of rapidly designing ad hoc instruments.

(3) A research design specialist capable of drawing carefully defined samples, designing experiments, and directing the statistical analysis of data.

(4) One or more technical writers familiar with educational jargon and evaluation concepts.

(5) A data processing unit with the capacity for data storage, retrieval, and statistical analysis as directed.

(6) Subject specialist consultants.

(7) A status figure capable of communicating directly with the superintendent of schools and all program directors.

There must be maximum involvement of program staff in every step of the evaluation process. Further, it follows that the evaluation staff must establish a continual rapport with the program staff based on communication of affect as well as publicly acceptable verbalizations. The relationships to which an evaluation unit submits itself are binding and pervasive. It does not follow, however, that evaluation operates at the administrative discretion of the program unit. Evaluation is the handmaiden of program development and quiet counselor to administrators, but it operates in accordance with its own rules and on an authority independent of the program unit.

An organizational paradigm that makes these intricate and demanding relationships understandable is an action system containing a feedback loop. The processing of input is at the discretion of the program unit. The definition of output and the shaping of input is at the discretion of the parent organization. The management of the feedback loop is in the hands of evaluation staff. The feedback consists of discrepancy between performance and standard. There can be no evaluation without discrepancy information. There can be no discrepancy without a standard; therefore,the first task of any evaluation is to obtain program standards.

A feedback loop of discrepancy information based on standards derived from the program staff will necessarily be of interest to a program staff that has been given responsibility for the success of its program.

Implementing the Model

What are the specific questions to be raised by an evaluation unit concerned with adequately executing its own functions as they are defined here? How does it know how to apply criteria governing the adequacy of standards and the conditions that must be established for the evaluation unit's success?

Only after the program's antecedent conditions, processes, and purposes have been clearly described in the program definition can the evaluator be reasonably confident of what he is evaluating. His second concern is for the clarity, comprehensiveness, internal consistency, and compatibility of the program definition.

Clarity is the common sense judgment exercised by an experienced writer or editor. The "comprehensiveness" of a definition is determined by the evaluator and his supervisor after careful reference to the program content taxonomy. There is a face validity for the exercise of this criterion based on the observation of omissions in the program definition. Internal consistency is often determined by the entire evaluation team including one or more consultants as well as the program manager. Their task is to consider the logical relationships of program components to discover if inconsistencies exist. Compatibility is judged by the program manager working with the evaluator to determine whether the program as defined conflicts with established programs or their support conditions.

Inevitably in the course of an evaluation an evaluator will ask: "Is the organization created to conduct the new program healthy?" "Does it appear capable of executing the purposes of the project? Pertinent concerns will be (1) staff competence, (2) communication apparatus, (3) flexibility of the program unit, and (4) commitment to a shared vision. The evaluator will ask: "Is there compatibility between the purposes and anticipated procedures of the program unit and the parent school system?" "Is there a political and economic base available to the school system that is adequate to support the program unit and the attainment of its purposes?"

These questions will be best answered from an attitude of patient optimism, no matter how haggard the evaluator. Much of the process work of evaluation is aimed at improving the health of the patient; no matter how sick he is, his involvement in a meaningful task, i.e., his goal-oriented behavior, may have a remarkable effect on his general condition. Even new resources can be found when public commitment is sufficiently strong.

Most important to the evaluator are his answers to the questions, "Do both the program unit and the parent organization understand the developmental stages any new program must go through before it can be effective?" and "Does the administration of the school system recognize the responsibility of the evaluation unit independently to monitor program unit activity in order to provide information pertinent to management decisions that must be made at each stage of program development?"

A negative answer to the first question requires general inservice training for program staff at the initiative of evaluation staff. The dramatic presentation of causes of past system program failures and the value of feedback information may be useful parts of a program staff workshop. A negative answer to the second question generally spells the failure of the evaluation unit. If the unit has not been specifically given authority to make its own management decisions independent of program staff and authority, its reports will ultimately fail to be objective and, whether positive or negative, will be suspect.

Given the pressure of school board members and community groups for product evaluations, the time constraints placed on evaluations are generally unrealistic regardless of the acceptance of these limitations by an evaluator. Evaluations must go through the same progressive steps that characterize the development of a project. Too often evaluators agree to do product evaluation within one or two years. They employ an experimental design borrowed from research methodology and thereby short circuit the natural stages of program development that provide the only sound basis on which to do evaluation work. The result is an evaluation beset by the classic design problems of inadequate sampling, faulty instrumentation, faulty design, lack of knowledge of critical independent variables, and lack of treatment stability.

The purpose of experimental design is to establish a relationship between treatment and effect. Design represents a method of securing the experimental and statistical controls necessary to obtain evidence of these relationships. Controls can be exercised only when a treatment is stable, the conditions of the treatment are under the control of the experimenter, and most of the important factors bearing on the outcomes are known to the experimenter.

Certain conditions are necessary for the use of experimental design in a school setting, and one of the purposes of the early stages of an evaluation is to secure these conditions—just as the early stages of program development form the base on which later program growth may be realized. In actual practice it turns out that movement through the stages of an evaluation requires frequent recycling through stages that precede the stage under negotiation at any point in time. Successive reappraisals of program operations and the program standards from which they are derived are generally a consequence of the decisions made by program staff on the basis of discrepancy information reported at Stage 2, 3, and 4. If a decision is made to reformulate standards rather than to revise program performance, there are immediate implications for the renegotiation of all subsequent evaluation stages. Hence, the soundness of program decision-makers' judgment and the support they derive from their organizational milieu is of prime importance to evaluators.

Stage 1 Work

In the first stage of evaluation, a documentation of the program staff's description of their program provides the best estimate of the conditions of the experiment. The evaluation unit facilitates this description by working with the program staff in accordance with small group techniques. The evaluator uses the design criteria to elicit from program staff a comprehensive program description including

(1) A description of the client population and their selection criteria as they are reflected in the program staff's understanding of the program;

(2) A description of staff, their selection criteria, level of preprogram competence and expected level of competence following any inservice training;

(3) The major terminal objectives of the program, i.e., the behaviors clients will be expected to demonstrate on completion of the program;

(4) The enabling or intervening objectives that must be negotiated before terminal objectives can be realized, i.e., the intervening behaviors or tasks students must complete on which terminal behavior is predicated;

(5) The sequence of enabling objectives and the nature and sequence of learning experiences that will lead to the attainment of enabling objectives (generally takes the form of an ordinal list at this first stage of evaluation);

(6) Characteristics and entry behaviors of clients, i.e., the characteristics or behaviors students should exhibit on entry into the program;

(7) A descriptive list of administrative support requirements, facilities, materials, and equipment;

(8) A description of staff functions and number and type of positions; and

(9) The casting of all program activity in a time frame to position events relative to each other over time.

The program staff must provide these definitions. It is the responsibility of the evaluation staff to ensure that the definitions are obtained.

Perhaps the most difficult part of defining a program for the first time is knowing how much detail is needed in the formulation of educational objectives. The adequacy of criteria for statements of educational objectives have for many years been a controversial question in the literature of evaluation. For most purposes it is still considered essential that program objectives be stated in behavioral terms. This constitutes the beginning point for most evaluations. However, the complexity and scope of any new program determines the level of specificity at which its objectives can be initially stated. Most ongoing school projects are sufficiently complex that in the early stages of evaluation definitions should be oversimplified. There is a relationship between the specificity with which objectives can be stated and the level of understanding of program staff at various time points in the ongoing program. To define all the objectives of an educational program with complete specificity at the beginning of a program is recognized as patently impossible by anyone who is engaged in a large and complex program worthy of federal funding.

Objectives must be arrived at by a method of successive approximation. In the early life of a new program, only the terminal objectives of a project and the major enabling objectives needed to reach the terminal objectives are understood by the program staff. As the staff works in the program, it discovers new terminal purposes as well as many intermediate or linking objectives that must be negotiated if ultimate goals are to be realized. Therefore, the definition of any new program is a continuous and increasingly detailed effort resulting from program staff operations experience.

As goals and program antecedents and processes are gradually better defined, the project moves from a stage of limited and tentative definition to comprehensive and reliable definition. This natural evolution of a developing program from adolescent self-discovery to mature self-determination eventually permits Stage 3 evaluation activity to occur in which the relationship between project outcomes and processes can be systematically studied.

After a comprehensive blueprint of the new program has been obtained from the program staff, the evaluation staff submits the program specifications to rigorous analysis. This analysis provides the program staff with new information about the resources required, internal consistency, compatibility with other programs already in existence, and comprehensiveness. Information is presented in the form of a series of judgments that the evaluation staff ensures have been based on well-defined criteria used by appropriate persons. Judgments may be made by program staff, parents, students, authoritative consultants, or others. All may contribute to a synthesis of judgment, or only those closest to a particular question may provide a judgmental answer.

In any event, the administration can eventually decide with some certainty whether there is justification for sustaining a program

through its next developmental stage. When the human and mone-
tary resources available to a program are obviously below the level
required to sustain it, when the program's operating components are
inconsistent with one another or with other activity already under
way in the school, or when a program defies repeated efforts at
comprehensive definition, administrators may terminate a program
with some confidence about the soundness of their decision.

It is important to note that the feedback of discrepancy between
program definition and standard is necessarily information with
negative affect. The program staff is told what it has failed to do.
Because these reports are always given to all members of the program
staff and all the superordinates to whom they may report, it is vital
that the purpose as well as the tone and intent of the report be
understood and accepted. The following cover page has been used to
achieve these ends.

EXPLANATION OF THE PROGRAM DEFINITION

What Is the Program Definition?

The program definition is a detailed description of an educational program as
it is perceived by the staff of that program. The definition is divided into three
essential components: (1) the objectives of the program; (2) the students, staff,
media, and facilities that must be present before the objectives of the program
can be realized; and (3) the student and staff activities that form the process
whereby the objectives are achieved. These components are referred to in the
definition as OUTCOMES, PRECONDITIONS, and PROCESS.

How Is the Definition Obtained?

The definition is obtained at a meeting attended by all levels of program staff.
The participants are divided into discussion groups where they contribute
information about the three essential components of the program. The Office of
Research compiles the comments into the program definition, which is then
mailed to all members of program staff with a request for further comments.
These comments are incorporated into the definition, which is continually
subject to updating and modification as the program develops.

What Is the Purpose of the Definition?

This definition is used as a standard against which to evaluate the program.
After the definition has been obtained, the Office of Research attempts to
determine whether the program is operating as the definition specifies. If not,
there are two alternatives: (1) The definition can be modified, or (2) the program
can be brought into line with the definition. Only after a definition has been
obtained and the adjustment between the definition and the program has been
made, can the Office of Research attempt to assess the impact of the program on
students.

Have Any Changes Been Made Since the Last Program Definition?

This definition contains a more comprehensive description of the program's objectives for students, teachers, and administrators. The last program definition did not describe any ENABLING OBJECTIVES, i.e., skills, attitudes, and information that students must acquire during the program to ensure the accomplishment of the major program objectives. These objectives have been specified in this current definition.

Staff functions and duties have been modified and are now stated more precisely. Other minor alterations have been made in the following areas: general description of staff, administrative support, time constraints, and communications.

Stage 2 Work

When an evaluation goes through its program installation stage, it is necessary for the evaluation unit to observe student and teacher activity to compare it with program standards for each activity.

Evaluation designs in widespread use today call for the comparison of student and teacher activity in a new program situation with activity in "other" program or control schools. The usual conclusion is that if the level or quality of activity is the same in both types of schools, the new program is not effective. This reasoning assumes that "other" program school activity is ineffective (which may or may not be true), and, more important, it ignores the importance of the only reliable standard against which program school activity may be compared: the program specifications themselves. Of course, when these specifications have never existed and the evaluator has not forced them into existence as a prerequisite to his evaluation, then other less meaningful standards of program activity must be used.

Once the standard for comparison has been determined, the enormous problem of collecting and analyzing reliable and valid information remains. Some standards call for comparisons of nonquantified information such as visual verification of described conditions or behavior. In such a case, the criterion problem is solved simply by referring to the program definition. Other standards require the quantification of comparative data on at least an ordinal scale. In this event, it is possible to encounter psychometric problems that require more time and energy than are available for the entire evaluation. Particularly when one is interested in documenting the nature of student-teacher transactions, the available instruments relevant to the information needs of the program leave much to be desired. Yet this does not mean that estimates cannot be obtained. Reliable judges making repeated observations in carefully defined classroom situations are perhaps the most effective, expeditious means of studying complex human interactions. These techniques are best used to verify the existence of unexpected variation in teacher activity rather than the nonexistence of differences, since the latter assumes an exhaustive classification system.

It is noteworthy that when the fidelity of teaching associated with a new program has been the topic of careful investigation, the results have almost always shown as much variation within the program as between disparate programs. It is possible to argue that this finding is due to inadequate and arbitrary schema for classifying teacher behavior. However, the more precise an investigator is in classifying his data and the more discrete he is in narrowing his observations to specific types of behavior, the less likely is this result of extreme variation to be due to the artificialities of measurement. That is, the greater the classification constraints imposed on data in order to meet minimum instrumentation standards, the less likely it is that within treatment groups variance will be exaggerated due to instrumentation inadequacies.

Instead, we are left with every reason to believe that great variation in teacher behavior exists within many experimental programs and that these behaviors reflect the pretreatment characteristics of teachers. When this variation exists, it is obviously a major responsibility of the evaluation unit to document the discrepancy between staff behavior and program specifications. Decisions to be made by program staff on the basis of this information may direct the retraining of teachers, the redesigning of program specifications, or the termination of the project.

At this point in the life of a project it is often necessary to build an ad hoc staff training design to compensate for lack of reliability in teacher behavior. When this project activity is initiated, it immediately becomes the responsibility of the evaluation unit to design a training program evaluation that is predicated on the same stages of program development as those underlying the original program evaluation strategy.

A study within a study and a program within a program are thus undertaken respectively by the evaluation and program units. Sometimes it is evident that staff must be expanded to support unexpected training activities. If, as a result, available resources are exhausted, the project's infeasibility is demonstrated.[4]

Stage 3 Work

Stage 3 generally requires greater specificity in the part of the program design dealing with instructional process than has been possible or necessary in previous stages.

In seeking an answer to the question, "Is the program achieving its enabling objectives?", the evaluator must enlist the aid of program staff in flow charting the relationship between learning experiences, enabling objectives, and terminal objectives. Figure 5 shows one format that can be used for this purpose. The steps in constructing a flow chart are.[5]

(1) List student activity (SA) and teacher activity (TA) associated with each learning experience (LE).

(2) Show the sequence of learning experiences leading to each enabling objective.

(3) List the sequence of all enabling objectives (EO).

(4) Show the structural relationships of all enabling objectives to each terminal objective (TO).

(5) Repeat (1) to (4) for all terminal objectives.

(6) Estimate the time between each node on the flow chart.

(7) Group teacher activities over time into teaching functions. Aggregate functions to define teaching positions.

(8) Estimate facilities (includes equipment and media) needed to support teaching activity, and list them.

(9) Cost out facilities and staff requirements relative to nodes on flow chart. (It is possible to prorate fixed staff and facilities cost on a proportional time basis.)

(10) Identify entry behaviors of students.

(11) Throughout Stage 3 correlates of student entry behavior and inprocess student and teacher behavior will gradually be secured. These correlates are listed as they are identified and may serve as independent variables in Stage 4.

The resource columns shown to the right of the flow chart in Figure 5 facilitate the careful aggregation of program resource requirements relative to process activity. The student behavior correlates shown at the extreme left of the diagram provide for the collection of information that may prove valuable to the solution of program remediation problems, which often arise at Stage 3, and the improvement of quasi-experimental designs used at Stage 4. The basic purpose of the flow chart however, is to afford careful description of enabling and terminal objectives based on the interaction of students, teachers, and resources.

Figure 5: Program Design Analysis

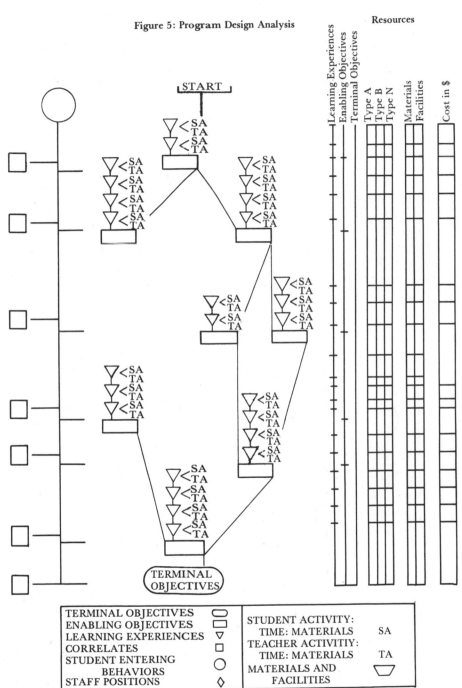

Figure 6: "Enabling Objective" Attainment and
Interim Product Flow Analysis

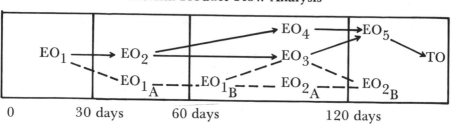

Figure 6 shows a simplified example of the designed flow of
"enabling objectives" (solid lines) compared with the actual flow of
"enabling objectives" as determined by evaluation field work (dotted
lines). The time line at the bottom permits a comparison of actual
attainments with expected attainments at some of the target dates
defined in program specifications. Such a chart is an essential aide to
Stage 3 evaluation procedure. The activities included in this procedure are described in Figure 7.

Figure 7: Enabling Objectives Evaluation Activity Sequence

Sequence of EO's / Sequence of Evaluation	A: Verify administrative feasibility of pre and postinstruction	B: Administer pretest and describe performance	C: Determine performance levels criteria	D: Administer learning sequence for EO_1	E: Administer posttest and describe performance	F: Evaluate data relative to performance level criteria	Proceed to next EO	G: Identify EO_{1a}	H: Identify learning sequence for EO_{1a}	I: Administer learning sequence for EO_{1a}	J: Subjective approval of EO_{1a} learning sequence
Steps	1	2	3	4	5	6	◇ Complete Steps 7-10	7	8	9	10
EO_1											
EO_2											
EO_3											
EO_4											

Column A includes a description of who administers what, when, and to whom and details the activity needed to support administration of both pre and postinstruments for an evaluation of program sequence relative to enabling objective. Column B includes the administration of the pretest and description of results in terms of levels for each valid subscore. Column C establishes performance level on the instrument to be used as program success criteria. This level is determined as a function of pretest performance estimates of the effectiveness of treatment and estimates of the importance of the enabling objective in the overall structure of objectives contributing to terminal objectives. Column D represents the administration of program treatment in the form of learning activity sequence. Column E calls for the administration of the posttest and data descriptions comparable to column B. Column F compares posttest with pretest and performance level criteria defined under column C. As a result of this comparison, a determination is made to either move to EO_2 or to reexamine EO_1. On the assumption that student and teacher activity has been monitored through the continuous operations research design to remain consonant with program specifications, it follows that the predicted relationship between treatment and enabling objective has been faulty. An analysis of EO_1 takes the form of the identification of subobjectives (EO_{1a} and EO_{1b}) subsumed in EO_1 for which learning experiences must be devised. This faulty relationship is generally due to a lack of adequate analysis of student behavior relative to task completion. Having just completed an attempt to produce learning experiences conducive to EO_1 and having information as to the pre and postperformance of students on criterion tasks, the teacher is in the best possible position to intuitively postulate new behaviors that must be learned to enable achievement of EO_1. These new behaviors become a new set of objectives (EO_{1a} in column G) for which new learning experiences must be devised (column H) and administered (column I).

Since no instrumentation is available to measure the attainment of EO_{1a}, evaluation of this second alternative learning sequence must be conducted subjectively by the classroom teacher (column J). Limited resources and time generally mitigate against the employment of criterion measures at this level of program development work in a public school setting.

The program staff's discovery of new objectives subsumed under previously stated enabling objectives will be a consequence of teaching problems arising from unexpected reactions of students, insights gained from introspection and/or task analysis, and insights gained from successful teaching. This will no doubt have a bearing on the teacher's incentive to engage in curriculum analysis, and a desire to increase staff initiative may be an important consideration in any administrator's determination to do curriculum development work.

Staff may be aware of many layers of underlying enabling objectives but fail to state them because of limited time and energy. Failure to use existing knowledge of curriculum and student interaction before teaching, causes enormously inefficient programs.

It seems necessary to establish a delicate balance between spending time and effort on curriculum analysis *before* the teaching sequence and *after* feedback about the success of the sequence. Cost and staff satisfaction requirements seem to dictate that minimum resources be used to achieve student performance standard levels. Since in most cases this minimum cannot be identified before feedback is received about the success of learning experience, it seems wise to use the staff's collective judgment in defining objectives at whatever levels of complexity are possible and in estimating appropriate learning experiences. Unfortunately collective judgment is often not a part of planning and inprocess program development work.

There is obviously a relationship between the specificity of a set of objectives, the time required to meet the objectives, and the time expected to be required. When enabling and terminal objectives are first defined in Stage 1, time estimates for their completion are given. However, as teaching difficulties are encountered in Stage 3 and new subobjectives are discovered or employed, the time dimension of the project must be warped to accommodate them.

An important inprocess set of administrative decisions deals with setting time limits for the attainment of new subobjectives. Here lies a dilemma. A program can fail to reach terminal objectives because it bogs down in subobjectives, or it can fail to achieve its terminal objectives, even though it finishes its entire planned sequence of activity, because of inattention to the achievement of enabling objectives.

Again, administrative decisions about use of resources during the program are critical to program success. Obviously, program administrators need periodic information about movement toward terminal objectives as well as feedback on enabling objectives in order to make wise resource allocation decisions.

In summary, decision whether to move forward to the next enabling objective (EO_2) or to a subobjective (EO_{1a}) is based on the following considerations:

(1) The validity of performance data concerning EO_1;

(2) The time estimated to complete EO_{1a};

(3) The time available to reach terminal objectives;

(4) The staff's ability to identify more efficient learning experiences to reach EO_1;

(5) The staff's ability to identify alternatives to EO_{1a}, such as EO_{1b} or EO_{1c}, and to estimate their relative time requirements; and

(6) The staff's ability to identify and locate necessary support requirements, such as materials and trained personnel, as well as evaluation requirements, such as instruments and student's time.

The problem-solving effort at this point requires careful teamwork between evaluation and program staff. The criteria required consist of models of learning and curriculum structure appropriate to the particular program under study. These models are derived from the principles of curriculum analysis suggested by such theoreticians as Gagne[6] and Bloom.[7]

The value of this type of structural analysis is now obvious; but a serious question remains about the feasibility of its being done by a public school staff. Clearly, a research center or university is best equipped to do this work in conjunction with a public school system. Ultimately, public schools may be the recipients of packaged curriculum programs containing precisely defined relationships between instructional process and pupil performance. Then, school systems can devote their evaluation resources more properly to such installation activity as pupil selection, inservice teacher training, and conditions of administrative program support.

Stage 4 Work

At Stage 4 the evaluator may cast an experimental design that answers the question: "Has the program achieved its terminal objectives?" This calls for the kind of designs we have long employed in educational research and have more recently employed incorrectly in evaluation—"Employed incorrectly," not because quasi-experimental designs of the type described by Stanley and Campbell[8] do not belong in an evaluation strategy, but because they have consistently been used at the wrong stage of a program's development.

In Stage 4, many of the relationships between treatment, conditions, and effects discovered in Stage 3 can be properly expressed as independent variables in the experimental design. The administrative control secured over the new program in Stages 2 and 3 insures treatment stability. Problems of sampling, instrumentation, and analysis are more likely to be solved because of increased staff knowledge of factors interacting with treatment.

Stage 5 Option

A word about cost-benefit analysis may be in order here. A lot of "econometrics" talk can be heard these days about applying cost-benefit analysis to school system outputs as a method of identifying efficient programs. This is fine if the following conditions can be met:

(1) The programs that produce measurable benefits are sufficiently well defined to be replicable.

(2) There is agreement on both the value and measure of benefit.

(3) Antecedent conditions can be sufficiently well defined and measured to determine their effect on output.

Generally speaking, these conditions are not met when so-called cost benefit studies are reported in the literature, and in the author's experience it has not yet been possible to meet these conditions in any public school program setting. That is not to say they will be unattainable in the future. It is likely the day will come when they will be routinely mandated.

Information for Decision Makers

By assumption, those responsible for making decisions about one or more programs are the first and primary audience for evaluation information. The feedback given may be characterized as formal or informal.

After each cycle of evaluation activity, members of the program staff are provided with formal feedback in the form of a cycle report. The report contains information about the problems in program design or operation that require adjustments.

The cycle report is always given to and discussed with the program administrator, who has the courtesy of a preview of each written report before it is issued. Since it is assumed that all strata of program staff have some decisionmaking powers, the criterion used in further distributing reports is whether a given group or level of staff can make decisions to effect program change on the basis of given information. Thus, if the findings concern only teacher activities, the report is distributed to teachers, but not to paraprofessionals. In addition, reports are distributed to adults in the system, whether or not they are members of the program staff, who have contributed to evaluating findings.

Informal feedback is provided to program staff by the evaluator, who interacts almost continuously with both administrative and field personnel. The degree of interaction is determined both by the size and scope of the field to be covered and by the number of scheduled activities. Program activities such as inservice training meetings and group planning sessions, as well as scheduled evaluation activities, provide opportunities for informal contacts. The evaluator seizes every opportunity for communicating recent evaluation findings. The timeliness of feedback is important. Thus, it is provided as promptly after each set of evaluation activities as is consistent with care and accuracy of data handling and may be presented orally while written reports are in preparation.

The crucial factor in a program's ultimate chances for success is the program administrator's receptiveness to evaluation information. The first evaluation efforts within a program may produce a vague design and serious discrepancies between design and operation. However, given the program manager's cooperation and sufficient time, these problems can be solved. Another program may have a superior first design and fewer discrepancies between design and operation. In either case, if the program manager is not receptive to information provided, the program will not mature to the point where a product evaluation is tenable.

The program administrator's ability to make use of evaluation information is a second aspect of the program's chances for success. It may be that the administrator is not sufficiently imaginative to devise solutions to problems identified in findings. On the other hand the problems may be inherent in the system and beyond the administrator's control. This is the case with insufficient budget allocations or variations in program implementation due to conditions in the schools.

The ultimate audience for evaluation information is at the policy-making level of an entire school system. Although providing information to this audience may appear to violate the relationship established with the first audience, the fact remains that policy makers need evaluation information in order to make rational decisions to retain or terminate programs and to allocate resources among them.

As a great deal of time is required to implement all of the evaluation stages described here, policy makers of the school system may ask for information relevent to a program's chances for success before the completion of the program. They will want indications of risk before the program product has been measured and a cost-benefit analysis performed. The provision of such information by the evaluation staff may irreparably damage cooperative staff relations.

However, the decision to jeopardize evaluation staff work must be at the discretion of the chief school administrator.

Generally, information on program risk *is* requested by policy makers. This information can be provided to the policy makers by using the Program Interim Assessment Profile shown in Figure 8. This profile includes information about the program administrator's amenability to program improvement and receptivity to discrepancy information. This amenability to improvement is measured by comparing the number of changes in the program with the number of evaluation reports received.

The first three criteria relate to the adequacy of program design and have been discussed at length under Stage 1 of the model. "Program Implementation" is a summary of all Stage 2 discrepancy information, and "Relation of Process to Outcomes" is a summary of all Stage 3 discrepancy information. Criteria 6 and 7 are not based on evaluation staff work: "Program Effectiveness" information deals with the adequacy or importance of program outputs in terms of the changing goals and values of a school system, and "Program Efficiency" asks whether the purposes of the program are of sufficient value to warrant the use of resources identified in the program design as necessary to achieve program outputs.

An interim assessment of a program is achieved by collecting the information needed to satisfy the first six criteria. The information collected to satisfy this profile should be helpful to the decision maker in deciding whether a program should be continued or terminated.

The estimate calls for a study of program performance relative to the number of times information has been reported for each of the first five factors in the profile. The factor of program efficiency, calls for some kind of administrative determination of cost relative to the value of service being rendered. The chart is merely a convenient way of comparing and reviewing pertinent information about each program in a system.

One other important aspect of providing information to decision makers is communication. All audiences entitled to evaluation information are relatively unfamiliar with the terms and concepts of evaluation work of this type. Although evaluation activity such as design meetings and informal contacts provides a kind of inservice training for staff, the effort must be made to communicate with program staff at their extant level of understanding and sophistication. It is incumbent on the evaluation staff to do this successfully. Evaluation findings must, therefore, be presented as concisely and

Figure 8: Program Interim Assessment Profile

Age of program ———

Age of evaluation ———

Number of previous reports ———

Program Adequacy Criteria	Information Available from Evaluator	Number of Previous Mentions in Cycle Reports	Criteria Level of Performances		
			Low	Median	High
1. Comprehensiveness					
2. Internal Consistency					
3. Program Compatibility					
4. Program Implementation					
5. Relation of Process to Outcomes					
6. Program Effectiveness (Adequacy)					
7. Program Efficiency					

clearly as possible—concisely to ensure that they are read and clearly to ensure that they are understood. Although the time-consuming task of searching for the right word in the right place may be a source of frustration to the evaluation unit, it is imperative. Evaluation findings not read and not understood are not used. Technical information will generally be reported in state and federal reports, with a different audience in mind. Evaluation units should consider at least three audiences for reports: (1) technical personnel representing the interests of a funding authority, (2) the program staff for which the evaluation report has feedback utility, and (3) the public that supports the program and the parents of the children who must benefit from it.

Footnotes

1. Much of this material was first presented in Chapter 11 of the National Society for the Study of Education 1969 Yearbook, *Evaluation* (University of Chicago Press, 1969).

2. See *Educational Evaluation and Decision-Making* by the Phi Delta Kappa Commission on Evaluation: Daniel L. Stufflebeam, Walter J. Foley, William J. Gephart, Egon G. Guba, Robert L. Hammond, Howard O. Merriman, and Malcolm Provus. Published by F. E. Peacock Publishers, Inc., Itasca, Illinois, 1971.

3. Matthew B. Miles, "On Temporary Systems," in *Change Processes in Public Schools* (Eugene: University of Oregon, 1965).

4. The importance of teacher training in support of almost any conceivable new program and the readiness of evaluation staff to determine the effect of that training cannot be overemphasized. Inservice training evaluation is, if anything, more complex than preservice training evaluation, which has been the source of considerable uncertainty among professors in teacher-training institutions. Clearly, this topic is worthy of further discussion elsewhere.

5. A number of flow charting references are available. See for instance Desmond Cook, *PERT Charting*, Office of Education Monograph, 1965.

6. Robert M. Gagne, *Factors in Acquiring Knowledge of a Mathematical Task* (Princeton, N.J.; Princeton University, 1962).

7. Benjamin S. Bloom, J. Thomas Hastings, George F. Madaus, *Handbook on Formative and Summative Evaluation of Student Learning* (New York: McGraw-Hill, 1971).

8. Donald T. Campbell and Julian C. Stanley, "Experimental and Quasi-Experimental Designs for Research on Teaching," in *Handbook on Research on Teaching*, ed. N. L. Gage (Chicago: Rand McNally and Company, 1963).

9

Application to
Public School Programs

Chapter 4 contains an example of the application of the model to a project. This application followed the procedure customary in Pittsburgh when conducting the evaluation of an ongoing program. While this is an excellent example of the usual approach used with the model, it is not the only type of evaluation possible. The model is equally applicable to projects that have not yet been installed, or to projects under development. The following discussion describes the application of the Discrepancy Evaluation Model to several other projects in the Pittsburgh public school system.[1]

The Opportunity School

In February 1969 an educational and rehabilitation project called Opportunity School was established in one Pittsburgh neighborhood. The project was designed to serve emotionally disturbed, delinquent boys, and was intended as an alternative to the institutionalization often ordered by Juvenile Court, or to the continual disruption of the schools by these boys.

Planning began several months in advance with the careful gathering of information through consultants, site visits, and conferences with administrators of similar schools. Goals were set early in the planning. At this point design work began within the framework of the Discrepancy Evaluation Model. Planning within the framework meant, for example, that all members of the project staff assisted in designing the project and in implementing their own design. The criteria for completeness of design under the model were used to be sure that no dimensions of planning had been overlooked. And, finally, the design was planned to be compatible with all spheres of school and community with which it interacted.

The section of the annual report devoted to assessing compatibility brings this out very well:[2]

Since this program is a joint effort between the Pittsburgh Public Schools and the Juvenile Court, the Court played an integral role in the planning of the program from its inception. In addition, the Court has made the following contributions to program operation:

1. Assigning a full-time probation officer to make home visits, to help participants effect a better adjustment, to find jobs for those students of working age and to coordinate program activities with those of the Court.

2. Screening students referred as potential candidates by the Pittsburgh Public Schools and the Catholic Schools of the Diocese of Pittsburgh.

3. Assigning students to the program at a formal Court hearing.

4. Making records of student participants available for program staff information immediately following selection.

A second cooperating agency is the YMCA of Pittsburgh. The YMCA offers its facilities at the North Side Center at a nominal rent. It further provides three meals a day for participants, making it possible to extend the regular school day to 12 hours.

The YMCA has agreed to provide three classrooms, a gymnasium, and a swimming pool for the school's use, five days a week, Monday through Friday, for a 12-month period beginning February 1969. Other recreational facilities are made available at such times during the day as may be mutually agreed upon. The YMCA provides all utilities and custodial services and supplies, as well as a private telephone. It also makes available its lunchroom facilities for use by the students assigned to the Opportunity School at such times during the day as are mutually agreed upon.

In addition to cooperating community agencies, a number of departments in the Pittsburgh Public Schools have offered specialized services. For example, the Division of Pupil Services identifies potential candidates for the school; the Communication Skills Office provides resource persons for difficult diagnostic problems and aid in materials selection; the Division of Mental Health Services provides consultants to the program staff bi-weekly; the Director of General Services makes arrangements for student transportation to and from school; and Allegheny High School handles official records for the school and makes arrangements for use of its facilities and courses as necessary.

And, as the report concluded:

The Opportunity School Program represents an innovative attempt by the Pittsburgh Public School System to tailor a curriculum and physical plant to meet the specialized needs of proto-delinquent youth. It incorporates an individualized academic and counseling program for emotionally disturbed boys with delinquent records at the Pittsburgh Juvenile Court.

Of particular importance is the care that went into the planning of this project. This project and its development represent the first occasion on which the Pittsburgh evaluation model was used before installation of the project. A design for the program was derived before the program was begun in February 1969.

Several problems have arisen involving the interface of the project with other institutions involved in this joint endeavor. To some extent, the fact that these problems and that of staff-student ratio were so quickly identified can be attributed to the preparation of a program design. It may prove instructive to examine a part of the design to get an idea of the detail involved in the preplanning. Since role-conflict is often a source of difficulty in implementation of a new project, let us take for our example the "Staff Functions and Duties" section:

Position	Functions	Duties (Variables)	Criteria
Coordinator-teacher	Administration of the program (50% of time)	Schedules teachers	
		Schedules students after consulting with each teacher	Class size limited to 7 pupils
		Schedules activities of paraprofessionals	
		Schedules staff conferences	Daily for half-hour
			Weekly for 3 hours
			As needed
		Requisitions supplies and materials	
		Turns in attendance record to Allegheny High School	
		Provides liaison with supportive agencies for facilities and services	
		Makes decisions on behavior problems	
		Provides instructional direction	
		Makes recommendation when student is ready to return to appropriate school on a full-time basis	
		Fills out transfer forms	
		Schedules transition of students to appropriate school	

Position	Functions	Duties (Variables)	Criteria
Coordinator-teacher (cont'd)	Diagnosis, planning, motivation, instruction, and record-keeping (same functions and duties as for special education teacher) (50% of time)		
Counselor-teacher	Adjustive counseling (50% of time)	Interviews student and gets him to express difficulty Administers tests Keeps counseling record on each student Keeps permanent record card on each student up to date Refers students to psychiatrist and communicates salient points in students' records to him Works closely with probation officer	
	Liasion with Allegheny High School counselor, appropriate schools, and Board of Education	Provides information to counselor on students in program Makes arrangements for students participation in group tests at Alleghany High School Follows up on students returned to an appropriate school	As required by couselor If to be taken
	Diagnosis, planning, motivation, instruction, and record-keeping (same functions and duties as for special education teacher) (50% of time)		
Reading specialist	Diagnosis of individual learning problems (particularly in reading) (70% of time)	Consults permanent records on each student Runs student through tele-binocular instruments Administers formal and informal reading inventories	

Position	Functions	Duties (Variables)	Criteria
Reading specialist (cont'd)	Planning, motivation, instruction and record-keeping (same functions and duties as for special education teacher)		
Special education teacher	Diagnosis of Individual learning problems	Arrives at diagnosis	
	Planning for instruction of individual students	Selects appropriate materials for remediation (textbooks, exercises, games, self-made) on basis of diagnosis Prepares lesson plan	
	Motivation of individual students	Makes home visits Knows and relates to student on an informal basis Provides a pleasant atmosphere for learning Provides a model for student	
	Instruction of individual students	Holds small classes Tries various approaches to subject matter If student incapable of learning during a given class, devises an alternate activity using resources of other staff members if necessary	
	Record keeping for instruction	Keeps information sheet on each student Consults information sheet in planning, motivating, and carrying out instructional activities Plans and accompanies students on field trips Plans parents' night	
Physical education teacher			
Shop teacher			
Art teacher			

Position	Functions	Duties (Variables)	Criteria
Music teacher			
Probation officer	Liaison with Juvenile Court	Receives, investigates, and adjusts police complaints	
		Files recurrent petitions	
		Reports to Court on individual students	At least once a week
	Guidance of students	Makes home visits	
		Investigates use of free hours by students	
		Holds group therapy sessions with students as part of regular curriculum under "Guidance"	
		Follows up on students returned to an appropriate school	Once a week for a least six months
	Job placement	Ascertains needs (financial and emotional) of students	
		Keeps informed of community resources to help student	
		Contacts prospective employers (Armed Services, government agencies, Job Corps, Neighborhood Youth Corps, and private)	
	Community relations	Makes speeches to community groups	
	Assistance with instructional program	Assists in physical education program	
		Supervises meals	
Paraprofessional	Assistance with instructional program	Rides bus to school with students	
		Accompanies students during school hours when they are out of building	
		Proctors halls	
		Passes out towels in gym	
		Provides lifesaving services for swimming	
		Assists in group activities at direction of teachers	

Position	Functions	Duties (Variables)	Criteria
Paraprofessional (cont'd)	General duties	Answers phone in office and takes messages	
		Types	
		Files	

Such a complete delineation of each staff member's role provides good guidelines for those who actually have to do the work. Not only does each staff member have a clear idea of what his duties are, but, when unexpected duties arise, a logical framework exists into which they can be fitted. And finally, when disagreements arise a clear design exists to which reference can be made in order to settle the issue.

The high quality of this design in terms of completeness, internal consistency, and compatibility with the environment made it possible to use the design as a basis for the implementation of a slightly different program for younger, predelinquent boys in a second neighborhood a year later. At this time, both projects are operating smoothly. Adjustments to the design are made as the need for them arises, or as new ideas are evolved.

With a new and somewhat circumscribed project such as the Opportunity School, fairly complete planning can be done in advance, the appropriate staff hired, materials ordered, facilities found, and so on for a relatively easy implementation of the project. (Note that the completeness of the planning is a large factor in the ease of implementation.) Often, however, projects operate under constraints that make this type of approach impossible.

Early Childhood Education Program

Early in 1969, money became available for early childhood education in Pittsburgh. In the course of planning, it was decided to begin a double project, one part of which would be the dissemination of a carefully structured curriculum already operating in one public school under the guidance of the Board of Education and University of Pittsburgh personnel; the other, an installation of a "free-learning environment" with the help of consultants from the Carnegie-Mellon University Child Development Laboratory. In the case of the "free-learning" or "discovery learning" environment, there was no clear curriculum or list of materials. Staff could not be chosen; it was limited to those teachers and aides already teaching in the selected schools. Objectives had been set only in the most general of terms.

As is often the case, it was necessary to take an incremental approach to installation of the project: a series of successive approximations to a desired condition. Early in the 1969-1970 school year, a series of workshops designed to orient staff to the theory and practice of discovery learning were instituted. As the year went on, objectives for student achievement, use of materials and facilities, and staff facilities were gradually "firmed up." At each step, instruments were designed to monitor the degree of achievement of each of the set of objectives. For example, room arrangement, an important feature of the project, was monitored monthly by an independent observer. As might be expected, the degree of achievement of objectives varied from school to school, so that by the middle of the year, one of the five schools was operating very close to the objectives, and the rest ranged on a continuum to one that was still very close to the original program traditional in the schools.

The operation of the evaluation in several stages at once is clearly illustrated here: In Stage 1, design work proceeds with the setting of objectives for use of facilities and materials, staff activities, staff training, and student achievement. In Stage 2, operation of the program is continually compared with the desired form of operation, as far as it has been defined. This makes it possible to change strategies rapidly when it is apparent that the one in use is not working. In Stage 3, interim products—results of staff training, changes in room design, changes in teacher attitude, and progress of children in self-direction—are continually observed. And, in June, after only one year of project operation, a preliminary and pilot Stage 4 product assessment will be run. None of the stages is complete. Nevertheless, all are proceeding in tandem without difficulty.

Program for Pregnant Girls

In Pittsburgh there is an educational and medical program for pregnant school-age girls. One of the peculiarities of this project is that the funding and organization change from year to year. The program was begun in 1964, in association with the Urban League of Pittsburgh, with the intent of providing continuing education, medical care, and social counseling to students during and immediately following pregnancy. Funding for the first years of operation came through the Office of Economic Opportunity. These funds were terminated in 1967. The following school year, the program was operated by the Pittsburgh Board of Education and the medical portion of the program was necessarily curtailed. In the 1968-1969 school year, however, a grant was made to the Maternal and Infant Care Project, a program of the Allegheny County Health Department, that made it possible to add a business manager and two social workers to the program staff. Social workers from the Board of Education then confined their connection with the program to making referrals and helping students return to regular school after delivery of the infant. The board continued to provide teachers and a counselor, paid through ESEA funds.

Each of these changes in funding and organization was reflected in changes in the project operation. At present, the Board of Education provides only the educational part of the program and this is the portion being evaluated. However, the existence of a design for the program for each of the funding stages would provide a clear record of change over time. The model would then function as a framework for recording historical change, and a series of successive evaluations would show which of the several organizational structures operated most efficiently. Unfortunately, a clear design has only been obtained since ESEA funds were granted to the project, so that this type of comparison cannot be made except in retrospect.

School Lunch Program

Another type of evaluation of an ongoing project might be termed a "blitz" evaluation. The North Side Lunch Program in the Pittsburgh Public Schools provides a good example of an evaluation performed in this way. The evaluators, armed with a series of questions derived from the model, went into the field and conducted interviews with the project staff. A comprehensive design for the project was derived from answers to the questions asked (the interviews took the place of the usual design meeting). The evaluators also observed operation of the project and made comparisons with the design. Compatibility of the program with the school environment was assessed through interviews with connecting personnel, which yielded the discovery that several problems—lack of facilities, lack of space for all children to eat lunch, conflict over who would take lunchroom duty—had arisen and had been resolved on a school-by-school basis by the principals.

The interesting thing about this evaluation is that it was performed in the space of three weeks. As an example of the amount of detail that can be gathered in that amount of time, the design for the program follows.

Northside Lunch Program Design

I. GENERAL

A.   Overall Statement of Objectives and Rationale for the Program

The Program is designed to ensure that children bussed from the Columbus Area to elementary schools on the North Side have an adequate lunch and/or a place to eat their lunch.

B.   Scope

1.   Number of Schools Involved

The lunches are prepared at Oliver High School and served at seven elementary schools on the North Side[3] and the Educational and Medical School (added to the program in the fall of 1968). An average of 500 lunches are served in these schools daily.

2.   Grades or Ages of Participants

Any children in these elementary schools may participate in the lunch program. Educational and Medical students and school staffs may also participate in the program.

3.   General Description of Staff

Director of Food Services (1)
Food Service Manager (1)
Cafeteria Personnel (15)
Lunch Aides (At least one per school)
Truck Driver and Helper (one of each)

II. INPUT AND OUTPUT CRITERIA

Student Variables—those behaviors or characteristics that the program is attempting to change. The input criteria specify the level on entry into the program and the output criteria specify the goals of the program.

Variables	*Input Criteria*	*Output Criteria*
a. Possession of lunch or milk	Student has no lunch or milk	Student has lunch or milk (purchased)
	Student with no means to purchase lunch or milk	Student has lunch or milk (provided free)
b. A place to eat lunch	Student has no place to eat lunch	Student has a place to eat lunch

III. PRECONDITIONS

Preconditions are the things required for program operation that the program does not intend to change.

A. Student Conditions

Preconditions	*Criteria*
1. Attendance at school	Student must be in one of the participating schools
2. Economic level	Needy students (established by social service exchange) get free lunches
	Other students pay for their lunches

B. Staff Qualifications

Position	*Qualifications (Preconditions)*	*Criteria*
Director of Food Services	Education	Graduate level training in food management
	Experience	Experience as a food manager
Food Service Manager	Education	An undergraduate degree in food service management

Position	Qualifications (Preconditions)	Criteria
Food Service Manager (cont'd)	Experience	Experience accumulated through inservice training of Pittsburgh Board of Public Education
Cafeteria Personnel	Experience	Experience as general service workers and on-the-job training
Lunch Aides	Education	High school diploma (preferred)
	Economic Level	Below poverty level as measured by local neighborhood center (OEO)
	Residence	In a poverty neighborhood (OEO)
Truckdriver and Helper	Education	Eighth grade or more
		Pennsylvania Driver's License with no points
	Experience	Experience with Board Labor Division
		Knowledge of routes and school locations

C.   Support

1.   Administrative

Preconditions		Criteria
a.	Principal provides lunchroom	Daily
b.	Principal establishes policy concerning service of lunches	Yearly
c.	Principal elicits support and cooperation from teachers and staff for collecting money giving out tickets, communi-	Daily

Preconditions	*Criteria*
cating with Oliver cafeteria, and assisting in the lunchroom	

d. Teacher determines the number of lunches, collects money and gives out tickets for these lunches, or assists in some portion of these duties — Daily

2. Nonadministrative

Preconditions	*Criteria*

a. Associate Superintendent for elementary schools collects and transmits to Assistant Superintendant for School-Community Affairs a list of applicants for free lunches — Yearly

b. Assistant Superintendant for School-Community Affairs provides list to Community Action Program for verification of need to receive free school lunches — When requested

c. Community Action Program verifies student need — When requested

D. Facilities and Media

Preconditions	*Criteria*
1. Lunchroom in the schools with tables and chairs	One place per table per student
	One seat per student
	Lunchroom should be large enough to handle all bussed students
2. Cafeteria (at Oliver)	Adequate to prepare class A lunches[4]

Preconditions	*Criteria*
3. Truck	Adequate to carry heavy carts (200 pounds each)
	Equipped with built-in lift
4. Carts to hold the food and maintain hot and cold temperatures	Insulated
	Equipped with heating unit
	Mobile
	Large enough so that two carts are sufficient for each school
5. Packaging materials and utensils for all phases of lunch	Disposable

E.   Time Constraints

Preconditions	*Criteria*
1. Time allowed for lunch	½ hour daily for each child
2. Time to prepare lunches (at Oliver)	4 hours daily (before noon)
3. Time to prepare room, serve lunches, and clean up (at each school)	2 hours daily
4. Time for delivery and pickup of empties	7 hours daily
5. Time for teacher to order lunches and collect money	15 minutes daily

IV. PROCESS

Variables	*Criteria*
A. Student Activities	

Variables	*Criteria*
1.	Students submit applications for free lunches	Yearly
2.	Students order lunch or milk and receive lunch ticket	Before 9:30 a.m., daily
3.	Students come to lunch room	At specified time, daily
4.	Students receive lunch or milk and sit down and eat	Daily

B.   Staff Activities

    1.   Functions and duties

Position	*Functions*	*Duties (Variables)*	*Criteria*
Director of Food Services	Coordination and direction of program	Plans and integrates program within schools	Yearly
		Experiments with new devices and food for improvement of program	Regularly
		Visits schools where program is operating and samples lunches	Periodically
		Bids, buys, and supplies food for program	Weekly
		Keeps complete record of free lunches and milk for ESEA and NSL	Monthly
Food Service Manager	Coordination of preparation and distribution of food	Plans menu	Weekly
		Supervises cooks and staff	Daily
		Organizes working time of cafeteria staff	Daily
		Sees that lunches are prepared and delivered on time	Daily
		Collects money from truck driver	Daily
		Has full clerical duties	Daily
		Records amounts received from each school	Daily

Position	Functions	Duties (Variables)	Criteria
Cafeteria Personnel	Preparation of lunches	Cook and package lunches	Daily
		Load lunches in carts	Daily
Lunch Aides	Service of children	Wash and set tables before children arrive	Daily
		Collect tickets from and serve food to students	Daily
		Maintain order in the lunch-room	Daily As needed
		Wash tables and clean up after children leave	Daily
		Record number of lunches and cartons of milk given out	Daily
Truckdriver and Helper	Delivery of food	Load and unload truck	Daily
		Deliver carts to each school	Daily
		Pick up empty carts from each school	Daily
		Pick up food supplies from warehouse before first trip to Oliver	As needed
		Collect money from schools	Daily

2.   Communication

(a)   Intrastaff

Variables	Criteria
Director of Food Service discusses program operation with program staff during visits to preparation center and school lunchrooms	Periodically

(b)   Program staff with others

Variables	Criteria
(1) School clerk telephones preparation center to order lunches	Daily
(2) Food manager sends menu to principals of participating schools	Weekly

In a clear-cut program like this, many man-hours can be saved by knowing in advance what questions are most relevant to determining the extent and objectives of a program, and simply going and asking. The efficiency of the evaluation, however, depends directly on the quality of the questions. One way to ensure the relevance of the questions is to have a tested conceptual framework on which to hang them, and this is what the model provides.

In addition to providing a framework for evaluating a project, the model can be used as a guide for staff training. Most of the projects evaluated in Pittsburgh have gone through several design revisions as a result of program changes or panel judgments. Revision of objectives has been in the direction of increasingly precise definitions of behavioral objectives. For example, compare the following analyses of end of the year objectives set by the Kindergarten Program in 1968 and again in 1969. In 1967-1968 students were expected to show only "certain cognitive understandings and skills."

In 1968-1969 students were expected to show:

Area	Variables	Input Criteria	Output Criteria
Cognitive skills	Recognition of similarities and differences in:		
	Color		Child can name primary and secondary colors
	Shape		Child can identify square, circle, triangle, rectangle, sphere, cylinder, cube, and brick
	Size		Child classifies objects as big or little, long or short, bigger, biggest, etc.
	Detail		
	Sound		Child can identify relative pitch and volume; identify sounds by timbre
	Taste		Child can identify sweet, sour, salty, and bitter tastes
	Touch		Child can identify objects by the way they feel: texture, density, size, and shape
	Recognition of relative positions		Child correctly applies terms such as above, on, under, beside, in front of, behind, between, right, and left
	Recognition of patterns		Child recognizes recurring patterns

Area	Variables	Input Criteria	Output Criteria
Cognitive skills (cont'd)	Reproduction of patterns		Child can imitate patterns (rhythmic, mathematical, and design)
	Set matching		Child can match sets one-to-one
	Verbal knowledge of cardinal numbers		Child recognizes and uses numbers 1 to 20
	Verbal knowledge of ordinal numbers		Child correctly applies *first* and *fifth* relative to position

As can be seen from this example, the project staff in 1968 had become more sophisticated in the setting of objectives as the design proceeded through several revisions. Some project managers who have been working on design for several years may not recognize that stating behavioral objectives is often a matter of refining nonbehaviorally stated objectives. When confronted with a program outcome such as "increasing self-esteem," program staff sometimes say, "We can't define it, and you can't measure it." However, if the concept of observation of behavior is introduced,[5] it is generally possible to secure clear statements of measurable behavior.

The effect of training project staff in the explication of behavioral outcomes is to allow them to set for themselves well-defined tasks that can clearly be seen to be achieved. If the objectives are not achieved, the natural reaction is to try a different approach. When objectives are vaguely stated, achievement is not discernible and the motivation for change in the event of either failure or success is not so strong.

Gradual changes in project design lead to the recognition that a project is an iterative process. The development of this concept is fostered by the form the model gives to the project design: The activities or processes of a program change as the program staff achieve a better understanding of the relationship of preconditions and entry level on change variables to exit levels on change variables. In refining the design of the program, project staff must then develop the capacity to analyze the relation of their program activities to the objectives they have set.

Footnotes

1. Lorie Dancy is the major author of this chapter. She is Field Research Associate in the Office of Research of the Pittsburgh Public Schools.

2. Pittsburgh Public Schools, "Annual Report of the Opportunity School" (Unpublished 1969).

3. Horace Mann, John Morrow, Halls Grove, East Park, Schiller, Spring Garden, Spring Hill.

4. Two ounces of cooked protein, ¾ cup fruit and/or vegetable in two separate dishes, bread, butter (2 tsp.), ½ pint milk, something rich in Vitamin C, and Vitamin A twice a week.

5. J. C. Flanagan, "The Critical Incident Technique," *Psychological Bulletin* 51 (1954): pp. 237-258.

10

A Statewide Application

Purpose

The purpose of this evaluation system (developed for the Chief State School Officer of New Jersey[1]) was to provide those concerned with education at every level of authority in a statewide education program with the information needed to develop better programs and to periodically assess their effectiveness.

Certain assumptions underlie the design of the information system. To ensure the success of the system, these assumptions must be understood by all users of the system and should be subject to periodic review. For this reason the statewide training of users, from local district personnel to state legislators, must begin even before the system is operational.

This chapter examines the assumptions of a proposed state management information system. It raises some basic questions, suggests the planning and action necessary if the questions are to be answered, and shows the necessity of using research and evaluation findings as a basis for successful institutional planning. In other words, it provides state officers with an explicit rationale for adopting a management information system.

The process of management is a five-step cycle of (1) defining one's objectives relative to resources, (2) selecting processes for achieving objectives within resource limits, (3) monitoring those processes, (4) determining their effects, and (5) redefining objectives. Each of these five steps contains a cycle of activity that must occur if the next step is to be negotiated. Taken together, these activities and steps constitute management's functions. An intimate relationship between evaluation, research, and planning is necessary at every level of management authority, because plans are made on the basis of knowledge derived from evaluating successes and failures. The broader our knowledge of where we have succeeded or failed—our planning base—the more likely it is that we will record a greater number of future successes.

To use research and evaluation to improve one's predictive power as the basis for sound planning requires a well-understood management information system, which in turn requires an elaborate technology.

Concern for the individual student arises because American society rests on a technological foundation that steadily demands increased skill from each successive generation. The ordinary citizen must develop his talents to the fullest extent possible simply to fill his place in society. Public education agencies have responded to the needs of their citizens by designing many plans and programs to extend the individual's education. Concurrently a demand for efficient evaluation techniques has arisen, so that the programs may be more effectively managed and more quickly adjusted to the educational needs of the community.

As education and technology change, however, they interact with the existing educational structure and produce new, different, and continuously changing needs. These needs cannot be assessed or even identified until enormous masses of information have been collected and analyzed. In order to be able to manage complex information needs, many states have implemented high-speed data-processing systems to obtain better information about their schools more quickly and with more reliability. How could such a system benefit New Jersey? To get some idea of the possibilities, let us look at some of the aspects of education in the state.

Education as a Complex System

Education may be broadly defined as a set of processes that more or less permanently alter an individual relative to certain objectives. At a certain stage of alteration relative to these objectives, the individual becomes what we call "an educated man." Educated men themselves then decide which objectives will be selected for the next generation of students and may induce change in institutions and educational processes. Education, therefore, is an example of a complex, feedback-oriented system, amenable to systems analysis.

Education involves many variables: the individual's characteristics, those of the context in which the school operates, the teaching processes used, and the materials with which the processes proceed. The extent to which analysis is successful in identifying and measuring these variables will determine the success with which rational decisions can adjust the system to produce the desired effect.

The successful operation of this system depends on the cooperation of many people. The State Department of Education is charged with coordinating this work as well as the following standard functions: (1) regulation (set minimal standards for professional staff, students, and facilities); (2) stimulation (inspire, encourage innovation, and disseminate ideas); and (3) support (consult to facilitate the attainment of local purposes).

In order to carry out most of these functions, state department staff must be in a position to see that necessary information is available at the local and state level. This information tends to be of a compound nature, as illustrated by the following four questions,[2] each of which can be broken into many parts:

1. How much money should be spent on educational programs?

How much is being spent now? How much benefit is received from this expenditure? What benefits have high priority? What areas of benefit are not being met at the present time? What resources are now being devoted to programs showing little or no benefits? How much present resource can be reallocated to serve new or neglected programs? How much new resource is needed?

2. How can we identify better educational programs?

Where do our most obvious local, regional, and statewide educational program failures lie? Why do these failures occur? What people or groups are already engaged in research to avoid these failures? What specific questions need to be answered before a solution to the problems can be formulated? What people are available to plan the research needed to answer these questions? Roughly what will be the cost of planning and executing the research in terms of facilities, media, staff consultants, and time? If information is available bearing on the problem as identified, is the planning of an educational project indicated? What will the project cost in terms of facilities, media, staffing, etc.? What target population is to be selected for the project? What community attitudes is the project likely to encounter? What administrative resistence is the project likely to encounter? What sort of cooperation is necessary from the community before the project can be implemented? What sort of cooperation from administrative personnel in the school system is necessary before the project can be implemented?

3. How can the State Department of Education initiate greater program innovation within the state?

What is the standard type of program in the field in question, as offered by school districts in the state? What innovative programs have already been implemented? What resources are necessary for further implementation? What sort of student would be turned out by new programs? How would he compare with the student typical of the standard program? What innovative programs are being planned or implemented in other states? How do they seem to compare with programs of a more standard type? What community attitudes will an innovative program encounter? Is this community apathetic? Involved? Demanding? Educated? What precise target population is involved in new projects? What educational needs do not seem to have been met? What consultative expertise is available for new ideas? Planning? Implementation? What new ideas are being generated at the local level? Can they be applied in other localities? Are there special conditions in the locality for which a program is planned that will affect its efficient operation?

4. How can a State Department of Education provide better management consultant assistance to local districts?

What techniques of school business management have proved most efficient in the past? What new techniques of school business management are being tried? What techniques have been proposed but not tried? What techniques have proved least effective or efficient in the past? What techniques are most acceptable to the type of community involved? What expertise is necessary on the part of administrative personnel to implement the techniques considered? What new methods of planning facilities and construction have been tried? Are there certain layouts of facilities that have been shown most efficient and effective, and if so, what are they? What minimal construction criteria must be met? What are the state recommendations on facilities as to space allotments per pupil, etc.? What personnel management problems have been encountered in other school districts? How were they solved? What solutions were tried and didn't work? What personnel management practices used in other systems appear applicable in an educational setting? (This category can be extended to include a host of other questions about insurance, transportation, bond issues, community relations, etc.)

To collect, tabulate, analyze, and interpret this amount of data by hand in anything approaching a reasonable amount of time with a staff of reasonable size is simply impossible. The problems of communicating this volume of data alone are sufficient to cause a management breakdown. If New Jersey is to improve its educational system, then it must establish a management information system based on the most recent developments in electronic data processing and systems analysis. A discussion of the characteristics of such a system should make its usefulness clearer.

A Theoretical Basis for a State Information System

At present there is no universally acceptable way of obtaining a complete and formal description of a general complex system. If one restricts oneself to multiple observations of an existing system, then its internal dynamics may be missed. That is, a purely empirical approach to systems analysis is tantamount to assuming that a complex system is quite simple. On the other hand, a completely rational approach may produce an analysis having little or no correspondence to the actual system.

Most theorists employ a mixed strategy of empiricism and rationalism for describing a system. That is, they accept the phenomenology (or *protocol*) of the system as a base (but not a determinant) for modeling the dynamics of the system. Newell provides an excellent description of this method of protocol analysis where the technique is applied to model the human problem-solving system.[3] A summary of this method follows:

(1) Observation of Phenomenology. The analyst selects from the entire array of data some portion (or subset) of the behavior of the system he wants to study, using some selected observational methods.

(2) Rational Partition. The analyst then divides (or partitions) his observations into the following categories: (a) Inputs (things entering processes); (b) Processes (whatever operates on the inputs); and (c) Outputs (things emerging from processes). The analyst is free to define and choose these in any convenient way subject to the following restrictions:

(a) Exclusiveness. If a data element is in one of the categories, it cannot be in any of the others.

(b) Coherence. A hypothesis relating particular inputs to particular processes to particular outputs must have been formulated. The set of coherence hypotheses constitutes a model of the system's behavior.

(3) Model testing. Another subset of the possible data is drawn and compared to what would be predicted by the set of coherence hypotheses. Should a discrepancy arise between hypothesis and data, the analyst chooses from the following alternatives, using a pure or mixed strategy:

(a) Alter one or more of the coherence hypotheses.

(b) Select more data from the total array of data.

(c) Choose alternative modes of measurement.

Phases 1, 2, and 3 are repeated until the analyst is satisfied with his set of coherence hypotheses (*i.e.,* he decides that he will get no more information by repeating the cycle).

The contribution of a statewide information system requires the statewide observation of educational phenomena, an analysis of protocol, and model building and testing. Obviously the data chosen for analysis will place restrictions on possible coherence hypothesis and ultimately on the form of some ultimate model of the system. Since we cannot look at all education phenomena, on what basis shall we choose data for analysis?

It should be apparent that our choice will be governed by our theory of education, and for this reason our theory should be explicit. A dynamic theory will direct our attention to phenomena associated with changes in students, staff, programs, and conditions that in turn change the purpose of education. A static theory will give less attention to phenomena associated with changes in means and ends.

On arbitrary, but it is hoped acceptable, philosophical tenets, we choose the dynamic theory of education as the starting point for a systems rationale. The people most likely to know which phenomena to analyze are those who work in institutions subscribing to a dynamic theory of education. Therefore, a statewide information system should consult available experts and relevant literature for descriptions of

(1) Variables (measurable quantities that may be either inputs, outputs, or the contexts in which they occur);

(2) Processes (operations on the set of variables that hold some variables constant (context) and manipulate others (inputs) to produce measurable changes (outputs)); and

(3) Boundary conditions (statements that are used to measure the

effects of processes and/or to determine which processes are applied. The descriptions of these three masses of information constitute *taxonomies* of variables, processes, and boundary conditions. At this time we will simply define a useful taxonomic organization as one that has these properties:

(1) Proximity (items that are conceptually similar to one another are measured in similar fashion);

(2) Implementability (the organization lends itself quickly to representation of a digital computer); and

(3) Adequacy (the taxonomy is broad enough to classify all present examples and is adaptable to classify any new ones).

The most general form of statewide information system is one that provides a useful taxonomic organization of variables, processes, and boundary conditions. Any particular implementation of the system will depend on such factors as:

(1) Whether or not to include (and measure) a variable on a statewide basis vis-a-vis cost and relevance;

(2) Which of many machines and programs to house the system in; and

(3) How and who to poll and for what to obtain the boundary conditions.

On the basis of analysis completed to date in New Jersey and elsewhere, the design of the management information system most useful to administrators seems to require attention to at least five major areas of information:

(1) The changing purposes of education (goals);

(2) Changes in student performance relative to these purposes (performance);

(3) Changing programs relative to performance and goals (program);

(4) Changing resources and their reallocation (resources); and

(5) Changes in messages about information (communication).

These five dimensions are served by the system through capacities to

(a) Derive statements of education goals and to resolve differences or conflicts in the statements over time;

(b) Record student performance on scales derived from statements of goals and to measure differences in performance over time;

(c) Derive descriptions of programs sufficient to insure their installation with fidelity or their modification over time in accordance with intent;

(d) Describe educational expenditure and define a reliable basis for resource allocation in accordance with specific desired benefits over time;

(e) Collect information and convey it quickly and accurately to describe operations or solve problems.

An Example of Assumptions

For this example, we view the establishment of a hypothetical information system by the Department of Education of a large eastern state. This office oversees the operations of 500 legally incorporated school districts in 20 counties. The population and socioeconomic densities of these school districts range from inner-city urban to wealthy suburban to isolated rural. There are large concentrations of both non-English-speaking citizens and families dependent on public assistance.

To complicate matters, the state department has no direct power over the individual school districts. The state has a long-established tradition of autonomy in education, precluding a central authority or the rapid development of one. The state department has several indirect sources of power such as:

(1) The disbursement of state-allocated resources to the locals;

(2) The administration of federal funds allocated under Titles 1, 3, 4, and 6 of the ESEA etc.; and

(3) Statutory powers such as teacher certification, accounting and auditing, and others.

For this example, we have presented a weak department of education. Any information system that suffices here will also be adequate for a stronger department.

Need for the System

The department decided that it needed some form of computer-based information system for the following reasons:

(1) It was responsible for the evaluation of almost 2,000 federally funded programs. Mechanical filing of these reports alone became prohibitive in terms of staff and space costs.

(2) Purely mechanical methods had proved inadequate to do a thorough job of teacher certification. Merely checking to make sure that each of the 2,000 annual applications was *complete* took four staff members almost three weeks.

(3) Information had snowballed to the point that no individual had a broad overview of what was actually going on. Conversely,

certain individuals acquired inordinate power because their jobs and/or memory capacities enabled them to know one area in depth.

(4) The lack of adequate computational facilities prohibited the proper statistical evaluation of data from many sources.

(5) Due to local autonomy, one normative test was not used, making comparisons between schools and districts virtually impossible even in those rare instances when the state could obtain and assess student performance data.

It became evident that there was not a lack of data, but rather a lack of systemization of data. The result of this "information barrier" was that program assessments, resource allocation, and teacher certification were based on only a fragment of the available data. While local agencies experienced similar difficulties, they invariably were closer to their own data than the state, and were hence able to dispute some of the state's decisions. Thus, information handling problems often spilled into the political arena. Since the state could not organize sufficient data to make completely objective allocation decisions, it was forced to make them on other grounds, thus often enraging the community.

After many years of struggle, the state decided to do something to channel the fervor of political argument into productive educational change. They accomplished this by bringing more objectivity into the process through a statewide educational information system grounded in the principles of a general systems analysis of education.

Establishment of the System

The state faced two problems:

(1) The construction of a useful taxonomic organization to represent the educational phenomenology of the state; and

(2) The establishment of a data collection and storage center using high-speed digital computers and relevant peripheral equipment.

In order to create taxonomies of variables, the department had to specify a universe of requests, which amounts to a theory of education in the state. Next, they had to review existent techniques of measurement and relate them to the universe of discourse by means of taxonomy. They did this by hiring a group of educational theory specialists who did the following:

(1) They interviewed many individuals possessing expertise in broad substantive areas to find constructs that could be used to redefine "education" more specifically. Some partial results of this were:[4]

Education:: = (Community, School)
School:: = (Student, Staff, Facilities)
Student:: = (Background, Cognitive Behavior, Affective Behavior)
Cognitive:: = (Knowledge, Analysis)
Knowledge:: = (Particulars, Universals)
Particulars:: = (Facts, Terminology)

(Note: This is presented only as an example of hypothetical results.)

A tentative version of this universe of requests was reviewed by a blue ribbon panel of educators from all over the nation and adopted as the state's official phenomenology of education.

(2) A search was made of a large number of existent measurement instruments. Trained psychometricians selected tests, subtests, and items and produced a tentative taxonomy by relating these to the constructs of the universe of requests. Another blue ribbon panel was convened to discuss and revise this to produce an official taxonomy.

(3) Since local autonomy precluded the establishment of standardized tests, definition of the universe of discourse was complex. At this point, each construct in the taxonomy had been specified in terms of measurement techniques that were in fact tests of one form or another. The psychometricians proceeded to expand each of these tests into an item pool. The goal of this effort was to construct this pool so that any large subset of these items was a measurement instrument for its taxonomy-related construct. By this device, each local agency could tailor make its tests, but the results from each district could be comparable. Thus, the universe of discourse was defined in terms of subsets of the item pools.

(4) "Student," "staff," and "facilities" were chosen as elemental files (categories for storing information in the machine), since they represent discrete sources of information. The columns of the array associated with each elemental file represented scores of instruments for each of the offspring of the construct naming of the file. A staff of programmers translated this conceptual framework into a machine configuration.

(5) The final version was rechecked and found to satisfy all the properties of a useful taxonomic organization. The result was a useful taxonomy of educational variables. Similar procedures were used to develop a useful taxonomy of processes. As we shall see in the section on evaluation, the boundary conditions taxonomy will be defined during the assessment process, and will be isomorphic to the variables taxonomy.

The next problem facing the department was the development of data collection, storage, and reporting facilities and procedures. Since taxonomy development was primarily conceptual, it proceeded under minimal interaction with locals. In this phase, the local agencies became a factor. The state realized that locals could not be commanded to participate in the system, and therefore enticed them to join by the following:

(1) The state offered to design and score tailormade instruments for each individual district. This would aid local agencies in monitoring their own students and would give them access to instruments that they have neither time nor staff to develop. Further, local autonomy would be preserved. To accomplish this, the state set up a network of regional test development and scoring stations. Each of these has access to the main data base and item pools. Further, they have mechanical scoring machines that produce information in a form compatible with the central data base. Each of the stations confers with its associated locals to produce instruments, which are administered and returned to the station where they are scored and forwarded to the central computer. The scores are incorporated into the main data base; they are also summarized in a separate report to be returned to the local.

(2) The state also offered assistance to the locals in meeting the evaluation requirements of their Title 1 and 3 programs. Without state help here, the locals were hard-pressed to find staff and resources to conduct these assessments. On the other hand, given state assistance, they had the possibility of attracting more resources by the increased knowledge of alternatives and the increased rigor of evaluation reports. A detailed discussion of this procedure is presented later in this chapter. Here it suffices to point out that by means of participation in program evaluation the system's processes taxonomy is used and updated.

(3) The state also used our section of the variables taxonomy to improve and simplify the process of teacher certification. Since the main data base contains much background and performance data, regression equations were constructed to yield predictions of teacher success in various contexts in the same way that many universities predict student success in academic contests. Local agencies benefit by saving time and guesswork in their staff selection and assignment duties. The state benefits by establishing a rationale for selection and assignment of teachers and by updating and refining its staff file.

(4) Local agencies often find class scheduling a perplexing problem. Once again, the state is able to trade a service (scheduling) for

the privilege of obtaining relevant data (*i.e.*, completing and updating the facilities file).

Thus, the state information center is established on the principle of local-state tradeoff. In a context of strict local autonomy this system flourishes because locals save staff and resources that they can put back into the classroom while the state benefits by conducting its business on a more rational basis.

Use of the Discrepancy Model

Recently new methods of evaluation have been developed that parallel Simon and Newell's work in problem-solving.[5] They make use of the idea that an educational program goes through several well-defined stages, and that evaluation machinery must be present in all of these. Provus produced an operationalized version of a dynamic interaction model; it seeks to compare program performance in each of four stages with a standard of expectation.[6] A discrepancy between performance and standard is a clue that the program is not working as it should be and should be corrected. The dynamic model requires much staff effort, but may result in overall savings, since program faults may be diagnosed in time for possible remedial action. The standard for the present stage under consideration is derived as a result of the previous stage (except for the initial one for judging the program's design). The development of this initial standard is a result of pooling the expertise of program staff and consultants. Once again, we run into the same considerations of objectivity, and the need for a large body of information with which to judge the program design.

This method has a broad scope in that it views the entire time-path of the program. It also has provisions for incorporating the use of quasi-experimental techniques after program design and installation have been investigated. It has more power than traditional quasi-experimental design, because it allows hypotheses to be rejected as explanations of aberrant data. This is to say that program design analysis should enable one to be sure that the dependent variable is sensitive to the treatment and that the program installation enables one to be confident that the treatment was applied properly.

Discrepancy evaluation is desirable since it provides a means of attack on alternative explanations of deviant experimental results. It seems to fit quite nicely into the entire systems approach to education. It is well mated to the Statewide Information System concept being advanced here.

An Emotional Climate for Evaluation

An evaluation rationale must encompass more than a methodology; regardless of technique, evaluation always exists in a human setting—an emotional climate. Evaluation should be a double-edged sword in the sense that it should offer praise for a job well done as readily as censure for slovenly performance. Unfortunately, most individuals do not see things in this light; the evaluator is viewed as an outsider and a threat to job and prestige. In many instances, this may indeed be true; the evaluator often is a man who enters the classroom for an hour, gets some test data, and pontificates in statistical language without any inquiry about the history of the program or the problems of the individual staff menber. Under these circumstances, it is no wonder that evaluators are mistrusted.

A complete discussion of emotional climate is inappropriate at this time since the topic has been treated in great detail by several industrial psychologists, the best of which are Gilman[7] March and Simon[8] and Homans.[9] Although it may seem odd, a book by Whyte[10] entitled *Human Relations in the Restaurant Industry* is probably the most useful source in this context; a large chain of restaurants and a school system possess many similarities:

(1) If we consider that the aim of food service is to produce a contented customer and the aim of a school system is to produce an educated child, production and distribution are virtually inseparable.

(2) Both institutions require the services of trained personnel and must add a considerable amount of intuition to the basic formulation of their job.

(3) The basic processes of each institution are only vaguely defined. Education and cooking both proceed by recipes based on experience not by general theory.

Whyte found that the management of a large chain of restaurants was virtually impossible: A full 80 percent of these businesses failed, usually because of emotional climate problems. In other words, managers were unable to get their staff to work together harmoniously and efficiently to meet outside competition. Here the analogy seems to stop: School systems do not go bankrupt. This, however, is due to the fact that there is usually only one public school that a child can attend. If we consider the fact that 20 to 50 percent of inner city students fail to graduate, it can be argued that schools too have a relatively high failure rate.

The point of this digression is not to prove that schools ought to be run like good restaurants, but to show that Whyte's observations about emotional climate may be used to help design a good evaluation rationale. Three of Whyte's major findings follow:

(1) For a large system, success was a direct function of the introduction of objectivity into the basic system. The rise of many successful restaurant chains can be attributed to improved techniques of menu planning, portion control, and automation. It is to be hoped that this is also true in education: As we define the basic processes more carefully, we hope to gain sufficient control over their effects to ensure that more children acquire better skills.

(2) Successful restaurateurs followed a "golden rule" of sorts: Only give criticism to an employee if you can suggest positive ways of remedying the defect.

The study showed that it was not sufficient to show that customers didn't like a particular dish; employees were likely to attribute this to faults in the customer rather than admit inadequacy on their part. This attitude is actually defensible to some degree, since the entire operation is only vaguely defined. Again, we note a parallel with education: Program staff and management do not want to admit failure; it is much more satisfying for them to attribute deviant results to faults in the students or community. They find support for this attitude only to the extent that evaluation is not capable of providing meaningful alternatives.

(3) Successful restaurateurs always maintained communication through a well-defined chain of command. Further, the extent of their success was directly dependent on maintaining this structure of authority. The same thing is obviously true in education; much resistance to evaluation is encountered because program managers feel that the evaluator will undercut their authority. This type of resistance can destroy the "team spirit" required by the cooperative venture of education. Thus, evaluation should involve program management and staff in a fashion that reinforces the chain of command; each team member should see the evaluator as a resource who will help him do a better job.

If evaluation is to be considered in the general context of a systems analysis of education, it must not have a punitive character. It is to be hoped that we have gotten away from the concept of the test as a punishment for the lazy student; we also ought to move away from the idea that evaluation is a "scientific" way to trim the budget. Any program assessment technique should be a tool that not only identifies deviant performance but also provides constructive suggestions for improving programs. A systems oriented evaluation rationale ought to involve rather than alienate program staff and managers. They should seek out evaluation, rather than fear "Big Brother's" surveillance.

A recent article by Egon Guba underscores this argument.[11] He too, feels that anxiety is a symptom of an inadequate evaluation rationale, and that assessment ought to be present throughout the life of a program.

Implementation Strategies

Let us now consider several implementation strategies that will encourage local staff to approach their respective evaluation tasks with enthusiasm and creativity.

District Evaluation

Under this strategy, the state would initially communicate only with the school district, which would have primary evaluation responsibilities. Individual program managers and staff members would come under state scrutiny indirectly through district supervisors. Unfortunately, this system prevents local access to the state information system, and local communication with experts in the state staff. The system places financial burdens on the school district itself, since staff would have to be hired to assume evaluation responsibilities. The state would have fewer contacts to maintain, but the information it received would be filtered through two sources, local and district managers.

Further, this strategy must contend with evaluation-based anxiety among district managers and officals that they may pass on to their local subordinates. District evaluation may be a first step toward a state evaluation and assessment rationale, but in the long run it is only a means for putting off emotional climate problems rather than solving them.

Target Group Evaluation

Another strategy might involve the evaluation of programs initially by target groups. In this method, the state would designate representatives to evaluate all programs with common targets, such as English as a foreign language, remedial reading for underprivileged children, and school lunch programs for the disadvantaged. Individual program managers would escape scrutiny by being pooled into a group report.

This strategy places a financial burden on the state; each target group representative would have to possess considerable educational credentials to accept the responsibility. Further, he would incur considerable expense in traveling from one district to another. With all this, the local agencies would still be deprived of the benefits of direct access to state information and experts. Again, it seems that his strategy avoids emotional climate problems rather than solving them.

Pilot Evaluation

Under this strategy, the state would begin an in-depth evaluation of programs in one school district. This would be done initially on a voluntary basis; the district would serve as a laboratory for perfecting the evaluation rationale so that it could be easily installed in other districts. This strategy would deal directly with emotional climate problems.

The state information system should be in a fairly mature state of development before a pilot attempt; without this, the state would not be able to provide the information resources that make the evaluator a valuable tool rather than a feared watchdog.

The key to making this strategy work is the principle of local state tradeoff. In other words, if the program staff member feels that the presence of the state evaluator represents a cost, in terms of prestige and/or authority, this must be offset by a benefit in terms of information and/or assistance that will eventually enable him to do a better job. Further, the evaluator and program staff should determine future action on the basis of consensus, so as not to disrupt the chain of command. Thus, the evaluator exists outside the authority structure in a consultative role.

A principle of accountability should also be instituted that would require each individual in the chain of command to be responsible for thorough reporting of programs under his jurisdiction. Thus inpetus for evaluation would flow through the normal authority structure.

A pilot study would also enable the state department to determine fully the kind of public relations activity that would be necessary to alter the image of the evaluator from foe to friend.

Since this strategy deals most thoroughly with emotional climate, and since emotional climate is the major obstacle to a state evaluation rationale, it seems to be the logical place to begin. With this in mind, the next two sections give more details about the structure of a pilot evaluation rationale.

A Dynamic State Evaluation Rationale

This section constitutes a general extension of the Discrepancy

Evaluation Model to the state level. It assumes a considerable amount of independence and autonomy on the part of local educational agencies. It also presumes the existence of a state information system meeting the requirements discussed in the third section of this chapter. There are six major divisions of effort in the evaluation rationale:

Goal Definition.

Given generally stated goals, the evaluator should be able to provide local educational agencies with concrete educational objectives. Under this formulation, locals would be free to develop specific goals for future programs and receive assistance from the state in terms of instruments for measuring them and advice about possible programs that are relevant to them.

In this division, state representatives would meet yearly with responsible local officials to discuss goals. They would develop a standard form for reporting these meetings to translate the stated goals of the locals into the language of the variables taxonomy. That is, the state representative would suggest taxonomic categories to the locals as a means of clarifying goals; the categories acceptable to the locals would be forwarded to a central location; and information about each, including schemes for measurement, would be extracted from computer files associated with each taxonomic category. Since the processes taxonomy is cross-indexed with reference to variables, a list of programs relevant to these goals (taking into account known context information about the local district) may also be generated. Once the locals receive instruments to measure achievement, they must meet again with a state representative to define their goals completely in terms of scores on these tests. Note that this is one method for filling in parts of the boundary conditions taxonomy. Thus, the state benefits by specifying local goals in common terminology while locals are saved the expense of searching for instruments and programs to define and reach their goals.

Need Assessment

After locals have defined goals in terms of scores and instruments, they must determine how much they deviate from these standards. State specialists would meet with local officials to work out the logistics of a testing program, including printing, administration, scoring, and interpretation. It would probably be feasible to hire

specialists in these areas on a statewide basis, since each local agency
could not afford to do so.

After test results are gathered and scored at state-run centers, the
local would be informed about the disparities between the present
system and the specified goals. This constitutes the educational need
of the local agency. Given this, local and state representatives would
meet again to discuss which of the particular needs can be met, given
existing theory and resources. Once again, the statewide information
system is necessary to provide both kinds of information. From this
meeting will come a list of need priorities that will be a time schedule
for the application of resources to reduce needs. Locals benefit from
this type of analysis since they can now define their needs clearly
when they ask their taxpayers for more money. The state benefits,
because it will have a clearer picture of statewide needs and thus will
dispense its resources more rationally and effectively.

Program Design

As local agencies seek to meet their needs, they will design new
programs or adapt existent ones. Again, it is not feasible for a local
agency to hire personnel specifically trained in this area. Probably for
this reason alone, it is a sad fact that many of the programs in
operation today are not of the best design. Some are inconsistent,
others are ill specified, and many do not reflect a broad knowledge
of the educational research field. A statewide evaluation system can
remedy this by

(1) Conducting regular seminars and training sessions in program
design for local officials.

(2) Preparing a manual that standardizes the reporting of program
design. This should bring many local designs together in a form
compatible with the taxonomic classifications of the state information system.

When a program design is received at the state level, it is compared
with other programs in the processes taxonomy, to see if it omits
important concepts or includes extraneous ones. Since the processes
taxonomy is indexed by independent and dependent variables, it is
possible to see if the program is properly controlled by listing the
variables known to have an effect on the program's independent and
dependent variables and comparing them with the stated assumptions
and controls of the program. Thus, the program design is judged
relative to the standard of previous knowledge. Should discrepancies
arise, the information is returned, in detail, to the local agency for a

redesign of the program. This process continues until the program is in accord with past knowledge (as determined by the state information system) and the standards of good research design (as determined by state staff using technical criteria).

Local agencies benefit in that they receive assistance in program design that they could not normally afford. The state benefits in that it is assured of funding programs that are consistent with theory and design principles and thus have a good chance for success.

Program Installation

It is mandatory that programs be installed according to the specifications of the approved design. Often, however, this is not the case; many times the program design is inconsistent with the realities of the school situation or suffers from errors or vagueness in instructions. In any case, the design must be changed to monitor this possibility, the state should require reports from locals about program installation, according to a standard form. The written reports on current programs would also be codified and placed in a special computer file to mark their progress vis-a-vis the design specifications. Thus, an administrator could summarize statewide educational program behaviors by ordering appropriate printout. Further, the state should spot check at least one program in each district each year to determine whether program installation is in accord with program design. This should be done on a random basis to keep everyone on their toes.

The statewide monitoring of educational program installation and progress data is a force for great efficiency. To keep a healthy emotional climate among local agencies, all feedback should be constructive. It should offer alternatives to remedy discrepancies between performance and design standards. If something goes wildly astray, the state department should have an "emergency squad" to come to the aid of the local agency. Once again, both state and local agencies trade resources for the eventual benefit of education in general.

Program Effects

After (1) the program design phase insures that the dependent variables are sensitive to the treatment and that all relevant context variables are accounted for, and (2) the program installation phase assures that the treatment is being applied properly, the program will be subjected to evaluation by a quasi-experimental design. Thus, another measure in the relevant need area will be taken and analyzed at the state center. Given steps (1) and (2) above, significant and reliable change in the direction of reducing the need can be attributed to program effect. All statistical operations should be performed under the supervision of a trained psychometrician, using a state library of computer programs.

Once again, local agencies benefit from the availability of services and expertise that they could not possibly afford, and the state benefits by a standardized analysis of program effects.

Cost-Benefit Analysis

The State Department of Education will now have compatible information about many programs that may be grouped according to the processes of taxonomy. Since this taxonomy satisfies the property of proximity (similar programs classified near each other), an analysis of the costs (resources expended) compared to the benefits (need reduction) of similarly classified programs may be conducted. On the basis of these comparisons, the state administrator may reach the conclusions of the form "for a given context, the XYZ Reading Program provides the most improvement on the M test of reading achievement." Analyses of this nature will aid state decision makers in funding future programs and, conversely, will aid local agencies in the selection of future program designs.

This entire state evaluation and assessment rationale may be summarized as a mixture of evaluation by dynamic interaction and emotional climate control by local-state tradeoff of benefits. The preceding discussion is only a general description of this rationale in its broadest sense. Decision makers may choose to stress some of the stages of this rationale more than others in light of available resources. The point to be made is that this rationale appears to be adequate to all aspects of evaluation.

The Evaluation Applied: An Example

In this section, we follow an idealized path of one program through the entire evaluation and assessment process. In most instances we have simplified matters by drastically reducing the number of alternatives at each decision point. The case involves the school system of Bay City, located in an Eastern state that has implemented a state information system and used the evaluation rationale discussed in the preceding section. Among other things, Bay City has the following characteristics:

Statistics on Race and National Origin

Total adult population:	30,000
White:	20,000
Black:	7,000
Hispanic origin:	2,500
Oriental:	500

Income Statistics

Median Income: $5,000/year

	White	Non-White
Over $15,000/year	1,000	100
$10,000-$15,000/year	3,000	900
$6,000-$10,000/year	6,000	1,000
$3,500- $6,000/year	8,000	5,000
Under $3,500/year	2,000	3,000
	20,000	10,000

Educational Level of Adult Population

	White	Non-White
Completed Ph.D, M.D.	150	2
Completed Masters	850	48
Completed Bachelor's	2,000	500
Completed High School	7,000	2,000
Completed Grade School	8,000	4,000
Less	1,900	3,450

School-Age Population

	White	Non-White
High School	1,500	900
Junior High	1,900	1,000
Elementary	2,600	1,000
Pre-Primary	1,000	1,100
	8,000	4,000

Student Population by School and
Per Capita Expenditure

	White	Non-White	$ Per Capita
Wilson Jr./Sr. High	2,000	400	400
Lincoln Jr./Sr. High	1,000	1,450	300
Central Parochial	400	50	400
Field Elementary	600	100	400
Smith Elementary	800	50	500
West Elementary	700	250	300
Carver Elementary	150	900	250
North Elementary	400	350	300
South Elementary	350	400	300
Holy Name Parochial	600	50	400

Percentage of High School Graduates
Entering College

	White	Non-White
Wilson High	53%	42%
Lincoln High	40%	27%

On the basis of these statistics and numerous complaints in the community, the Bay City School Board decided to improve education relative to eight broad goals: (1) increased knowledge of science, (2) increased knowledge of mathematics, (3) increased knowledge of social studies, (4) increased ability to read, (5) increased ability to communicate in writing, (6) increased appreciation of music and art, (7) increased knowledge of health and physical fitness, and (8) increased interest in education.

The board found that it was unable to realize these goals without assistance from state and federal sources, in terms of both financial and staff resources. They then applied to the newly formed state evaluation center for assistance. A state team visited Bay City and collected more background information (in accordance with the variables taxonomy) and produced statistics about community and student attitudes, as well as more detailed information about the teacher and student populations. The team also assisted the school board in systemizing its available resources along lines of "who teaches what, where, and when."

With this information, the school board met with the state team to discuss the elaboration of goals. Our discussion will focus on the goal of increasing reading ability. The first task was to define this goal clearly in terms of operations. The state team obtained a list of all variables subsumed under the heading "Reading" from the variables taxonomy. They were able to inform the local agencies that reading ability is actually a constellation of factors, including, among other things:

(1) Readiness to read, as measured by the Murphy-Durrell *Reading Readiness* Analysis (New York: Harcourt Brace and World, 1965);

(2) Rate of reading, as measured by the speed and accuracy subtest of the *Gates-MacGinitie Reading Test* (New York: Columbia University-Teachers College Press, 1965);

(3) Reading comprehension, as measured by the *Kelley-Greene Reading Comprehension Test* (New York: Harcourt Brace and World, 1953);

(4) Word recognition, as measured by the *Gates Advanced Primary Reading Test* (New York: Columbia University Press, 1958);

(5) Oral reading, as measured by a subtest of the *Gates-McKillop Reading Diagnostic Test* (New York: Columbia University-Teachers College Press, 1962); and

(6) Silent reading, as measured by the *Iowa Silent Reading Tests* (Chicago: World Book Company, 1961).

(The reader should note that the above do not comprise a definitive analysis of factors affecting reading ability or instruments for testing reading ability; they are to be considered as examples of outputs from the variables taxonomy heading "Reading." Our present variables taxonomy includes over 60 instruments in this category.)

The local board studied these instruments for a month, after which they met with the state evaluation team to discuss the feasibility of administering a combination of these instruments, in light of available resources and context factors. At the same time, the local board reviewed information about past administration of the tests and arrived at standards of achievement, defined in terms of scores on the particular test.

We now consider a concrete example of a part of these determinations. (Again, this discussion illustrates only method and is not to be evaluated by its content.) The local board decided that on the basis of community attitudes and parents' educational data that children might come to school illdisposed to read. Thus, one specific goal might be to diagnose readiness to read and take proper action based on the diagnosis. In this light, the Murphy-Durrell Reading Readiness Analysis was investigated. Statistics reported from the state center showed that this test had a split-halves reliability coefficient of .98 overall, and was able to explain 65 percent of the variance in

predicting the three reading subtests of the Stanford Achievement
Tests (actual reading ability). Since the Murphy-Durrell test is administered and scored by the teachers in the classroom, it was estimated
that it would cost a total (including teacher's time) of $1.25 per
student. Further, the test had been standardized on a population
similar to that of Bay City. Published norms for the test were
accepted as standards for Bay City. Thus, part of the general goal of
improving reading has been completely specified in terms of scores
on an existent instrument. Of course, decisions such as these would
have to be made for each of the stated goals. Once again, the
important point to be made is the process of goal definition and
performance standard specification by means of the variables taxonomy.

When goals and standards were specified, the state team proceeded
to conduct a program of test administration to assess the needs of
Bay City relative to the stated goals. In the case of the reading
readiness test, the team would conduct training sessions in administering the test, distribute them, collect results, and prepare reports.
In Bay City the results were:

Percentage of Students in Normed Stanine Categories on Murphy-Durrell Test

	Stanine	Bay City	Comparable Norm
(Poor)	1	10%	4%
	2	12	7
	3	15	12
	4	20	17
	5	19	20
	6	10	17
	7	8	12
	8	6	7
(Superior)	9	2	4

It was clear that Bay City children were far below the norms in
reading readiness. Thus, a need in the area of reading readiness has
been established.

Given this need, the Bay City School Board sought means to
reduce it. The Murphy-Durrell Test has been analyzed in the research
literature. Summaries of this literature were obtained from the processes taxonomy by sifting out the studies that mentioned the test as
"inputs." One study[13] showed that children with low scores on this
test benefitted greatly from systematic instruction in phonemics. The

processes taxonomy was again sifted using Bay City context statistics and "Phonemics" as the treatment variable. One program met these specifications: It involved the use of the Initial Teaching Alphabet (a phonetic device) on beginning readers. The program was observed to have beneficial effects in its past application.

Thus, the Bay City schools instituted a program of reading instruction using the Initial Teaching Alphabet. The state evaluator was called in after planning had begun, but before installation of the program. On examining the materials presented to him and comparing them with design criteria, he found several oversights in the design of the program. While academic objectives had been spelled out quite clearly, and the instruments that would measure different types of reading achievement had been listed with expected performance levels, there had been no clear attempt to specify how teachers would be trained to use the new materials; materials had been specified only as far as the books to be used (no allowance had been made for written material or blackboards in the classrooms). Further, the teaching process to be used in the classroom had been sketched in with virtually no detail.

In response to questions from the evaluator, the program staff attempted to fill in these blanks in the design. It was found that by the use of consultants the teaching process could be defined well enough that workshops could be set up for instructing the teachers. The added cost of the workshops (three two-day workshops and one inservice training day came to $3,300) was not prohibitive and the program design was modified to include them. An investigation of available time and facilities showed that the program could be implemented without conflict with existing programs.

When September came, the program staff was ready to implement the program as designed. In this case the design used in evaluation was the original proposal with the modifications prompted by the evaluator's examination.[14] In order to communicate the specifications to all concerned, a copy of the revised design was sent to all program personnel and other interested parties.

With the program in operation at Field, Carver, and South Elementary Schools, the evaluator set out to see that it had been properly installed. Questionnaires sent to teachers showed that in Field and South Elementary Schools all materials and facilities had been supplied according to the program design, but that in Carver Elementary, because of a mixup by the school clerk, the books had been randomly distributed among the first grades instead of given to two classes as had been the original intent. It was decided to modify application of the design so that all first grades at Carver would have the ITA books.

In order to get the feel of a well-functioning classroom, the evaluator observed and interviewed teachers at Holy Name Parochial, using instruments obtained through the state information system. (Holy Name had had a similar program for three years and had been used as a source for training personnel.) Classroom activities were consistent with the process section of the public school design, and the evaluator decided to use the same observation schedules in his evaluation. The evaluator then observed first grade teachers in Field, South, and Carver Elementary Schools. One of the teachers at Carver had not had the workshops or inservice training specified by the design and was having little success understanding the new materials herself, let alone teaching them. An ad hoc remedy was supplied by allowing her to observe the trained teachers in her school. This was not written into the official program design, because had it not been for the clerical mixup about the books that teacher would not have been considered part of the program. Instead, provision was made in the design for assuring that the proper books got to the proper classes.

The evaluator continued monitoring the classroom process throughout the school year. As refinements of teaching techniques were discovered and disseminated, they were written into the design of the program. Refinements in curriculum were also made to suit certain circumstances; for example, in Carver, which had an 85 percent black population, it was decided to attempt to obtain materials with illustrations of black people in everyday situations.

A meeting of the program staff at this time to discuss community demands on the program resulted in adding an objective of "self-esteem" to the program design. No one knew how to measure it, but processes likely to produce it were written into the design: notably, the acquisition of black-oriented materials at Carver. Reference to the state information system showed that no one else had thought too much about measuring self-esteem, and this idea was given priority for the following year's program.

Measurement of reading achievement at the end of the first year of program operation showed that Field, Carver, and West were about equal in reading achievement, the mean lying near grade level achievement. This was a great improvement over the previous year, but did not bring the mean reading achievement test score near that of Smith where the students were predominately white middle class.

Since the program had been so succesful, it was decided to install

it in North and West the following year. The evaluator monitored
training of staff and installation. In general, the program was installed according to the design. At one school, however, the principal
was obstructive, and the problems became so severe that the following year it was decided to return to teaching the conventional
alphabet at that school.

Reading achievement scores for the second year showed a higher
mean than the previous year at all three of the original project
schools. This might have reflected additional expertise on the part of
the staff. Interestingly, however, means at the new school in which
the program was successfully implemented matched the increase over
the two-year period at the original three schools.

Questions and Answers About a Statewide Evaluation System

The following is a composite of two different conversations held
between the author and each of two Chief State School Officers
interested in installing an evaluation system.

1. What are the purposes of the evaluation system?

The first purpose of an evaluation system is to conduct a need
assessment, that is, to determine the discrepancy between educational
goals of the state as derived from some authoritative or representative
source and actual attainment of these goals by students in selected
school grades.

The second purpose is to conduct evaluations that

(a) measure changes in student performance over time at both
school district and state levels of authority,

(b) determine the educational purposes being served by the
expenditure of local and state educational funds,

(c) estimate the effect of educational programs on student
performance,

(d) identify weaknesses in local and state educational programs,
and

(e) establish a basis for the reallocation of educational funds
for specific educational purposes.

2. How long will it take to achieve these purposes? How long does
it take to determine state goals?

The lengths of time vary. Defining the educational goals of a state
can take a lifetime. Pennsylvania has been at the job for more than
five years.[15] On the other hand, Colorado a few years ago created a
study committee that completed the job in a few months. As a
result, Colorado has been in a position for some time to move
forward promptly with a statewide assessment plan.[16]

3. What is statewide assessment and how does one go about it?

The states that are careful to define educational goals will be able to determine the education needs of their state. Need assessment, as it was first called under the Title 3 ESEA Guidelines, consists of comparing performance with a standard in order to identify discrepancies or shortcomings in performance.

Assessing the educational competency of a state's citizens depends on the existence of measures of performance. All state programs presently committed to assessment are measuring the performance of students, not adults. However, some are concerned only with a determination of performance. This is a little like taking a reading on the depth of water in a channel without regard to how much water your boat draws. These states will know how their students perform but will decide only after the fact what the performance signifies. When standards of performance are set before measurement rather than afterward, the results are more likely to be objective.

4. How much time may be needed for a state need assessment study?

To assess need requires a set of performance measures for each educational goal. Obviously, if state goals are numerous and complex this may take a very long time. However, it is possible to determine specific needs such as statewide reading performance relative to expected levels of performance in the length of time it takes to administer, score, and analyze the results of a standardized reading test, that is a few months.

5. Isn't the reference to "state goals" in the previous answer a threat to our traditional American principle of local autonomy in education?

By statute and federal mandate, the state department of education has responsibility for the disbursement of resources for various programs; it is altogether proper for the state to explicate in detail the reasons for making these allocations. The state desires an information and evaluation system so that it can operate objectively, rather than subjectively on the basis of incomplete information.

6. This is commendable, but what if locals do not agree with state goals? Is the department going to operate by fiat?

Any responsible state official realizes that he cannot survive for long if he is at cross-purposes with local education agencies. We seek to establish a state information system on the basis of local-state tradeoff. This means that the local trades some of its autonomy for essential professional services that it could not possibly afford alone. The state is aware of the emotional climate in which the system must function; it is prepared to work with locals during all stages of the evaluation process.

7. How long will it take to measure changes in student performance?

To measure changes in student performance requires comparable measures at at least two, and preferably three, equidistant points in time. Fluctuations in test scores can make trend analysis of this data grossly misleading. The primary methods of eliminating misinterpretation depend on obtaining many points in a series, which requires still more time. However, compromises are again in order. Two measures over time are better than one, and when standardized tests are used, a year is generally the shortest acceptable interval.

Another consideration affecting time is a choice of instruments that ensure at least minimum comparability at two or more time points. Where statewide achievement tests were administered the previous year, it may be possible to measure changes in student achievement as soon as a decision to assess is made. However, this statewide testing with a single instrument is the exception, and even then careful attention must be given to test levels, forms, and batteries to ensure comparability across grade levels. Given most tests, it is usually possible to find only a few grades where student performance can be compared with the previous year. Hence, for most state assessments, considerable time before the first measurement point will be required to select or redesign an appropriate instrument for even such widely measured behavior as reading.

8. Is it possible to attribute positive changes in student performance to the effectiveness of educational programs?

Not unless the programs have been carefully described and meaningful relations have been established between program variables and performance variables. Even then, of course, the scientific method leaves us without "proof positive." However, modern technology and scientific business practices rest on assumptions of causation, and those of us in education would be the last to spurn this evidence. The trouble is, we rarely have it. Accurate descriptions of programs, their resource requirements, their outputs, and analyses of how resources are converted to outputs are generally unavailable.

9. Well then, how long will it take to know the effect of educational programs on students?

We will estimate the effect based on a systems analysis of each educational program in the state and a benefit analysis of all programs in a state. Nothing less than a comprehensive evaluation system is required. A great deal of information is needed to make this kind of system work, but it can be collected locally. And it will be provided willingly and rapidly once local administrators understand its value. Hence, a massive training program is needed to make a sound statewide evaluation program work. For statewide training of administrators to occur there must be crash staff development programs for state departments of education. The ingredients of the training are analytic skills and interpersonal competence. The flock of statistics, measurement, and experimental design courses taught at universities under the evaluation rubric are of little value to practitioners who must install and maintain a statewide evaluation system. The design of such a system requires considerable sophistication derived from the more precise and quantitative social and natural sciences, but the maintenance of the system requires the construction of interdependent human relationships based on precise definitions of information needs and values. In this latter area, verbal skills transcend quantitative ability.

10. The importance of finding out what programs our educational funds are buying and what goals these programs serve is clear, but isn't this what Program Planning and Budgeting Systems (PPBS) is all about and won't these efforts take a long time?

Yes, stating purposes carefully and identifying the time and money needed for the goods and people that can accomplish these purposes is what PPBS is mostly about. And there are places such as the Baltimore schools, Dade County schools, and Yale University, that have been working on these programs for many years. However, such management skills as administration by objective, program control by exception, and communication based on information feedback are critical to the operation of PPBS. And very little staff training work is visible in places struggling to install PPBS. Again before an evaluation system or a PPBS system will work, a strategy of tradeoff must be established between the administrators who wish to improve and better manage their local programs and state department personnel who wish to determine program effects on students. Once local managers recognize the utility of the evaluation information they receive from a state department, they will quickly learn the skills they must have to generate the data on which the information is based.

11. How much money will this information management system cost?

Development costs will run about $1.5 million. After the first two years of initial investment we should be able to run the system for about $400,000 per year.

12. Is education so backwards in this state that we need this large capital investment immediately?

Education is a complex discipline, involving millions of people and thousands of variables. The public constantly demands better education, which means that we must engage in research to find ways of doing the job better, and this means that we must collect, handle, and interpret a lot of information. In fact,there is so much information that computers are absolutely necessary to help manage it all.

13. We realize that computers are helpful and that good research is desirable; the question is why do we need this system *now*? The school system seems to be working; why should we spend this large amount of money to change it?

The school system functions now by sacrificing much important information on the altar of expediency. Often data is so collected as to give only summary statistics without data on individual cases. If we want the data summarized in another way, we must go out into the field and start from scratch. The office of statistical services has found 698 forms used to report basic educational data; about 30% of these overlap in information requested. Since there are about 600 school districts in the state, we can see that a considerable amount of time is wasted filling out forms.

698 forms x 30% redundancy x 600 school districts x X manhours per form = 125,640 X wasted man-hours.

We have sampled some of the forms in general. Each requires someone in the local district to summarize files of individual students according to some criterion. Thus we find the same file of students being combed on separate occasions to find all dropouts or to make racial or numerous other classifications. It is a considerable understatement to say that ten man-hours are required for each of these searches. At the federal minimum wage of $1.75, a gross understatement of the waste incurred by the state in needless effort is:

125,640 x 10 man hours per form x $1.75 = $2,198,700.00

Thus we see that the state information system would probably pay for itself if it merely eliminated effort wasted in filling out forms.

Remember that information requirements can only increase in the future; the only way to meet these needs economically is with the aid of electronic equipment.

14. The TECH staff has submitted a proposal to support the ABC Corp. in developing the system. Why are they necessary for this project? ABC is a big company and should be able to do the job without this other expense.

First, although ABC is indeed a large corporation, the bulk of its experience lies in systemizing fields that lend themselves readily to quantification; they are a relative newcomer to the field of education. Their initial effort in Puerto Rico has been continuously plagued by problems that might be classified as resulting from insufficient educational experience. On the other hand TECH's primary business is education, and its staff has considerable training and experience in educational research and evaluation.

Secondly, there are several clauses in the ABC contract that imply that this state should advise ABC about initiating work or the sufficiency of completed work. At this time, the state department cannot spare staff to do this, thus the need for TECH.

15. The report paints a rosy picture for the future of education in this state. How much of this can we expect in the first year of the project and in the second, and so forth?

The development of these systems takes much time, and they should always be viewed as a capital investment rather than a purchase for immediate consumption. Since the state must discuss the system in detail with local educational agencies, the task becomes even more difficult. Several benefits may be achieved, however, even in the first year:

(a) Identification and systemization of the state's information needs;

(b) Computer adaptation of state accounting and finance procedures in terms of a functional budget,

(c) Elimination of costly redundancies in basic reporting forms;

(d) Foundation work for the pilot project such as instrument development, staff training, and the like;

(e) Simulation of the management information system; and

(f) Development and experimental test of the item-pool statistical machinery.

In the second year we may achieve:

(a) A test of the goal development and specification process in the pilot district;

(b) Dynamic evaluation of programs in the pilot district;

(c) A field test of item-pool statistical machinery; and

(d) Groundwork for extending the system to an entire region, including development of a regional statistical services center.

In the third, fourth, and fifth year we may expect:

(a) Extension of the system to the entire state; and

(b) Alteration of the system in light of pilot evidence.

If the project were adequately funded we could probably expect the system to be working in its most general form in six years.

16. Are there any other needs for the information system?

Yes. The primary need for the system is to give the state department more information to perform its duties on a more objective basis. Often, the state cannot manage the information that it already has, and this information is not enough to help make sound management decisions. For instance, there are about 2,000 programs funded under Title 1 of the ESEA alone. The state cannot possibly find time to do an in-depth analysis of each one, and local agencies cannot afford to do the job. As a result, much misinformation is produced, which breeds dissatisfaction at the local level and spills over into the state political arena as well. A computer-assisted information and evaluation system can make local and state information compatible with the public information needs of management.

Also, since there is no central repository of information, communication within the state department is hampered, resulting in costly duplication of effort. A state information system would facilitate concerted action by the state department.

Many federal grants will also be awarded in the future on the basis of needs assessment. The states that write the best-detailed reports will get the lion's share of the funds. This state can get the jump on the rest of the states by implementing a computer system now.

17. What is the evaluation information that will be useful to administrators in local school districts?

It is information describing the strengths and weaknesses of specific programs. It is given to the managers of the programs, periodically, from the time the program is planned through its installation phase and its output of short term and long-range benefits. On the basis of this information the program manager can change his program to improve it, maintain it at a steady state, or recommend that it be terminated. If the information is made public, the manager may prefer to terminate a program and use its resources for some more constructive purpose, rather than continue to operate an ineffective program. Obviously these decisions are needed if American education is to improve at every level. Ultimately, school superintendents from the smallest town to the largest city stand accountable to their boards for improvement, and a wise administrator welcomes information that ensures his accountability.

18. Can administrators really afford to make evaluations public?

Educational leadership can only be based on an honest appraisal of what is wrong in a system. Courageous leaders will want to know where weaknesses in new programs exist so they can be modified as necessary. They will want an informed public that shares both the risk of developing new programs and the inevitable frustrations of failure. Public evaluation as an education reform strategy could create a new basis for joint public and professional effort. On this base new programs can be launched that may yet meet the critical needs of our times.

Footnotes

1. Frank Morra, Assistant Professor, San Bernadino State College is the coauthor.

2. These four questions were raised at a Governor's Conference on Education held in New Brunswick, N.J. April 2, 1966.

3. Allen Newell, "On the Analysis of Human Problem Solving Protocols" (Paper given at the International Symposium of Mathematical and Computational Methods, Rome, July 4-9, 1966). (Available from Department of Computer Science, Carnegie-Mellon University, Pittsburgh, Pennsylvania 15213).

4. Note: Read "::" = "as" defined as "equal to."

5. Allen Newell and Herbert A. Simon, "GPS, A Program that Stimulates Human Thought" in *Computer and Thought*, ed. E. Feigenbaum and J. Feldman (New York: McGraw-Hill, 1963).

6. Pittsburgh Public Schools, Office of Research, *The Discrepancy Evaluation Model* (1969).

7. Merritt Gilman, "Problems and Progress in Staff Training," *Crime and Delinquency* 12, no. 3 (July 1966): pp. 254-260.

8. James G. March, and Herbert A. Simon, *Organizations* (New York: Wiley, 1958).

9. George C. Homans, *The Human Group* (New York: Harcourt Brace, 1950).

10. William F. Whyte, *Human Relations in the Restaurant Industry* (New York: McGraw-Hill, 1948).

11. Egon Guba, "The Failure of Educational Evaluation," *Educational Technology*, May 1969.

12. Pittsburgh Public Schools, op. cit.

13. H. A. Murphy, "The Spontaneous Speaking Vocabulary of Children in Primary Grades," *Journal of Education* 140 (1957): 1-106.

14. Had the evaluator come into an ongoing program, the design would have been obtained by a structured interview with all the program staff.

15. State Board of Education of the Commonwealth of Pennsylvania, *Quality of Education Project (QEPS): A Plan for Evaluating the Quality of Education Programs in Pennsylvania*, 3 vols. (Harrisburg, Pa.: 1965).

16. Colorado Department of Education, Task Force of Assessment and Evaluation, "Technical Report" (Unpublished, 1969-70).

11

Application to a Federal Bureau

The Overall Design

At the time the work described here was done, the Bureau of Educational and Personnel Development encompassed 14 programs, each of which funded from 10 to 80 projects in American schools, colleges, and universities. The bureau is organized to fund programs with specific goals, and projects that serve these goals, under conditions defined by Congress. In all, over 750 projects are funded, from the training of university professors, to teacher, papaprofessional, and youth tutor training.

The general goal of the bureau is to marshal national resources in new ways to meet the critical training needs of students, teachers, schools, and the educational and social institutions that support them. The bureau also has the responsibility of ensuring that its programs and projects are well administered and that they operate and develop as expected. The bureau works to be reasonably assured that its money is well spent. Training programs have traditionally been unsuccessful in American education. The bureau wishes to be able to intervene to put faltering programs back on the track so that they are ultimately successful.

Purpose

The purpose of this study was to design and implement an evaluation system for the Bureau of Educational Personnel Development of the Office of Education. The major purpose of the evaluation system was to provide a general core of information that would enable the bureau and all its subdivisions to assess the impact of their programs, function as a cohesive, efficient unit, and meet the following objectives:

(1) Provide accurate and detailed descriptions of proposals, projects, and programs.

(2) Provide comprehensive statements of purpose at all levels within the bureau.

(3) Provide a measure of accomplishment of the purposes.

(4) Provide a comparison of processes across subdivisions with common purposes in order to identify and compare effective process elements.

(5) Identify factors conducive to the success or failure of various types of programs under varying and specified conditions. This information was to be available for developmental work on new training programs.

(6) Provide information about the effect of training programs on trainee performance and subsequently, of trainee performance on student achievement.

(7) Provide information about the impacts of the programs in effecting changes in existing institutions.

(8) Provide information on the subsequent use and career patterns of the trainees.

(9) Provide a comprehensive data base for research questions.

(10) Enable the establishment of cost-effectiveness analyses of various processes that produce the same products.

(11) Provide information that would permit modification or improvement of ongoing programs.

The evaluation system was to provide information that would help fashion new strategies for meeting the training needs of educational personnel. The evaluation system was designed to provide specific answers to questions that had long preplexed the bureau and the Office of Education.

(1) To what extent are bureau programs meeting their objectives?

(2) To what extent do various program components affect the accomplishment of objectives?

(3) What is the effectiveness of training programs in terms of trainee performance?

(4) To what extent are the improved training practices and organizational structures promoted by the bureau being institutionalized?

(5) What is the impact of programs in terms of the use and career patterns of trainees?

(6) What is the impact of federal money on school children's achievements in schools employing teachers trained under BEPD grants?

(7) What context variables influence the accomplishment of the objectives of the bureau?

Assumptions

The assumptions underlying the application of the Discrepancy Evaluation Model were specified: Foremost, perhaps, was the definition of *decision maker,* which included all the staff responsible for making a program serve its stated purposes. A second major assumption was that the standards of each program were to be set by the program staff within the boundary conditions installed by the bureau. The third major assumption was that the Washington program staff and project staff at the local level were to be free to revise their program and project standards as long as higher level conditions were not violated.

Other assumptions were:

(1) Evaluation is the act of explicating standards, comparing standards with performance (S-P) and reporting discrepancies to those concerned with performance (feedback). Evaluation is part of a general problem-solving paradigm that includes research, management, and analysis functions.

(2) The operations, roles, and purposes of an organization are derived from criterion models that explicate institutional values, providing specific referents for modeling performance and specific criteria for evaluating performance.

(3) Criterion models are derived from values and knowledge; choices between alternative criterion models are made on the basis of

    (a) Probability estimates of consequence,

    (b) Congruence between reality and constructs of model, and

    (c) Sufficiency or conservation of resources.

(4) Feedback (S-P discrepancies) can result in

    (a) Changes in performance,

    (b) Changes in standards, or

    (c) no change or action.

(5) An organization is most responsive to feedback if the stan-

dards used for S-P comparison are a reflection of the values of the organization's members.

(6) A distinction must be made between the function of evaluation in the problem-solving process and the role of an evaluator in an organization's institutional setting.

(7) The evaluator's role is to guide the decision maker through the decisionmaking process and to insure that information needs are recognized and met.

(8) An organization includes communication, control, and analysis systems that maintain the organization and support its operations.

(9) Institutional operations serve both internal and external values (such as social utility) recognized and endorsed by members of the institution.

(10) The goals of an organization and the conditions under which it operates are a function of the interaction of staff experiences, values, and knowledge with the larger environment in which institutional operations occur.

A final assumption dealt with the nature of evaluation and the states of evaluation as defined under the model.

Task

Our task was to complete the design of an evaluation system that would

(1) Develop for the bureau a systems design that
  (a) Specified conditions imposed on each program,
  (b) Clarified bureau goals relative to each program by fixing standards for each input and output; and
  (c) Detailed the bureau report structure.

(2) Develop for each program in the bureau a systems design that
  (a) Specified conditions imposed on each project and provided appropriate instrumentation for ensuring that these conditions were met,
  (b) Clarified program goals relative to each project by fixing standards for each input and output, and
  (c) Detailed the program report structure for each program by providing a simulated report structure.

(3) Verify the installation of all report structures and data input procedures by field testing.

(4) Use a data-processing system to carry out the evaluation.

(5) Provide appropriate training and procedural manuals for all staff involved in the evaluation.

(6) Provide for the monitoring of design operation for one year.

The design of a program monitoring information system for the bureau would make possible the collection and storage of data essential to periodic discrepancy reports on installation, operation, and ultimate impact of bureau programs. But the evaluation of the bureau itself would have to depend on the formulation of an overall bureau design replete with definitions of major purposes, operations, and resources. To accomplish the explication of design, enabling legislation was studied, the goals of programs were elicited and compounded, the management structure of the bureau was reviewed, and its resources and resource allocation procedures were studied.

As a result, considerable documentation on bureau inputs, processes, and outputs was amassed and shared, first at the program level and then at the bureau level with policy-making staff. A basic mission statement was agreed on, and when shortly thereafter division and program budgets were established, it was possible to draw up the overall expectations of the bureau with respect to the impact of defined resources on specific targets. As a consequence, program managers became more aware of the boundary conditions of the system for which they were responsible and in some cases were able to transmit more specific conditions of funding to projects and project applicants in the field.

To conduct the bureau evaluation, it is necessary to set program standards for operating projects. These standards must take into account both the goals of the program and the conditions under which it must operate. At the bureau level goals and conditions, as defined by Congress, the Office of Education, and the Associate Commissioner for the bureau, established the standards for evaluating the bureau program. These standards are in the form of criteria for input, process, and output. The input standard is based on conditions; the output standard on the bureau's goals, and the process standard remains undefined. At the program level, the input standard is defined by the bureau's conditions together with new conditions that may be laid down by the program manager to ensure that his projects will have essential resources and support. The output standard is defined by the selection of relevant bureau goals. The process standard is undefined. At the project level, the input standard encompasses both the program conditions and any local conditions affecting the project. The output standard is defined by the program goals. The process standard is defined by the project manager, and constitutes a series of activities thought to be required for achieving the stated goals under the conditions identified.

The standards for evaluation at the level of bureau, program, and project are thus standards that specify the conditions, processes, and outcomes of projects. At the project level, outcomes are specified in terms of goals, objectives, and enabling objectives; input, in terms of the local and federal conditions; and process, in terms of installation and operation of the project. These standards should be related in the project proposal submitted to the program director. The standards can then be used as the basis for evaluating project performance. Only when the proposal meets program standards should the project be funded. After contracts have been awarded, program directors should ensure that the project conditions have been met, that is, that the project input standards have been met in the operationalized project. This can be done by the submission of data from project. Data on change variables (the conditions that are to be changed to meet project goals) can be collected in Washington and stored for later comparison. An assessment of those conditions being met at the project, program, and bureau levels can then be prepared in Washington to determine the necessity for changes in project performance or in project design. At some later time, new data based on the current design of the project can again be collected in order to make the comparison between standard and performance. At that time, an analysis of project operations, or process, as well as products, can be made and fed back to the project, program, and bureau staffs.

It is an assumption of the whole system that evaluation of the bureau's effectiveness in reaching its goals cannot take place unless projects are properly managed and large amounts of valid information are available to the bureau. This data will be compared to expected outcomes delineated in the proposal or design, leading to an evaluation of each project. The only source of this information is the project director. The director is unlikely to provide the information unless he too benefits from its collection. His benefit is the reports that help him manage his project better and increase its likelihood of success.

Given the cooperation of the project directors, the major cost of the bureau's evaluation system, that of data collection, can be almost eliminated. Hence, the real cost of the system becomes that of data analysis, report generation, and instrument preparation.

The Information Structure of the Evaluation

The initial information structure of the system consists of conditions in the form of inputs and outputs imposed on lower level subsystems and processes that can be defined initially.

Definitions at each level within the system are a function of definitions at all higher levels plus those conditions required to insure successful operations at any given level. These constraints do not apply to processess because process is free from the influence of higher level process definitions. For that reason, even though higher level processes may be undefined, lower order processes can still be defined and made part of the initial information system.

For any given program, inputs may be broken down into the various levels of participants in projects. Each level may be subject to conditions imposed from above. A clear definition of relations between levels is essential to adequate program design and a working information system. For any program in the bureau, variants of their condition descriptions will be required relative to program development events and the time they occur. For example, Figure 1 shows six condition descriptions (row headings) at seven points in time (column headings). The first column in the figure represents information describing conditions prerequisite to funding. The second column represents information on installation activities before actual program operations, such as recruitment etc. The remaining columns represent output information of various kinds necessary to achieve the short term and long term processes and products or projects and programs. Using structures of this sort, it becomes possible to generate most of the information required to evaluate each BEPD program. Figure 1 is of such a construction for the Career Opportunity Program (COP). The numbers in each cell refer to the variables listed in Figure 2 and represent the information requirements of the system.

Figure 1: Variables from Systems Levels at Various Stages for the COP Program

	Funding Conditions	Preprogram Activities	June 30, 1970	Sept. 30, 1970	Nov. 30, 1970	Jan. 30, 1971	June 30, 1971
Clients	11-16		104-121	122-125, 125a		122-125	122-125, 125a
Local Agency		48-101	102, 103	137-145 199-219		137-145 199-219 48-85	137-145 199-219 48-85
Institutions for Higher Education	126-129	130-136		196			147-149
Linking Agencies	24-47						
Youth to Youth Project	17-23			155-195		155-195	155-195
Community	1-10		15-154	198, 198	150-154, 198		150-154, 198

Figure 2: Variables Taxonomy For COP

1. Percentage of families in LEA district below OEO-established poverty limits in income
2. Number of bilingual homes in LEA district
3. Number of Black or Afro-American children served by the district
4. Number of Spanish-surnamed children served by the district
5. Number of Oriental children served by the district
6. Number of American Indian children served by the district
7. Number of Chicano children served by the district
8. Number of migratory workers' children served by the district
9. Number of Caucasian children served by the district
10. Estimated number of Vietnam era veterans in the area served by the district
11. Percentage of certified teachers who will work directly with COP participants
12. Percentage of certified administrators who will work directly with COP participants
13. Percentage of certified pupil services personnel who will work directly with COP participants
14. The salary to be paid at each level of the career lattice
15. A brief summary of the duties and responsibilities assumed in each cell of the career lattice
16. Statement of the experience and training required for each cell of the career lattice
17. Total expected number of tutees in YTY program
18. Total expected number of tutors in the YTY program
19. Checklist describing compensation that tutors will receive
20. Dollar estimate of cost to train tutors
21. Dollar estimate of cost to supervise tutors
22. Total estimated cost of tutor compensation
23. Dollar estimate of cost of equipment and materials to be used in YTY program

EXISTENT TRAINING PROGRAMS

	Amount of Funding	Number Trainees	Number Dropouts
Model Cities	24	25	26
New Careers	27	28	29
Title I, ESEA	30	31	32
Head Start	33	34	35
Follow Through	36	37	38
NYC	39	40	41
State Funded (B-2)	42	43	44
Locally Funded	45	46	47

BUDGET FOR 1970

	COP Funds	Other Funds
Director	48	49

Figure 2 (cont'd)

Other Staff	50	51
Secretarial/clerical	52	53
Consultants	54	55
Staff benefits/services	56	57
Tuition/fees	58	59
Books/supplies	60	61
Total trainee summer stipend	62	63
Total trainee stipend, regular year	64	65
Total school personnel stipends—		
summer and school year	66	67
Administrator stipends	68	69
Trainee benefits	70	71
Evaluation	72	73
Conferences	74	75
Recruitment	76	77
Travel	78	79
COP office supplies	80	81
YTY supplies	82	83
Other	84	85

SELECTION CRITERIA

Variable	Criterion	Emphasis
Income	86	87
Sex	88	89
Marital status	90	91
Ethnic background	92	93
Veteran status	94	95
Residence in school neighborhood	96	97
Educational level	98	99
Present employment as a paraprofessional	100	101

    102. For each cell in the career lattice the number of participants who were selected for that cell

    103. The total number of participants selected

Participant data—to be collected for each participant

    104. Participant's name

    105. Participant's street address

    106. City of residence of participant

    107. State of residence of participant

    108. Zip code of participant

    109. County of residence of participant

    110. Social security number of participant

    111. Congressional district of participant

    112. Sex of participant

    113. Age of participant

    114. Marital status of participant

Figure 2 (cont'd)

115. Number of dependents supported by participant
116. Income of participant
117. Ethnic background of participant
118. Veteran status of participant
119. Educational level of participant
120. Does the participant reside in the school neighborhood
121. Present employment of participant as a paraprofessional
122. School to which participant is assigned
123. Number of courses completed/number semester hours earned
124. Job performance rating
125. Career lattice position
125a. Testing results

IHE Data

126. Percentage staff members at each faculty rank who will work directly with COP participants
127. Percentage breakdown of these staff members according to highest academic degree
128. Percentage breakdown of staff members according to departmental affiliation
129. Percentage of staff members with prior experience with people with backgrounds similar to the COP participants
130. Estimate of the cost to the IHE in terms of staff salaries
131. Estimate of the cost to the IHE in terms of facilities
132. Tuition charged per COP participant
133. Additional fees charged per COP participant
134. Estimate of the percentage of time to be spent in college classroom
135. Estimate of the time to be spent in work-practicum
136. Extent of community involvement from checklist

LEA Outcome Data

Data requested is the mean for each school employing COP participants

137. Percentage teacher time spent on class preparation
138. Percentage teacher time spent lecturing
139. Percentage teacher time spent on class discussion
140. Percentage teacher time spent on clerical work
141. Percentage teacher time spent on diagnosis and prescription
142. Percentage time spent on maintaining discipline
143. Percentage teacher time spent on "other" activities
144. Checklist describing whether sufficient time is available for diagnostic and prescriptive activity
145. Checklist describing education-technological aids used during the last semester
146. Checklist describing areas in which teachers want help from in-class aides

IHE Outcome Data

147. Narrative description of new educational needs uncovered by the COP
148. Checklist describing resources necessary to meet this need
149. Cost of meeting this need

Community Outcome Data

150. Average attendance at PTA or similar meetings last quarter

Figure 2 (cont'd)

151. Number of community members, including parents serving on policy boards or councils
152. Number of community members, including parents serving as volunteer lay workers
153. Number of community members, including parents belonging to parent clubs or associations
154. Number of community members, including parents assisting and/or chaperoning at social functions or athletic events

YTY Outcomes
155. Total number of dropouts from tutoring program (tutors)
156. Total number new tutors recruited
157. Method of training tutors from checklist
158. Methods of tutoring from checklist
159. Supervisor estimate of amount of interaction between tutors and COP participants

RATINGS

	Supervisors	Participants	Tutors	Tutees
Tutor training	160	161	162	163
Materials and equipment	164	165	166	167
Achievement of tutors	168	169	170	171
Attitude of tutors	172	173	174	175
Achievement of tutees	176	177	178	179
Attitude of tutees	180	181	182	183
Teacher reaction to YTY Program	184	185	186	187
Parent reaction to program	188	189	190	191
Overall rating of YTY program	192	193	194	195

Other LEA Outcomes
196. Number of teachers and administrators who participated in summer training at IHE
197. Number of community people who participated in summer training at IHE
198. Aggregated community rating of COP as a whole

RATINGS

	Teachers	Administrators	Participants
Achievement of participant in academic skills	199	200	201
Attitude of participant toward school	202	203	204
Participant job performance	205	206	207
Attitude toward community	208	209	210
Attitude toward teachers	211	212	213
Attitude toward administrators	214	215	216
Attitude toward COP in general	217	218	219

Bureau

At the bureau level, information needs were defined in three categories: (1) program outcomes relative to student performance; (2) program outcomes relative to the behavior of professional and nonprofessional school staff having a direct influence on student behavior; (3) changes in behavior, institutional policy, and personnel affecting the behavior of professional and nonprofessional school practitioners. This latter category included descriptions or measures of increase in parent and community participation in the educational processes as well as the effectiveness of state departments of education and of such organizations as teachers' associations and unions.

The most general information structure of the bureau's evaluation system could be expressed in a bivariate table showing the relationship of student, teacher and institutional data to the time periods at which this information is collected. After the first year, the bureau's information needs would be on an annual basis.

A General Taxonomy

To insure the uniformity of information reported at program and bureau levels, a taxonomy of variables was needed. The taxonomy was used as the basis for all program descriptions of input, process, and output. Use of the taxonomy ensured design and instrument comparability across projects and programs to the extent that common variables were understood and shared.

BEPD General Taxonomy

The Elements of the Bureau Taxonomy

I. Job Category of Personnel: This component describes the present job category of the program participants.

    A. General Educational Personnel—applies to programs describing several different levels of professionals and nonprofessionals.

    B. General Professional—applies to programs describing several levels of professionals only.

    C. Administrators—applies to programs describing principals, general school administrators, or coordinators who serve more than one school or school district.

    D. Practicing Teachers—applies to programs describing preschool through secondary teachers including physical education teachers, vocational-technical teachers, and librarians with teaching duties.

    E. Supervisors—applies to programs describing supervisors, subject matter specialists who develop curriculum and work with teachers, and traveling teachers in a specific subject area who serve in an advisory capacity to other teachers.

    F. Preservice Professionals—applies to programs describing personnel not yet in service but being trained for a professional role.

    G. General Nonprofessionals—applies to programs describing aides and general community personnel.

H.   Preservice Nonprofessionals—applies to programs describing personnel not yet in service but being trained for a nonprofessional role.

I.   Instructional Specialists—applies to programs describing personnel with specialties that apply directly to instruction. Instructional specialists are further subdivided:

   1.   General Curriculum Specialists—applies to programs describing personnel who are specialists in curriculum development without regard to subject matter area.

   2.   Media Specialists—applies to programs describing personnel who are specialists in planning, development, and use of instructional media.

J.   Pupil Service Specialists—applies to programs describing pupil service personnel including all specialties where services are not directly related to instruction.

   1.   Counselors—applies to programs describing counselors only.

   2.   School Psychologists—applies to programs describing school psychologists whose functions are testing and diagnosis but not counseling and/or therapy.

   3.   Physical Health Personnel—applies to programs describing personnel whose functions are directly related to the physical health of the child but who have no teaching functions: doctor, dentist, nurse, etc.

   4.   Mental Health Personnel—applies to programs describing personnel whose functions are directly related to the mental health of the child. Includes personnel with teaching functions only if they are part of a mental health team.

   5.   Social Workers—applies to programs describing personnel who function as liaison between home and school and are not part of a mental health team.

   6.   Combination of Pupil Service Personnel—applies to programs describing more than one type of pupil service category or pupil service teams.

K.   Trainers—applies to programs describing trainers or teachers of any professional or nonprofessional category.

L.   Evaluation Specialists—applies to programs describing personnel engaged in research and evaluation.

M.   Others—applies to programs describing participants who cannot be classified in any other category.

II. Focus: This component describes the approximate range of the program's focus. The range can be as wide as the training of a secondary guidance counselor or as specific as training a secondary guidance counselor to encourage disadvantaged youth to go on to college.

A.   General—applies to programs whose focus is limited only by the restrictions placed by the characteristics of the other components.

B.   Specific—applies to programs in which the focus is further restricted than the restrictions placed by the characteristics of the other components. An exception may come under IVB where the deficiencies are quite specific and IIG3 where the change agent role may be a narrowly defined area.

III. Purpose of Training Program: This component describes the major goal for which the program exists.

A. General Professional—development or training in job category—applies to programs describing skills, knowledge, or general information for continuing professional development or training in job category without regard to subject matter, population, or special skills.

B. Professional Development or training in job category for work in specific subject matter and/or with special populations—applies to programs describing skills, knowledge or general information with regard to teaching specific subject matter, or working with special groups. This characteristic is further subdivided:

    1. Special Population—applies to programs specifying work with special groups (socioeconomic, minorities, regional, handicapped) without regard to subject matter.

    2. Specific Subject Matter—applies to programs describing specific subject matter (math, social studies, etc.) with which the participant will work after leaving program without regard to population or methodology.

    3. Specific Subject Matter and Special Population—applies to programs describing both specific subject matter and special population with which participant will work after leaving the program.

C. Training in Curriculum Development—applies to programs that have as their major purpose developing competencies in curriculum development. This characteristic is further subdivided:

    1. General—applies to programs training curriculum development competencies without regard to subject matter.

    2. Specific—applies to programs training curriculum development competencies in a specific subject matter area.

D. Training in Development of Media—applies to programs that have as their major purpose developing competencies in the development and use of media. This characteristic is further subdivided:

    1. General—applies to programs that specify developing competencies in the development and use of media without regard to subject matter or methodology.

    2. Specific Subject—applies to programs that specify development and use of media in a specific subject matter.

    3. Specific Methodology—applies to programs that specify development and use of media for a specific methodology such as individualized instruction or CAI.

E. Training in Implementation and Use of Special Instructional Methodology—applies to programs that have as their major purpose training personnel to implement and/or use a particular methodology such as individualized instruction, CAI, etc.

F. Training in Human Relations—applies to programs that have as their major purpose training in interpersonal relationships, group techniques, and increased competency in working with people of different cultures.

G. Training for Special Role—applies to programs that have as their major purpose training personnel to take on a new role not generally part of their functions. This characteristic is further subdivided:

    1. Training Role—applies to programs in which personnel not

generally trainers are instructed in the training of other personnel.

2.   Leadership Role—applies to programs in which personnel not generally holding leadership positions are trained to be leaders of other personnel.

3.   Change Agent—applies to programs in which personnel are trained specifically for the role of change agent.

4.   Unclassified—applies to programs that specify the training of personnel for new roles without specifications of the roles or any role that cannot be classified in the other categories.

H.   Research and Evaluation Specialists—applies to programs that have as their major purpose the training of research and evaluation specialists.

I.   Training of Indigenous Personnel for New Careers—applies to programs in which the primary purpose is to upgrade indigenous personnel.

IV. Student Unit in Training Program: Some programs are designed to train individuals, and others are designed to train teams of personnel who will work together in the field.

A.   Individual—applies to programs that train individuals.

B.   Teams—applies to programs that train teams.

V. Cultural Emphasis of Training Program: This component refers to the content of the training program itself.

A.   General—applies to programs that either do not specify any culture emphasis or to programs in which the emphasis of another culture would naturally be part of the content, such as foreign language programs.

B.   Minority Group—applies to programs in which the emphasis of the content is in the context of a minority group culture.

VI. Selection Criteria for Participants in Training Program: This component refers to the conditions on which the participant is selected for the program.

A.   Undetermined Beyond Job Type Category—applies to programs in which the conditions are either unstated or are those normally acquired for the job category.

B.   Special Deficiencies—applies to programs that specify that the program will attempt to correct a deficiency in knowledge or skills that the participant needs for his job.

C.   Special Educational Requirements—applies to programs that require participants to possess educational requirements beyond those secured for their job category.

D.   Special Experience Requirements—applies to programs that expect the participant to have particular experience that is not necessarily acquired in his job category.

E.   Socioeconomic Requirements—applies to programs that admit to the program only participants with certain types of socioeconomic backgrounds.

F.   Others—applies to programs with selection criteria that do not fit any of the other categories.

VII. Primary Target of Program Participants: The primary target is considered to be the group that is the direct beneficiary of the participant's services, in other words, the group with whom the participant works after he leaves the program.

- A. Students—applies to all children of public school age including preschool.
- B. College Undergraduates and Graduate Students—applies to students enrolled in an undergraduate or graduate course training for a profession but still preservice.
- C. Professionals—applies to any of the professional levels in which the professional serves.
- D. Students and Professionals—includes characteristics A and C.
- E. College Students—includes characteristics B and C.
- F. Nonprofessionals—applies to preservice and inservice nonprofessionals.
- G. Professionals and Nonprofessionals—includes characteristics C and F.
- H. Parents—persons with public school age children.
- I. Community Volunteers—persons from the community who will work in some volunteer capacity with the schools.
- J. General Community Adults—Persons enrolled in adult education courses who do not have any further connection with the schools.
- K. General—includes a number of the above categories. Will generally apply when the participants include a wide variety of job categories and therefore the primary targets will be diversified.

VIII. Characteristics of Ultimate Student Target: Usually the ultimate target is the child. A program participant who is a trainer may have as his primary target the teacher, but the ultimate target will be the child taught by that teacher. If the program participant is a teacher or any other job category in which the primary target is the child, then the primary target and the ultimate target are the same. An exception to the child as the ultimate target is the adult enrolled in an adult education course. The characteristics under this component are without regard to grade level.

- A. General—applies when the ultimate student target can be any child without regard to special populations.
- B. Socioeconomic, Minority Groups—applies when the ultimate student target is a special socioeconomic or minority group.
- C. General Geographical—applies when the program stipulates that the students eventually taught will be from a specific geographical area without regard to special socioeconomic or minority groups.
- D. Special Education—includes all student populations in which handicaps exist that can influence learning. This characteristic is further subdivided:
  1. General—applies to all subdivisions of special education.
  2. Physically Handicapped—applies to a physical disability such as blindness, deafness, etc.
  3. Mentally Retarded—applies to all levels of mental retardation.
  4. Emotionally Disturbed—applies to children in special classes for the emotionally disturbed or those being seen by a mental health team.
  5. Learning Disabilities—applies when a program particularly refers to learning disabilities as opposed to the other subdivisions or those children with perceptual problems.
- E. Technical-Vocational—applies to school dropouts or students in the

       first few years beyond high school participating in a vocational-technical program.

    F.   Gifted—applies to students with special talents and/or in advanced placement courses.

    G.   Adults—applies to persons participating in adult education courses not included under F. Does not include parents and community volunteers, since in those cases the ultimate target is the child.

  IX. Education Level of Ultimate Child Target: Since the ultimate target is usually the child, the child is at some grade level in the educational system.

    A.   General—applies when no particular grade levels are specified.

    B.   Early Childhood—applies when the upper limit of the grade level of the child is grade 3.

    C.   Elementary—applies when the grade level is K-6 or where the lower limit is grade 4 and the upper limit is grade 9.

    D.   Junior High—applies when the lower limit is grade 7 and the upper limit is grade 9.

    E.   Elementary and Junior High—combines characteristics C and D.

    F.   Secondary—applies when the lower limit is grade 7 and upper limit is grade 12 or one or two years beyond grade 12 when those years are in a high school.

    G.   Elementary-Secondary—combines C and F.

    H.   Not Applicable—applies when the ultimate target is technical-vocational or adult as defined above.

  X. Subject Matter Context of Service to Ultimate Target: The service to the ultimate target is often in the context of a particular subject matter.

    A.   General—applies when subject matter is not indicated or the service is not subject matter related.

    B.   Arts and Humanities—applies to art, music, drama, theatre, and creative writing when not in the context of English.

    C.   Social Sciences—includes all separate subdivisions of social studies, such as economics, civics, history, etc.

    D.   English—includes grammar, composition, etc.

    E.   English as Second Language—applies to all programs in which the approach to English is as a second language and to all bilingual programs.

    F.   Foreign Language—applies when the first language is presumed to be English.

    G.   Math—includes all branches of mathematics.

    H.   Science—includes all branches of the physical and biological sciences.

    I.   Science and Math—includes characteristics G and H.

    J.   Reading.

    K.   Combined Language Arts—includes reading, English, spelling, etc.

    L.   Health and Physical Education—includes all subdivisions.

    M.   Vocational-Technical—includes all subdivisions of vocational-technical training including home economics.

    N.   Others—applies when subject matter does not fit any of the other categories.

  XI. Types of Training Programs: Several different types of programs are funded.

    A.   Summer Institutes and Workshops—last only for some period of time during the summer. Full time during that period.

  B. Summer Institutes with Additional Part-Time Service—applies when additional time beyond the work shop is noted.

  C. Multi-Phased Institute—applies when a summer institute continues over several summers.

  D. Part-Time All Year—applies when participants meet on a part-time basis over the course of a year.

  E. Fellowship Full-Time, One to Two Years—applies when participants are full time students for one to two years.

XII. Responsible Agency: The agency in charge of the training.

  A. Institution of Higher Education.

  B. State or County Educational Agency—applies when county agency cannot be considered a local school board.

  C. Local Educational Agency—applies to local school boards.

XIII. Length of Program: Duration over time.

  A. Undetermined—applies when length is not defined.

  B. Summer Institute and Additional Undetermined—applies when the length of the summer institute is defined and the part-time portion is not.

  C. 4 Weeks.   H. 9 Weeks.
  D. 5 Weeks.   I. 10 Weeks.
  E. 6 Weeks.   J. One Year.
  F. 7 Weeks.   K. Two Years.
  G. 8 Weeks.

Staff Roles and Functions

Evaluation Coordinator. The overall management and direction of the bureau evaluation system was lodged in the Division of Assessment and Coordination. It was the responsibility of the evaluation manager to ensure that the system was installed and remained operational, that it maximized available resources, and that it responded to the changing needs of the bureau and its clientele.

In order to accomplish the above, the manager's role was defined as follows:

(1) Identify the existing sources of bureau information collection and processing. For example: (a) data on proposed and implemented projects that are currently processed by the OE Office of Management Information; (b) information on operational projects collected through individual program evaluation efforts; (c) interim and final project reports.

(2) Modify existing data sources so that yield is compatible with the overall system. For example, information on common elements required for decisionmaking at the bureau level would be collected uniformly across programs.

(3) Identify data gaps or insufficiencies and provide for appropriate fill-in.

(4) Ensure that the evaluation system and other related bureau activities support each other. For example, program guidelines, proposal rating criteria and LTI training and technical assistance activities should be compatible with and supplement the evaluation system.

(5) Identify other Office of Education activities related to the bureau system and tie in the pertinent bureau activities when appropriate. For example, ensure that the data generated through various components of the bureau system are compatible with and phased into the OE Management Information Systems; adapt the system to respond to the development of the HEW Management-by-Objectives effort.

(6) Provide direction to individual program managers in the initiation and management of supplementary assessment activities, such as studies conducted by LTIs or in conjunction with training efforts.

(7) Organize the contributing and supportive elements of the system to achieve a uniform effort.

The staff of the Division of Assessment and Coordination worked with bureau personnel and consultants from outside the bureau, as well as other Office of Education personnel concerned with evaluation.

The successful development of the bureau's evaluation system depended on the careful interfacing of program and division chiefs with one another and with design specialists. To effect this work, a special evaluator was assigned. She was responsible for explication of program designs and for working with the program staff in defining the variables they wished to evaluate, and for setting criteria on those variables. Once the variables were defined, the evaluator worked with the program staff to frame basic measurement questions. The evaluator had the responsiblity of rephrasing these questions to permit a technical evaluation staff to design appropriate instrumentation and analytic procedures. At the completion of the analysis the evaluator was to interpret the results of the analysis to the program staff and guide the program staff in modifying the program design using the evaluation information. Ideally, there should have been an evaluation for each bureau program, but it was not possible to effect this recommendation.

Qualifications for this evaluation role were: (1) knowledge and experience with group process techniques, (2) experience with component analysis or work breakdown, (3) a working knowledge of discrepancy evaluation, (4) instrument development skills, (5) ability to write clearly, (6) high tolerance for ambiguity, and (7) nondirective counseling skills.

Technical Support Staff: The technical staff consisted of a design specialist capable of flow charting, PERT charting, and process and product analysis. Also included were experimental design specialists capable of doing ex post facto work, time series studies, and appropriate statistical analysis for the purpose of detecting changes in output variables relative to program effects over time. Eventually a staff capacity must exist for validating instruments and for detecting sources of error as well as real changes in individual levels of performance on both cognitive and affective scales.

Educational Data Process (EDP) Staff. The EDP staff was to be directed by a system manager who directed and coordinated activities of the EDP function. A systems programmer would develop and maintain the necessary software for the information system retrieval and assist in preparation of special data displays and analyses. In addition, computer operators, keypunch and verifier clerks, and editing and coding personnel would all be needed.

A set of materials was to be prepared to explicate purposes and procedures needed to maintain the system. These would include operation manuals prepared for the data-processing staff and for users in both the Office of Education and the field. Auxiliary to the manuals were various sets of training materials used to ensure that all staff were properly trained and supervised in their designated roles. Staff was actually trained in the use of the variables taxonomy described previously. Finally, a complete set of input and output documents for information collection and report generation was to be prepared and updated as needed.

Orientation to Levels Problem

The Bureau of Educational and Personnel Development is charged with the responsiblity of producing educational personnel in sufficient quantities and with sufficient competencies to ultimately produce changes in students. A necessary companion goal was the goal of institutional change. To these ends there existed interrelated sets of inputs, processes, and products that defined the intrabureau system. An analysis of the system provided the basis for testing the efficacy of these relationships.

Figure 3 represents a diagram of the system. The intrabureau system consisted of four levels (Levels 1-4) with an additional level (Level 0) existing outside the bureau.

In reality Level 0 consisted of three federal levels, the legislature, HEW, and OE. Federal objectives determined the activities and

Figure 3

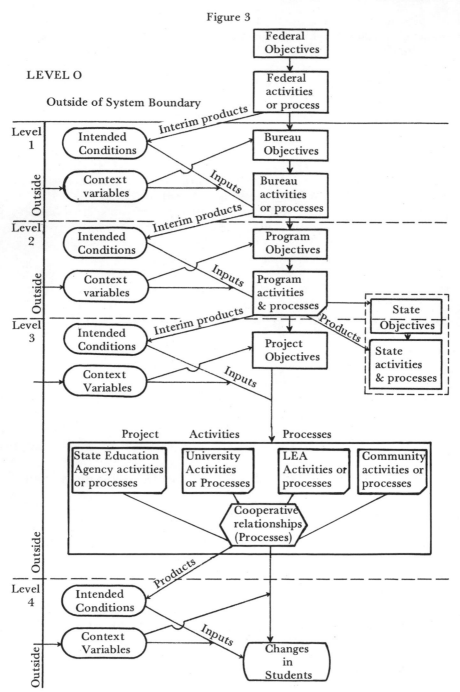

processes that were undertaken on that level in order to meet the objectives. These activities produced a set of interim products that became the basis on which bureau conditions were established. In addition, federal activities and processes influenced or determined bureau objectives.

At Level 1 the bureau objective determined the nature of the activities that led to the desired outputs. The enabling conditions, now outputs, enhanced the feasibility of these activities. In addition there existed a set of context variables defined by the environment outside the bureau that helped to define the bureau objectives and to enhance or restrict the bureau's activities. The bureau activities produced a set of interim products that are intended conditions or inputs at the program level.

At Level 2 a similar set of relationships existed, except that in some cases programs funded states directly rather than projects. In those cases, the state took over the functions of the program.

Again at Level 3 a similar set of relationships existed. Activities and processes were carried out by four units: state education agencies, universities, local education agencies, and communities. The activities of the four institutions led to the production of a set of cooperative relationships (institutional changes), which resulted in the production of the products that were the objective of the legislation. At Level 4 these products, together with the influence of the context variables, produced the ultimate product of the bureau changes in students. The institutional changes at Level 3 and all of the elements of Level 4 with the exception of the context variables constituted the total products of the bureau.

It can be seen that each level produced a set of lower level objectives more specific than the level above but always subsumed under it. It was therefore possible to build a hierarchical set of objectives with the possibility of assigning any objective of one level to a more general category at the next higher level. This system can be very useful for data reduction purposes.

On the other hand, the processes at each level were always necessary to but different from the processes of the next level down. Therefore processes were always defined and evaluated relative to the interim products of that particular level.

An overall bureau design could be described as a replication of identical designs at each level. In each case a plan was necessary to define the necessary inputs and processes that will produce the desired outputs relative to objectives. The direct products of Levels 1, 2, and 3 became interim products in the overall bureau design.

Two methods were available for creating the design. In the deductive approach, the objectives were set at Levels 0 and 1 and the necessary elements leading to the ultimate products were deduced from there. In the inductive approach, the objectives were still determined at Levels 0 and 1, but the analysis and design started at the level closest to the desired outputs and the designs of higher levels were induced from that point. Clearly, both approaches were necessary. The deductive approach increased the probability that programs would adhere to intent. The inductive approach increased the probability that realistic and meaningful outputs would be considered.

Three evaluation questions arose: (1) Were all the planned elements installed and operational? (2) Were the inputs and processes necessary and sufficient conditions to produce the interim products? (3) Were the interim products necessary and sufficient to constitute the enabling conditions of the next level? The first question was to be answered by a continuous monitoring and feedback at each level. The question of whether the inputs and processes produced the desired interim products required a process and product evaluation at each level. However, the question whether the interim products were necessary and sufficient to constitute enabling conditions required information from the next lower level and therefore required an inductive method. The inductive route, therefore, was to provide the necessary information for bureau improvement and change, and the deductive route was to provide the basis for the description and improvement of the bureau's own management.

Educational Data Process Specifications

The data flow diagrams (Figures 4-7) show the flow of data through the EDP system. Figure 4 shows the steps necessary to set up a tape file for each new program. This was necessary since the Program File Update System assumed a previous program file. The card input specified types and configuration of variables in order to determine file structure. The editor created on tape an empty file structure for the entire program.

Figure 5 shows the steps necessary to update an existing program file. From the project data reporting instruments, the values of variables were put on punched cards. The editor system added this data to the old file, producing a new file of the same format. This system contained provisions for correcting input errors from previous update runs.

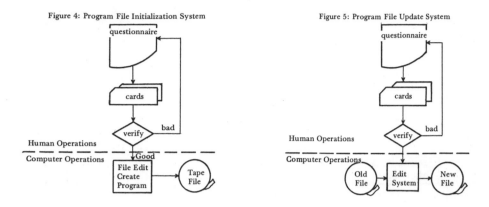

Figure 4: Program File Initialization System

Figure 5: Program File Update System

Figure 6 diagrams the Program File Analysis System. This system took the most recent program file and generated mandatory, exception, and special reports. Exception reports were examined to verify that the indicated discrepancy indeed existed. If errors were found, then the Program File Update System was used to correct them. Special reports were generated by subsystem programs, which were prepared for each special report. The analysis system encountered subsystem selection cards in the input data and called the appropriate subsystem. Subsystems may be added at any time.

Figure 7 diagrams the Bureau Analysis System. This system used the current program files from each program to prepare mandatory reports for bureau staffs and exception reports at the program level. This system handled special reports in the same way as the Program File Analysis System.

A rough estimate of the minimum configuration of the computer system was obtained by estimating the size of the program files. Each program had a maximum of 3000 variables for each project over a three-year period. If each variable required an average of 2 characters, and there were a maximum of 200 projects in a program, then a program file might contain 3000x2x200 = 1,200,000 characters. At 9600 characters per foot (on magnetic tape), these files require 125 feet of tape; each program file fits on 200 feet of tape allowing 75 feet for record gaps.

Data preparation and input required a trained staff to get values of the variables from the project data report instruments onto punched cards. This stage required keypunch and verifications staff. Reports were printed by the computer. Staff were also required to separate

Figure 6: Program Analysis System

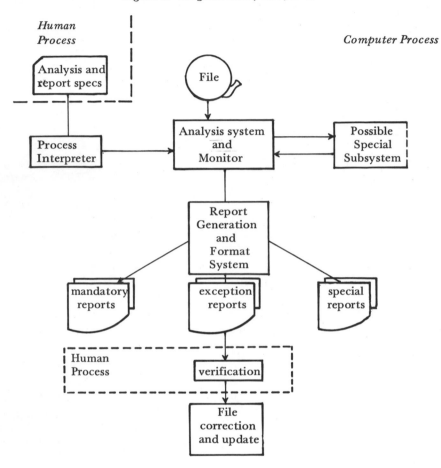

Figure: 7: Inter Project Analysis System

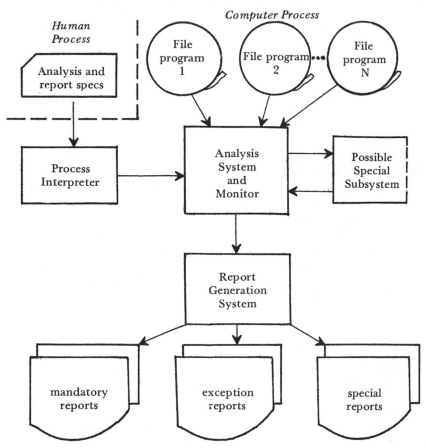

the reports and to distribute them to the proper recipients. The verifications staff examined the input to see if it was correct, and also verified correctness of exception reports. Verification of special reports was the responsibility of the development staff that requested the report.

The minimum hardware system to support the file maintenance and report generation would be: (1) a central processing unit— medium size, (2) a minimum of four magnetic tape drives, (3) a card reader and keypunch, and (4) a printer. Optional equipment for more efficient system performance would be: (1) a disc memory system and (2) two more tape drives. The total cost (on a purchase basis) of the hardware was estimated at approximately $400,000 assuming minimal reliability and versatility.[1]

TTT Program Evaluation

One program director who capitalized on the availability of the bureau design was the director in charge of the bureau's TTT Program. The program management staff made a decision in the summer of 1970 to use the Discrepancy Evaluation Model to evaluate their program at their level of interest and analysis, just as the bureau staff had made a similar decision at their level of operation. A description of this program and an indication of its intricate complexity is in order before we study its evaluation design.

Approximately five years ago, a few people in the Office of Education hit upon a teacher-training reform strategy that would require the participation of liberal arts college professors in the professional training program of teachers. A few such projects were launched and from this modest beginning, the inclusion of the community and student teachers themselves, as well as professors from various disciplines, was established as the basis on which teacher-training programs should be planned and sustained. Moreover, it was recognized that if large numbers of new teachers were to be affected, it would be necessary to retrain existing professors in teacher-training institutions; hence, a set of special conditions for the retraining of professors was established as the TTT Program. Today, the program provides money to public schools, state departments, and universities to train those who teach the trainers of teachers (thus the triple T), as long as clients and institutions at every level of effect are involved in the planning, administration, and assessment of the program.

Because teacher training had for a long time been rather parochial, the director of the new program was determined to establish a new body of teacher-training experience that would eventually prove useful to more institutions than those receiving OE funds. Therefore, he was careful to give project directors the widest possible latitude in the design and conduct of their projects. Their creativity and energy in meeting the unexpected would determine their success and that of the TTT Program.

The major problem to be faced in a program-wide evaluation of TTT was to obtain guidelines of program conditions as well as adequate project descriptions from which a program design could be distilled. If each university-based project operator was to retain initiative for the direction of his own operations and the discovery of new ones, he would have to be evaluated according to his own standards rather than those imposed from some higher authority.

Washington would establish minimal conditions to be met by each local program, but project directors and their staffs and their parity board would write the program design from which evaluation standards would be derived. This was no easy task. Triple-T projects ran the entire gamut of educational processes and purposes, in a startling array of educational settings, using a vast web of institutional resources.

In order to help TTT project directors design their projects in accordance with bureau specifications, a description of the major steps of project design was presented to project directors at design training meetings. There were eight basic steps involved:

(1) Identify the individuals and institutions involved.

(2) Identify the elements involved. An element is a basic major block of activities that brings individuals or institutions together in order to produce specified changes.

(3) Identify the subelements. Each element may be divided into a number of parts called subelements. A subelement should be a part of an element that has change variables different from those of the other subelements of the same element. Subelement acitivites always should contain a description of both behavior and content.

(4) Identify the change variables for each individual or institution affected by the element or subelement activity. A change variable is a condition the project seeks to change.

(5) Identify the receptors for all change variables. Receptors are individuals or organizations in which change is produced by project activities.

(6) Specify the input level for change variables. The input level is the observed condition of receptors before the operation of the element or subelement activity.

(7) Specify the output level for each change variable. The desired change or direction of change from input level to output level is the objective of the element or subelement activity.

(8) Identify the time-frame (beginning and ending dates) for each element and subelement and specify the time points at which outputs are expected to be achieved.

The data making up the design of each project was compiled by the project director and staff on four forms, so that the data received by the evaluating agency was consistent between projects. An extract from these executed design forms is presented on the following four pages. The evaluating agency prepared a detailed manual, with procedures, taxonomies, and glossary of terms, to facilitate project directors in the use of forms. The manual is found in Appendix A of this

FORM NO. 1 · ELEMENTS   PROJECT _____   PROJECT CODE ☐☐☐ PAGE _____ OF

Element Sequence Number (1)	Element Category (2)	Element Name (3)	Time-Frame Begin Date (4)	Time-Frame End Date (5)	Individuals And Institutions Involved By Taxonomy Category (6)
1	1 1 1	Planning for Teacher-Trainer Component	7/1/70	9/1/70	(taxonomy data)
2	1 5 1 3	TTT Advisory Board	7/1/70	6/30/71	(taxonomy data)
3	1 5 5	Recruitment of Triple-T Participants	7/1/70	6/30/71	(taxonomy data)
4	1 1 1	Planning and Development of Ph.D. Program	7/1/70	6/30/71	(taxonomy data)
5	1 2 4	Graduate Electives - MA Level	7/1/70	6/30/71	(taxonomy data)
6	1 2 4	Foundation Courses - Ph.D. Level	7/1/70	6/30/71	(taxonomy data)
7	1 2 4	Electives - Ph.D.	7/1/70	6/30/71	(taxonomy data)
8	1 2 4	Electives in Urban Affairs Courses	7/1/70	6/30/71	(taxonomy data)
9	1 4 5 2	Resource Centers	7/1/70	6/30/71	(taxonomy data)

FORM NO. 2 - SUBELEMENT ACTIVITY   PROJECT_____   PROJECT CODE [III] PAGE____ OF____

Element Sequence Number (1)	Sub-Element Number (2)	Subelement Name (3)	Time-Frame Begin Date (4)	Time-Frame End Date (5)	Individuals and Institutions Involved by Taxonomy Category
2	2.1	Parity representation	7/1/70	6/30/71	2 1 1 2 — No. 4; 2 2 2 4 — 1; 2 2 1 3 — 2; 2 5 2 2 — 1 / 2 1 1 3 — No. 2; 2 3 2 5 — 5; 2 3 1 1 — 2; 2 5 2 1 — 3 / 2 1 1 2 — No. 1; 2 1 1 1 — 1; 2 5 1 2 — 2 / No. 4 (9) (1)
	2.2	Developing orderly procedures -- regular meetings, recorded minutes mailed to members, prepared agenda, election of chairman	7/1/70	6/30/71	No. 1
	2.3	Communication to additional community leaders and educational personnel via invitation, use of media for publicity			3 8 — No. 7
	2.4	Select Chicago school district as focus for TT program	7/1/70	6/30/71	No. 1 (9)
	2.5	Parity sub-committee structure within advisory board	7/1/70	6/30/71	3 1 3 — No. 1; 2 2 2 3 / 2 1 1 2 — No. 1; 2 5 1 — 2 / 2 1 1 1 — No. 1; 2 5 2 1 — 1

FORM NO. 3 - ELEMENTS INPUT-OUTPUT _____ PROJECT _____ PROJECT CODE [| |] PAGE _____ OF _____

Element Sequence Number (1)	Receptor Category (2)		No.	Receptor Name (3)	Change Variable Category (4)	Description of the Change Variable: Input Level: Output Level: (5)
2	3 1	1	1	School of Education	5 1 1	Structures to facilitate community and schools substantial participation in teacher training. Input level - - little or no structure available. Output level - - systematic, structured, effective voice in decision-making
8	3 1	2	1	School of Education	5 1 2	Relations between graduate programs in education and Center for Urban Affairs. Input level - - casual, informal relations. Output level - - formal, mutually-beneficial relations
12b	3 8		1	TTT Project Staff	5 2 4	Input to decision-making from outside consultants. Input level - - little or no external inputs on decision-making. Output level - - increased information from external sources for project decision-making
13				TTT Project	5 1 1 2	Existence of a place for a summer orientation for new teacher trainers. Input - - no plan. Output - - a place for orientation with emphasis on community involvement

FORM NO. 4 - SUB-ELEMENTS INPUT-OUTPUT   PROJECT _____ PROJECT CODE ☐☐☐ PAGE ____ OF ____

Sub-Element Number (1)	Receptor Category (2)		No.	Receptor Name (3)	Change Variable Category (4)	Description of the Change Variable — Input Level: — Output Level: (5)
2.1			1	TTT Advisory Board	5 1 2	Representation in graduate program decision-making. Input level - - little or no representation outside education faculty. Output level - - shared decision-making by parity board
2.1			1	TTT Project at Northwestern	5 2 3	Policy-making in graduate programs. Input level - - unilateral decisions by the university. Output level - - shared decisions by parity board
2.2			1	TTT Advisory Board	5 3 2 2	Indicators of Board as a legitimate agency in educational planning. Input level - - board nonexistent and generally not credible. Output level - - functioning, credible, representative body with evidence of legitimacy (regular, scheduled, planned meetings)
2.3	3 5	1	1	Community-at-large	5 3 2 1	Communication with non-TTT groups. Input level - - project operating in isolation. Output level - - extensive communication network
2.3	3 4	2		Non-TTT Schools	5 1 2	Communications and influence on non-TTT schools. Input level - - they hardly know TTT exists. Output level - - increased knowledge and awareness of TTT programs

chapter. Although the completion of the forms was an arduous task, project directors found that by describing in detail the activities and goals of their project, they were helped to be better prepared for the installation of operation contingencies they would face in the near future and in many cases were already facing without adequate preparation. The design work forced many staffs to identify new and scarce resources (preconditions for which substitutes would have to be found) to better allocate staff time, and to be more precise about desired changes in individual and institutional behavior.

At this point in time, the design for each TTT project has been used as the basis for submitting proposals for refunding. As a result it will be possible to obtain comprehensive project designs and a program design that will specify performance information to be collected and compared with standards at various stages of the model. Considerable instrumentation work is already under way so that periodic assessment of performance on major program variables will be obtained only six months after the beginning of the evaluation. Comparisons of performance and standard, which are of interest only to a project director, will probably be made at the discretion of local management.

Drug Abuse Education Program

A program equally broad in scope but requiring more rapid evaluation is the Drug Abuse Education Program established in the summer of 1970.

Recent evidence has shown a great increase in drug traffic among the young people of our cities. Young people know how and where to get drugs—even those who are not users of drugs themselves. There are many different causes for drug abuse: Two clear causes are the availability of drugs on city streets and the lack of knowledge among young people of the hazards of drug use.

This lack of knowledge has been recognized and drug education programs have been instituted to fill this need for knowledge. In recognition of the need for clear evaluative procedures, the director of the federally funded National Drug Education Training Program has employed the Discrepancy Evaluation Model to assess the worth of the program. Projects are funded in 55 states and territories of the United States, and they undoubtedly have varying needs and methods for meeting both project and program goals. Again, a taxonomy of relevant variables was created and used as the basis for helping to shape statewide programs and standards and for identifying critical performance information to be compared with these standards. Resulting instrumentation is shown in Appendix B.

Appendix A: TTT Project Design Procedure Manual

This manual was prepared by the Evaluation Research Center of the University of Virginia: It gives much explicit information that is relevant to the TTT Program, but the general theory of evaluation and the structure of the manual can be easily generalized to any program to be evaluated under the Discrepancy Evaluation Model.

Table of Contents

Introduction

This material has been prepared to facilitate the design and evaluation of TTT projects. It is predicated on the assumption that sound evaluation is a means to both program improvement and program assessment. Unless TTT projects are carefully planned and rigorously installed, and monitored with fidelity, the risk of program failure will be high.

Before a program can be designed or evaluated, a considerable amount of information must be made explicit. This information will permit the construction of a specific project design suitable for describing individuals and institutions involved, the activities to which they are exposed, the purposes these activities serve, and the expected time during which the major events of the project will occur. Two separate designs will be submitted, one for '70-'71 and one for '71-'72.

To facilitate these descriptions four project design forms and five taxonomies have been prepared. These materials are complex rather than simple. They cannot be used without training. Yet they are essential to adequate program description, precise project design, and to both sound management and useful evaluation.

Project Design Procedure

Eight Basic Steps:

To execute the design of a project, eight basic planning activities are required. A brief description of these eight steps is given below. More detailed explanation is provided later. Since some steps are understandable only as they relate to other steps, it is desirable to survey the procedure before beginning the actual design of your project. It is also recommended that you study the Glossary of Terms prior to reading anything else.

1. *Identify individuals and institutions involved:* The individuals and institutions involved in the project activities must be named.

2. *Identify elements:* The elements of a project must be named. An element is a basic major block of activities which brings individuals or institutions together in order to produce specified changes.

3. *Identify subelements:* Each element may be divided into a number of parts called subelements. A subelement should be a part of an element which has change variables different from those of the other subelements of the same element. Subelement activities always should contain a description of both behavior and content.

4. *Identify change variables:* For each individual or institution affected by the element or subelement activity, all of the change variables which describe the effect of the element or subelement activity should be identified. A change variable is a condition which the project seeks to change.

5. *Identify receptors:* The receptors for all change variables must be named. Receptors are individuals or organizations in which change is produced by project activities.

6. *Specify input level for change variable:* The input level or initial condition of each person or institution to be changed should be specified. The input level is the observed condition of receptors before the operation of the element or subelement activity.

7. *Specify output level for change variable:* The expected output level for each change variable should be specified. The desired change or direction of change from input level to output level is the objective of the element or subelement activity.

8. *Identify time-frame:* The time-frame (beginning and ending dates) for each element and subelement must be identified and the time points at which outputs are expected to be achieved must be specified.

Design Procedure Materials

Taxonomies: In order to facilitate the design of a project, five taxonomies have been developed. The five taxonomies are:

1 — Element Taxonomy
2 — Individual Taxonomy
3 — Institution Taxonomy

4 — Individual Change Variable Taxonomy

5 — Institutional Change Variable Taxonomy

The categories of the taxonomies are identified by a single arabic numeral sequence. The first number in the sequence always refers to which taxonomy the category comes from; thus the category 1.1.1.1.20. refers to the Element Taxonomy, and specifically designates a course in the Psychology of Learning. The degree of specificity in the sequence increases from left to right; thus, 1.2.3.2. is a subdivision of 1.2.3. Where a taxonomy category is called for on any form, the column will be divided into an appropriate number of boxes in which to place the digits of the sequence.

The five taxonomies were created by organizing the information presented to the Office of Education by projects last year. Therefore, it is possible that as projects progress and change from one year to the next, the taxonomies may not cover all ranges of possible project details. It is planned that the taxonomies will be flexible and growing things. Therefore, if your project has an element, individual or institution, receptor, or change variable which does not fit in the taxonomy, then the space on the forms for the taxonomy category should be left blank, and complete information should be given in a footnote so that changes may be made and the category added later. In this way we can obtain the information we need concerning your project as well as discover and correct any deficiencies in the taxonomies.

Forms: Four forms have been developed to provide an orderly and systematic presentation of project designs. The forms are:

Form No. 1 — Elements

Form No. 2 — Subelements

Form No. 3 — Element Input-Output Design

Form No. 4 — Subelement Input-Output Design

All information submitted on these four forms should be typewritten. At the top of every form used in your project design, the name of your project, its three-letter project code, and the page number should be indicated.

Description of Elements: Form No. 1

Form No. 1 calls for information about elements, their time-frames, and individuals and institutions involved.

Several preliminary activities have proved useful in completing the Description of Elements form. First a list of proposed elements should be constructed by dividing the project into its major logical parts. An element, by definition, lasts only one year. This listing is an informal procedure, done on scratch paper. After this list has been completed, the Element Taxonomy should be applied to each proposed element. If the proposed element is too broad to fit in a single category, then it should be divided into several elements; if the proposed element is too narrow, several proposed elements should be combined to form a single element. When each element has been assigned a single category from the Element Taxonomy, then Form No. 1 may be attempted.

Column (1) calls for the assignment of a sequential arabic numeral to each element listed on the form. This number is supplied by the user. The first element is given the number one, and other elements are then numbered sequentially, according to the order in which they begin in your project.

Column (2) on Form No. 1 calls for a single category for each element as it appears in the Element Taxonomy. For example, if one element of the project is a field research project involving work in a community agency, the category would be 1.3.2.2.02.

Column (3) requires a descriptive name for each element which clarifies the element beyond the terms used in the taxonomy. This includes the name that your project uses for the element.

Columns (4) and (5) call for designation of the Time-Frame (beginning and ending dates) for each element. All elements of your project should be listed in the order in which they are expected to begin.

Column (6) requires that each individual or institution involved in each element be specified by listing an Individual Taxonomy category or an Institution Taxonomy category. Under the subheading "NO." in this column, there is space provided for designating the number (actual count) of each category of individual or institution involved in the element.

Description of Subelement Activity: Form No. 2

It may be necessary to divide an element further into smaller units called subelements, although not all elements will have identifiable subelements. *The smaller units of an element that have important and identifiable outcomes become subelements of the element.* There is no taxonomy to guide this effort; the success of the effort depends on logical analysis and knowledge of the activities which characterize an element. Indicate only those subelements deemed most important.

At this point a general example to indicate the level of specificity needed for subelements may be helpful. A typical element for a TTT Project is a course in some subject area. The teacher of the course may feel that the course material breaks down into five major areas, covering perhaps three weeks each. The teacher may also feel that these major areas break down further into sections covering about one week's work each. In this situation, the breakdown into five major parts is the level of specificity suggested, rather than the breakdown into the smaller parts.

Column (1) on Form No. 2 calls for the element sequence number from column (1) of Form No. 1.

Column (2) calls for the creation of a subelement number. This is the element number previously supplied by the user, followed by a period and a new number also supplied by the user. The new number is to be sequential for all subelements within an element. For example, the third subelement of element two is given the subelement number 2.3.

Column (3) requires the descriptive name used by your project for the subelements composing each element. See examples 1 and 2, following:

Example 1

If the third element has been identified as an academic seminar in Instructional Methods (1.2.3.8.), then four subelement activities might consist of:

3.1. Discuss the relationship of interaction analysis to Effective Classroom Teaching.
3.2. Discuss non-verbal communication in the classroom.
3.3. Discuss the effect of language used verbally and in textbooks on classroom teaching.

3.4.   Discuss the effectiveness of multimedia techniques for class-
       room teaching.

Example 2

If the sixth element is a practicum in which TTT's observe TT's in
the classroom and give feedback (1.3.2.1.01.2.) then three subelements might be:
6.1.   TTT's observe TT's in the classroom and meet subsequently
       with the TT's.
6.2.   TTT's observe TT's in personal help session with individual
       children and meet subsequently with the TT's.
6.3.   All TTT's and TT's meet together to discuss improvements
       in teaching methods.

Columns (4) and (5) call for designation of the time-frame (beginning and
ending dates) for each subelement activity. Subelement activities may fall in
sequential order, or they may overlap, or they may run concurrently. Subelement activities should be listed in the order in which they begin, even in cases
where there is overlap. If two subelement activities begin on the same date, the
one that terminates first should be listed first.

Column (6) calls for the identification of individuals and institutions (by
Individual Taxonomy category or Institution Taxonomy category) who are
involved in a subelement activity. As on Form No. 1, there is space provided for
designating the number (actual count) of each category of individuals and
institutions involved in the subelement activity. Although all individuals and
institutions involved in subelements should have already been listed on Form
No. 1, complete information must be given here.

Individualized Programs: If you have an activity in your project in which
services, resources, and/or experiences are *available* to individuals but not *required* by the project design then you should report it as an *Individualized
Element.* The procedure for doing this is as follows:

1. Separate out any *requirements,* either explicit or implicit, and make them
separate elements or subelements.

2. Look through the Element Taxonomy to find the appropriate "individualized" category. Category 1.2.4. is for individualized course offerings, and category 1.3.2.4. is for individualized practicum experiences.

3. Use this number to fill in the category in column (2) of Form No. 1.

4. Attach to the form as a footnote a list of
   a. the options available
   b. a rough estimate of the number of individuals choosing this option.

FORM NO. 1 - ELEMENTS   PROJECT EXAMPLE   PROJECT CODE [1][X][A] PAGE 1 OF 12

Element Sequence Number (1)	Element Category (2)	Element Name (3)	Time-Frame Begin Date (4)	Time-Frame End Date (5)	Individuals and Institutions Involved by Taxonomy Category (6)
1	1 5 1	Parity Board	9/1/70	9/1/71	2 3 1 1 No.3 / 2 1 1 1 No.1 ; 2 3 2 1 No.2 / 2 5 1 2 No.2 ; 2 2 1 1 No.3 / 2 5 2 2 No.2
2	1 2 1 1 20	Course in the Psychology of learning	9/1/70	2/1/71	2 1 2 1 No.10 ; 2 1 2 2 No.5 ; 2 1 1 3 No.3
3	1 2 3 8	Seminar in Instructional Methods	9/1/70	7/1/71	2 1 2 1 No.10 / 2 2 1 1 No.10 ; 2 1 2 2 No.5 / 2 2 1 8 No.3 ; 2 1 1 3 No.3 / 2 2 2 3 No.5
4	1 2 2 1 02	Course in Administration in the Urban School	2/1/71	7/1/71	2 1 2 1 No.10 ; 2 1 2 2 No.5 ; 2 1 1 3 No.3
5	1 3 2 1 02 4	TT supervise student teachers in primary and secondary education	9/1/70	7/1/71	2 2 1 1 No.10 / 3 2 1 No.18 ; 2 2 1 8 No.3 / 3 4 3 No.3 ; 2 2 2 3 No.5 / 3 4 2 No.3
6	1 3 2 1 01 2	TTT observe TT in the classroom and give feedback	9/1/70	7/1/71	2 1 2 1 No.10 / 2 2 3 No.5 ; 2 1 2 2 No.5 ; 2 2 1 2 No.10
7	1 3 2 1 02 1	TTT teach demonstration classes in local schools	9/1/70	7/1/71	2 1 2 1 No.10 / 4 1 No.540 ; 2 1 2 2 No.5 ; 2 1 1 3 No.3
8	1 3 2 2 02	TTT and TT do a field research project involving work in a community agency	2/1/71	7/1/71	2 1 2 1 No.10 / 2 2 3 No.5 ; 2 1 2 2 No.5 ; 2 2 1 2 No.10

FORM NO. 2   SUBELEMENT ACTIVITY   PROJECT _____   PROJECT CODE [LARMIL]   PAGE 2 OF 12

Element Sequence Number (1)	Sub-Element Number (2)	Subelement Name (3)	Time-Frame Begin Date (4)	Time-Frame End Date (5)	Individuals and Institutions Involved by Taxonomy Category (6)				No
2	2.1	Review and Discuss Research on the "self-fulfilling prophecy"	9/1/70	11/1/70	2 1 2 1 10	2 1 2 2	2 2 5	2 1 1 3	3
2	2.2	Review and Discuss Research on Learning Difficulties of Minority Group Children	11/2/70	1/1/70	2 1 2 1 10	2 1 2 2	2 2 5	2 1 1 3	3
2	2.3	Review and Discuss Research on the characteristics of Teachers for Minority Group Children	1/2/70	2/1/70	2 1 2 1 10	2 1 2 2	2 2 5	2 1 1 3	3
3	3.1	Discuss the Relationship of Inter-action Analysis to Effective Class-room Teaching	9/1/70	12/1/70	2 1 2 1 10 / 2 2 1 2 10	2 1 2 2 / 2 2 1 8	2 2 5 / 2 1 8 3	2 1 1 3 / 2 2 2 3	3 / 5
3	3.2	Discuss Non Verbal Communication In the Classroom	12/2/70	3/1/71	2 1 2 1 10 / 2 2 1 2 10	2 1 2 2 / 2 2 1 8	2 2 5 / 2 1 8 3	2 1 1 3 / 2 2 2 3	3 / 5
3	3.3	Discuss the Effect of Language used Verbally and in Textbooks on Class-room Teaching	3/2/71	6/1/71	2 1 2 1 10 / 2 2 1 2 10	2 1 2 2 / 2 2 1 8	2 2 5 / 2 1 8 3		
3	3.4	Discuss the effectiveness of multi-media techniques for classroom teaching	6/2/71	9/1/71	2 1 2 1 10 / 2 2 1 2 10	2 1 2 2 / 2 2 1 8	2 2 5 / 2 1 8 3	2 1 1 3 / 2 2 2 3	3 / 5
4	4.1	Relationships with Parents	2/1/71	4/1/71	2 1 2 1 10	2 1 2 2	2 2 5	2 1 1 3	3
4	4.2	Relationships with Teachers	4/2/71	5/1/71	2 1 2 1 10	2 1 2 2	2 2 5	2 1 1 3	3
4	4.3	Relationships with Community Organizations	5/2/71	7/1/71	2 1 2 1 10	2 1 2 2	2 2 5	2 1 1 3	3
6	6.1	TTT observes TT in the Classroom and meets subsequently with the TT	9/1/70	9/1/71	2 1 2 1 10 / 2 2 2 3 5	2 1 2 2	2 2 5	2 2 1 2	10
6	6.2	TTT observes TT in personal help session with individual children and meets subsequently with the TT	9/1/70	9/1/71	2 1 2 1 10 / 2 2 2 3 5	2 1 2 2	2 2 5	2 2 1 2	10
6	6.3	All TTT's and TT's meet together to discuss improvements in teaching methods	9/1/70	9/1/71	2 1 2 1 10 / 2 2 2 3 5	2 1 2 2	2 2 5	2 2 1 2	10
8	8.1	Prepare a Description of the Roles of Various Community organizations in School-Community Interaction	2/1/71	3/1/71	2 1 2 1 10 / 2 3 2 3 5	2 1 2 2	2 2 5	2 2 1 2	10
8	8.2	Analyze characteristics of Community Agency Leaders	3/1/71	4/1/71	2 1 2 1 10 / 2 2 2 3 5	2 1 2 2	2 2 5	2 2 1 2	10
8	8.3	Determine current and future community problems and needs	4/1/71	7/1/71	2 1 2 1 10 / 2 2 2 3 5	2 1 2 2	2 2 5	2 2 1 2	10

Description of Element Input-Output Design: Form No. 3

All of the change variables for each element should be listed before attempting Form No. 3. This should be an informal listing on scratch paper.

Form No. 3 permits an analysis of the change variables for each element at the same level of specificity as elements.

Column (1) calls for the identification of each element by the element sequence number indicated in column (1) on Form No. 1.

Column (2) requires identification of the receptor for each change variable. The receptor is the person or organization affected by the change variable of the element. Receptors will be identified either by Individual Taxonomy category or by Institution Taxonomy category. For example, if the receptor is a graduate student in education preparing to teach in graduate school, the taxonomy category from the Individual Taxonomy is 2.1.2.1. If the receptor is the Education Department of a University, the taxonomy category from the Institution Taxonomy would be 3.1.1. This column also provides space for indicating the number (actual count) of each category of receptors affected by the element.

For each category in column (2), a descriptive name for the receptor should appear in column (3). These descriptions should include proper names of institutions or accurate common names for groups of people which go beyond the taxonomy description.

Column (4) calls for the identification of change variables for the elements and for the assignment of a change variable category to each change variable. For this purpose the Individual Change Variable Taxonomy or Institutional Change Variable Taxonomy should be used. For example, if the project seeks to alter an individual's professional teaching skills, then the category from the Individual Change Variable Taxonomy would be 4.2.1.1. If the project seeks to alter the hiring policy of an institution, the category from the Institutional Change Variable Taxonomy would be 5.2.2.

Column (5) calls for elaboration on the change variable whose category is given in column (4). For each change variable category indicated in column (4), three lines of information should be given in column (5). The first line should give a written description of the change variable. This should be a brief description of exactly what change is expected to occur in each receptor as a function of each element. The second line of information should indicate the input level for the change variable; this is the level of performance prior to the effect of the element. The third line should indicate the output level for the same variable; this is the level of performance after the effect of the element.

FORM NO. 3 - ELEMENTS INPUT-OUTPUT   PROJECT EXAMPLE PROJECT CODE EXA PAGE 4 OF 12

Element Sequence Number (1)	Receptor Category (2)	No.	Receptor Name (3)	Change Variable Category (4)	Description of the Change Variable Input Level: Output Level: (5)
2	2 1 2 1	10	Grad. Students In Ed.	4 1 6	Understanding of teacher attitudes and characteristics and student characteristics that facilitate learning in the classroom. Input - Little or no Output - Increased understanding of and ability to discuss these factors
2	2 1 2 2	5	Grad. Students in Liberal Arts	4 1 6	Same as above
2	2 1 1 3	3	Grad. Faculty in Liberal Arts	4 1 6	Same as above
3	2 1 2 1	10	Grad. Students in Ed.	4 1 7	Understanding of communicative techniques available for use by teachers Input - Little or no Output - Knowledge of interaction analysis, techniques of non verbal communication, the effects of linguistic differences, and various media methods.
3	2 1 2 2	5	Grad. Students in Liberal Arts	4 1 7	Same as above
3	2 1 1 3	3	Grad. Faculty in Liberal Arts	4 1 7	Same as above
3	2 2 1 2	10	Cooperating teachers	4 1 7	Same as above
3	2 2 1 3	3	Undergraduate faculty in Ed.	4 1 7	Same as above
3	2 2 2 3	5	Grad. students preparing to be public school supervisors	4 1 7	Same as above

FORM NO. 3 - ELEMENTS INPUT-OUTPUT   *PROJECT* EXAMPLE *PROJECT CODE* [EXA] *PAGE* 6 *OF* 15

Element Sequence Number (1)	Receptor Category (2)	No.	Receptor Name (3)	Change Variable Category (4)	Description of the Change Variable: Input Level: Output Level: (5)
8	2 1 2 1	10	Grad. Students in Education	4 4 3 2	Improve relationships with community organizations and their leaders Input Level - No relationships Output Level - Establish monthly meetings with leaders of community organizations
				4 1 5	Develop an understanding of the problems and needs of the community Input Level - Little or no understanding Output Level - Awareness of the communities problems and needs
8	2 1 2 2	5	Grad. Students in Liberal Arts	4 4 3 2 4 1 5	Same as above Same as above
8	2 2 1 2	10	Cooperating Teachers	4 4 3 2 4 1 5	Same as above Same as above
8	2 2 2 3	5	Graduate students pre-paring to be public school supervisors	4 4 3 2 4 1 5	Same as above Same as above
8	3 1 1		Education Depart-ment of University	5 3 2 1	Develop communication channels between School of Education and various community organizations. Input Level - No formal channels Output Level - Monthly meetings between representatives of the school of education and representatives of various community organizations.

Description of Subelement Input-Output Design: Form No. 4

Form No. 4 permits an analysis of the most significant and relevant change variables for each subelement activity at the same level of specificity as subelements. Because this form is designed in the same fashion as Form No. 3, the procedural description here is skeletal. For elaboration on a particular point, refer to the procedure for completing Form No. 3.

Column (1) calls for the subelement number, given in column (2) of Form No. 2.

Column (2) calls for identification of the receptor by Taxonomy category.

For each receptor identified by taxonomy category in column (2), a descriptive name of the receptor should appear in column (3).

Column (4) calls for identification of a change variable category for each change variable.

Column (5) calls for further elaboration on the change variables identified in column (4).

FORM NO. 4 - SUB-ELEMENTS INPUT-OUTPUT   PROJECT EXAMPLE   PROJECT CODE [EXA] PAGE 7 OF 15

Sub-Element Number (1)	Receptor Category (2)				No	Receptor Name (3)	Change Variable Category (4)				Description of the Change Variable — Input Level: / Output Level: (5)
2.1	2	1	2	1	10	Grad. Students in Education	4	1	6		Awareness of research on "The Self-fulfilling Prophecy" / Input Level - Little or none / Output Level - Be able to discuss and cite this research
							4	1	2		Determine the relationship between "The Self-fulfilling Prophecy" and classroom learning / Input level - have no model / Output level - develop a conceptual model of the conditions under which "The Self-fulfilling Prophecy" is operative
2.1	2	1	2	2	5	Grad. Students in Liberal Arts	4	1	6		Same as above
							4	1	2		Same as above
2.1	2	1	1	2	3	Graduate Faculty in. Liberal Arts	4	1	6		Same as above
							4	1	2		Same as above
2.2	2	1	2	1	10	Grad. Students in Education	4	1	6		Identification of learning difficulties of minority group children / Input level - Inability identify / Output level - Be able to identify and describe learning difficulties of minority group children
							4	3	3	1	Attitude toward ability of minority children to learn / Input level - Neutral or Negative / Output level - Positive
2.2	2	1	2	2	5	Grad. Students in Liberal Arts	4	1	6		Same as above
							4	3	3	1	Same as above
2.2	2	1	1	3	3	Graduate faculty in Liberal Arts	4	1	6		Same as above
							4	3	3	1	Same as above

FORM NO. 4 - SUBELEMENTS INPUT-OUTPUT   PROJECT   Example   PROJECT CODE [EXA] PAGE 8   OF 15

Sub-Element Number (1)	Receptor Category (2)				No.	Receptor Name (3)	Change Variable Category (4)			Description of the Change Variable Input Level: Output Level: (5)
2.3	2	1	2	1	10	Graduate students in Education	4	1	6	Awareness of the variables predicting success in teachers of minority group students Input - Little or none Output - Be able to list the variables which are effective in selecting teachers of minority group children
2.3	2	1	2	2	5	Graduate students in Liberal Arts	4	1	6	Same as above
2.3	2	1	1	3	3	Graduate Faculty in Liberal Arts	4	1	6	Same as above
3.1	2	1	2	1	10	Graduate students in Education	4	2	1	Knowledge of interaction analysis Input level - None or little Output level - Be able to perform interaction analysis
3.1	2	1	2	2	5	Graduate students in Liberal Arts	4	2	1	Same as above
3.1	2	1	1	3	3	Graduate Faculty in Liberal Arts	4	2	1	Same as above
3.1	2	2	1	2	10	Cooperating teachers	4	2	1	Same as above
3.1	2	2	1	8	3	Undergrad. Faculty in Education	4	2	1	Same as above
3.1	2	2	2	3	5	Grad. Students preparing to be public school supervisors	4	2	1	Same as above
3.2	2	1	2	1	10	Grad. Students in Education	4	1	6	Knowledge of the function of non-verbal communication

FORM NO. 4 - SUB-ELEMENTS INPUT-OUTPUT   PROJECT Example   *PROJECT CODE* [EXA] *PAGE* 9 *OF* 15

Sub-Element Number (1)	Receptor Category (2)				No	Receptor Name (3)	Change Variable Category (4)	Description of the Change Variable Input Level: Output Level: (5)
3.2	2	1	2	2	5	Graduate students in Liberal Arts	4 1 6	Input level - None or little Output level - Understanding of the ways teachers communicate non verbally and the effect on students
3.2	2	1	1	3	3	Graduate Faculty in Liberal Arts	4 1 6	Same as above
3.2	2	2	1	2	10	Cooperating teachers	4 1 6	Same as above
3.2	2	2	1	8	3	Undergraduate faculty in Education		Same as above
3.2	2	2	2	3	5	Graudate students preparing to be public school supervisors		Same as above
3.3	2	1	2	1	10	Graduate students in Education	4 1 6	Awareness of linguistic differences Input level - Little or none Output level - An understanding of linguistic differences and their importance in the classroom
							4 3 3 1	Change feelings about the language patterns of minority children Input level - Neutral or Negative Output level - Positive
3.3	2	1	2	2	5	Graduate Students in Liberal Arts	4 1 6	Same as above
							4 3 3 1	Same as above

FORM NO. 4 - SUB-ELEMENTS INPUT-OUTPUT   PROJECT Example   PROJECT CODE [EXA] PAGE 10 OF 15

Sub-Element Number (1)	Receptor Category (2)			No.	Receptor Name (3)	Change Variable Category (4)			Description of the Change Variable — Input Level: / Output Level: (5)
3.3	2	1 1	3	3	Graduate Faculty in Liberal Arts	4 1		6	Same as above
3.3	2	2 1	2	10	Cooperating Teachers	4 1		6	Same as above
						4 3	3	1	Same as above
3.3	2	2 1	8	3	Undergraduate Faculty in Education	4 1		6	Same as above
						4 3	3	1	Same as above
3.3	2	2 2	3	5	Graduate students preparing to be public school supervisors	4 1		6	Same as above
						4 3	3	1	Same as above
3.4	2	1 2	1	10	Graduate Students in Education	4 2		1	Awareness of various media for use in the classroom — Input level - Little or none — Output level - Knowledge of the advantages and disadvantages of using various media in the classroom
3.4	2	1 2	2	5	Graduate Students in Liberal Arts	4 2		1	Same as above
3.4	2	1 1	3	3	Graduate faculty in Liberal Arts	4 2		1	Same as above
3.4	2	2 1	2	10	Cooperating teachers	4 2		1	Same as above
3.4	2	2 1	8	3	Undergraduate faculty in Education	4 2		1	Same as above
3.4	2	2 2	3	5	Graduate students preparing to be public school supervisors	4 2		1	Same as above

FORM NO. 4 - SUB-ELEMENTS INPUT-OUTPUT   PROJECT Example   PROJECT CODE [EXA] PAGE 14 OF 15

Sub-Element Number (1)	Receptor Category (2)	No.	Receptor Name (3)	Change Variable Category (4)	Description of the Change Variable / Input Level: / Output Level: (5)
8.1	2 1 2 1	10	Graduate students in Education	4 1 7	Awareness of the roles of various community organizations in school-community interaction / Input level - Little or none / Output level - Awareness of the roles of various community organizations in school-community interaction
				4 4 3 2	Relationships with community organization personnel / Input level - None / Output level - New formed relationships with community organization personnel
8.1	2 1 2 2	5	Graduate students in Liberal Arts	4 1 7 / 4 4 3 2	Same as above / Same as above
8.1	2 2 1 2	10	Cooperating Teachers	4 1 7 / 4 4 3 2	Same as above / Same as above
8.1	2 2 2 3	5	Graduate students preparing to be public school supervisors	4 1 7 / 4 4 3 2	Same as above / Same as above
8.2	2 1 2 1	10	Graduate students in Education	4 1 7	Understanding of the factors that contribute to leadership in community organizations / Input level - Little or none / Output level - Understanding of the factors that contribute to leadership in community organizations
				4 4 3 2	Relationships with leaders of community organizations / Input level - None / Output level - New relationships with leaders of community organizations

FORM NO. 4 - SUB-ELEMENTS INPUT-OUTPUT   PROJECT Example   PROJECT CODE [EXA] PAGE 15 OF 15

Sub-Element Number (1)	Receptor Category (2)				No.	Receptor Name (3)	Change Variable Category (4)			Description of the Change Variable Input Level: Output Level: (5)
8.2	2	1	2	2	5	Graduate students in Liberal Arts	4 1 7	4 4 3 2		Same as above Same as above
8.2	2	2	1	2	10	Cooperating teachers	4 1 7	4 4 3 2		Same as above Same as above
8.2	2	2	2	3	5	Graduate students pre-paring to be public school supervisors	4 1 7	4 4 3 2		Same as above Same as above
8.3	2	1	2	1	10	Graudate students in Education	4 1 5			Understanding of community problems and needs Input level - Little or none Output level - Increased understanding of community problems and needs
8.3	2	1	2	2	5	Graduate Students in Liberal Arts	4 1 5			Same as above
8.3	2	2	1	2	10	Cooperating Teachers	4 1 5			Same as above
8.3	2	2	2	3	5	Graduate students pre-paring to be public school supervisors	4 1 5			Same as above

Glossary of Terms

CATEGORY. The number of the line in any taxonomy which best describes the object being classified.

CHANGE VARIABLE. An observable condition which the project seeks to change. Successful performance of the element or subelement activity will alter the change variable from its input level to its output level.

CHANGE VARIABLE TAXONOMY. An organized description of the possible change variables in outline form.

EDUCATIONAL PROGRAM. An effort on the part of an educational agency which is based on a definite concept with stated goals. A program is a general theme which is manifested in its various projects.

EDUCATIONAL PROJECT. An actual expenditure of resources to implement an educational program. A project has individuals and institutions involved, elements, and objectives which are related to the concepts and goals of the parent program.

ELEMENT. A prescribed block of activities to bring individuals and institutions together under the design of an educational project. An element lasts only a single fiscal year. An activity continuing over three years would thus be three elements.

ELEMENT NAME. The name that your project gives to an element. This name should go beyond the general terms used in the Element Taxonomy.

ELEMENT SEQUENCE NUMBER. After all the elements in a project have been listed in the order in which they begin, they should be numbered in sequence. This is the element sequence number.

ELEMENT TAXONOMY. An organized description of the possible element classes in outline form.

FOOTNOTE. A method of drawing attention to an item on the forms, such as an especially unique or significant element or a place where the taxonomies do not fit. A footnote is to be marked by a circled number in the right-hand margin. An explanation should be typed on a separate sheet of paper.

INPUT LEVEL. The observed performance of receptors on the change variable prior to the effect of the element or subelement is the input level.

INSTITUTION. An identifiable group which is involved in or affected by the TTT project.

INSTITUTION TAXONOMY. An organized description of possible institution classes in outline form.

OBJECTIVE. A set of observable (or at least describable) conditions which mark the successful completion of an element or project.

OUTPUT LEVEL. The observed performance of receptors on the change variable after the effect of the element or subelement is the output level.

INDIVIDUALS. The individuals who are included in project activities.

INDIVIDUAL TAXONOMY. An organized description of the possible individual classes in outline form.

PROJECT DESIGN. For an educational project, a specification of (1) individuals and institutions involved, (2) elements, (3) subelements, (4) change variables, and (5) time-frame.

RECEPTOR. The individual or institution affected by the element or subelement.

SUBELEMENT. A part of an element which explicates the element beyond the description provided in the element taxonomy.

SUBELEMENT NUMBER. After each of the subelements of a given element have been listed in the order in which they begin, they should be numbered in sequence. The element number followed by a period and the sequential number of the subelement is the subelement number.

TAXONOMY. A system for organizing a body of information around concepts. The Individual Taxonomy in this document, for example, organizes the body of individuals around the concepts of "T", "TT", "TTT", "ultimate consumers", and "community".

TIME-FRAME. The beginning and ending dates for an element or subelement activity. This is the setting for an element or subelement in time.

1. Element Taxonomy Outline

Note. This is not the complete element taxonomy; only the major subdivisions are presented here so that the reader may comprehend the basic structure of the full taxonomy.

ELEMENT
CATEGORY

1.1.	PLANNING
1.1.1.	TTT PROGRAM COMPONENT
1.1.2.	NEEDS OF COMMUNITY
1.1.3.	NEEDS OF SCHOOLS
1.2.	COURSEWORK
1.2.1.	FORMAL UNIVERSITY COURSES
1.2.2.	SPECIAL COURSES, DESIGNED ESPECIALLY FOR TTT
1.2.3.	ACADEMIC SEMINARS
1.2.4.	INDIVIDUALIZED COURSEWORK PROGRAM
1.3.	PRACTICUM
1.3.1.	PERSONAL LEARNING EXPERIENCE
1.3.2.	CLINICAL EXPERIENCE
1.3.3.	RESEARCH STUDIES
1.3.4.	INSTRUCTIONAL TECHNIQUES
1.3.5.	CURRICULUM CONSTRUCTION
1.3.6.	GROUP DYNAMICS
1.4.	STAFFING ARRANGEMENTS
1.4.1.	EXPERIMENTS IN JOINT APPOINTMENTS
1.4.2.	EXPERIMENTS IN SUPERVISION
1.4.3.	EXPERIMENTS IN STAFFING IN THE CLASSROOM
1.4.4.	EXPERIMENTS IN JOINT PROBLEM SOLVING
1.4.5.	EXPERIMENTS WITH FACILITIES
1.5.	MANAGEMENT AND COORDINATION OF TTT
1.5.1.	DIRECTING BOARD ARRANGEMENTS
1.5.2.	COORDINATING ALL INTER- AND INTRA-AGENCY COOPERATION
1.5.3.	RESPONSIVENESS TO OUTSIDE AGENCY CONTROLS
1.5.4.	MAINTAINING ADEQUATE SUPPORT SYSTEM ARRANGEMENTS

Element Taxonomy Outline (cont'd)

1.5.5.	RECRUITMENT AND PLACEMENT
1.6.	EVALUATION AND ASSESSMENT

Element Taxonomy

1.1.	PLANNING
1.1.1.	TTT PROGRAM COMPONENT
1.1.2.	NEEDS OF COMMUNITY
1.1.3.	NEEDS OF SCHOOLS
1.2.	COURSEWORK
1.2.1.	FORMAL UNIVERSITY COURSES (*i.e.*, in college catalogue)
1.2.1.1.	Education Courses
1.2.1.1.01.	Abnormal Psychology
1.2.1.1.02.	Administration
1.2.1.1.03.	Adolescent Psychology
1.2.1.1.04.	Child Development
1.2.1.1.05.	Community Relations
1.2.1.1.06.	Counseling and Guidance
1.2.1.1.07.	Curriculum/Curriculum Development
1.2.1.1.08.	Educational Psychology
1.2.1.1.09.	Ethnic Cultures
1.2.1.1.10.	Evaluation
1.2.1.1.11.	Foundations of Education
1.2.1.1.12.	Group Dynamics
1.2.1.1.13.	Higher Education
1.2.1.1.14.	History of Education
1.2.1.1.15.	Human Behavior
1.2.1.1.16.	Human Growth and Development
1.2.1.1.17.	Language Arts
1.2.1.1.18.	Learning Theory
1.2.1.1.19.	Philosophy of Education
1.2.1.1.20.	Psychology of Learning
1.2.1.1.21.	Management
1.2.1.1.22.	Materials Development
1.2.1.1.23.	Media and Technology
1.2.1.1.24.	Organizational Behavior
1.2.1.1.25.	Planning
1.2.1.1.26.	Research Problems
1.2.1.1.27.	Research Design
1.2.1.1.28.	Special Education
1.2.1.1.29.	Statistics
1.2.1.1.30.	Supervision
1.2.1.1.31.	Tests and Measurement
1.2.1.1.32.	Techniques, Methods and Materials of Instruction
1.2.1.1.33.	Physiology
1.2.1.1.34.	Vocational Education
1.2.1.1.35.	Other (specify)
1.2.1.2.	Liberal Arts Courses
1.2.1.2.01.	Anthropology

Element Taxonomy (cont'd)

1.2.1.2.02.	Arts and Humanities
1.2.1.2.03.	Bilingual Studies
1.2.1.2.04.	Black Studies
1.2.1.2.05	Economics
1.2.1.2.06.	English and Language Arts
1.2.1.2.07.	English for Speakers of Other Languages
1.2.1.2.08.	Foreign Languages
1.2.1.2.08.1	Chinese
1.2.1.2.08.2	French
1.2.1.2.08.3	German
1.2.1.2.08.4	Italian
1.2.1.2.08.5	Russian
1.2.1.2.08.6	Spanish
1.2.1.2.08.7	Swahili
1.2.1.2.08.8	Other (specify)
1.2.1.2.09.	Geography
1.2.1.2.10.	History
1.2.1.2.11.	Health and Physical Education
1.2.1.2.12.	Industrial Arts
1.2.1.2.13.	International Affairs
1.2.1.2.14.	Language and Linguistics
1.2.1.2.15.	Mathematics
1.2.1.2.16.	Political Science
1.2.1.2.17.	Social Studies
1.2.1.2.18.	Sociology
1.2.1.1.19.	Speech and Drama
1.2.1.2.20.	Urban Affairs
1.2.1.2.21.	Science
1.2.1.2.22.	Other (specify)
1.2.2.	SPECIAL COURSES Designed especially for TTT
1.2.2.1.	Education Courses
1.2.2.1.01.	Abnormal Psychology
1.2.2.1.02.	Administration
1.2.2.1.03.	Adolescent Psychology
1.2.2.1.04.	Child Development
1.2.2.1.05.	Community Relations
1.2.2.1.06.	Counseling and Guidance
1.2.2.1.07.	Curriculum/Curriculum Development
1.2.2.1.08.	Educational Psychology
1.2.2.1.09.	Ethnic Cultures
1.2.2.1.10.	Evaluation
1.2.2.1.11.	Foundations of Education
1.2.2.1.12.	Group Dynamics
1.2.2.1.13.	Higher Education
1.2.2.1.14.	History of Education
1.2.2.1.15.	Human Behavior
1.2.2.1.16.	Human Growth and Development
1.2.2.1.17.	Language Arts
1.2.2.1.18.	Learning Theory

Element Taxonomy (cont'd)

1.2.2.1.19.	Philosophy of Education
1.2.2.1.20.	Psychology of Learning
1.2.2.1.21.	Management
1.2.2.1.22.	Materials Development
1.2.2.1.23.	Media and Technology
1.2.2.1.24.	Organizational Behavior
1.2.2.1.25.	Planning
1.2.2.1.26.	Research Problems
1.2.2.1.27.	Research Design
1.2.2.1.28.	Special Education
1.2.2.1.29.	Statistics
1.2.2.1.30.	Supervision
1.2.2.1.31.	Tests and Measurement
1.2.2.1.32.	Techniques Methods
1.2.2.1.33.	Physiology
1.2.2.1.34.	Vocational Education
1.2.2.1.35.	Other (specify)
1.2.2.2.	Liberal Arts Courses
1.2.2.2.01.	Anthropology
1.2.2.2.02.	Arts and Humanities
1.2.2.2.03.	Bilingual Studies
1.2.2.2.04.	Black Studies
1.2.2.2.05.	Economics
1.2.2.2.06.	English and Language Arts
1.2.2.2.07.	English for Speakers of Other Languages
1.2.2.2.08.	Foreign Languages
1.2.2.2.08.1	Chinese
1.2.2.2.08.2	French
1.2.2.2.08.3	German
1.2.2.2.08.4	Italian
1.2.2.2.08.5	Russian
1.2.2.2.08.6	Spanish
1.2.2.2.08.7	Swahili
1.2.2.2.08.8	Other (specify)
1.2.2.2.09.	Geography
1.2.2.2.10.	History
1.2.2.2.11.	Health and Physical Education
1.2.2.2.12.	Industrial Arts
1.2.2.2.13.	International Affairs
1.2.2.2.14.	Language and Linguistics
1.2.2.2.15.	Mathematics
1.2.2.2.16.	Political Science
1.2.2.2.17.	Social Studies
1.2.2.2.18.	Sociology
1.2.2.2.19.	Speech and Drama
1.2.2.2.20.	Urban Affairs
1.2.2.2.21.	Science
1.2.2.2.22.	Other (specify)
1.2.3.	ACADEMIC SEMINARS

Element Taxonomy (cont'd)

1.2.3.1.	History and Systems of Education
1.2.3.2.	Research Methods
1.2.3.3.	Area Surveys
1.2.3.3.01.	Child Psychology
1.2.3.3.02.	Learning/Behavior Theory
1.2.3.3.03.	Social Studies
1.2.3.3.04.	Math/Science
1.2.3.3.05.	Language/Communication
1.2.3.3.06.	Models of the Educational Process
1.2.3.3.07.	Bilingual Education
1.2.3.3.08.	Role of Arts and Sciences in Education
1.2.3.3.09.	Diagnosis of Learning Problems
1.2.3.4.	Curriculum
1.2.3.4.01.	Historical Perspective
1.2.3.4.02.	Innovative Curricula
1.2.3.4.03.	Curriculum Development
1.2.3.5.	Supervision
1.2.3.5.01.	Strata of Administrative Techniques
1.2.3.5.02.	Supervision of Pre-service Personnel
1.2.3.5.03.	Supervision of In-service Personnel
1.2.3.6.	Evaluation and Assessment
1.2.3.7.	Community and Contemporary Problems
1.2.3.7.01.	Minority Culture
1.2.3.7.02.	Community Organization and Needs
1.2.3.7.03.	Public School Problems and Needs
1.2.3.7.04.	University Problems and Needs
1.2.3.7.05.	Special Controversial Topics
1.2.3.7.06.	Medical Problems (including Drug Abuse)
1.2.3.8.	Methods of Instruction
1.2.3.9.	Teacher Training
1.2.3.0.	Development of Goals
1.2.4.	INDIVIDUALIZED COURSEWORK PROGRAM
1.3.	PRACTICUM
1.3.1.	PERSONAL LEARNING EXPERIENCE (i.e., the participant is to enter this experience without his "title," and let the situation affect him as a person)
1.3.1.1.	Residence in a Neighborhood composed of a particular ethnic/disadvantaged group.
1.3.1.2.	Interaction with the agencies of the community as a person (i.e., try to get welfare, treatment at a clinic, ride the bus, etc.)
1.3.2.	CLINICAL EXPERIENCE (i.e., the participant has his title on and interacts with the situation)
1.3.2.1.	Clinical Experience in the schools
1.3.2.1.01.	Observation
1.3.2.1.01.1	Classes/curriculum
1.3.2.1.01.2	Supervision of Teaching
1.3.2.1.01.3	Administrative Procedure
1.3.2.1.01.4	Facilities
1.3.2.1.01.5	Counseling

Element Taxonomy (cont'd)

1.3.2.1.02.	Participation
1.3.2.1.02.1	Responsibility for a class
1.3.2.1.02.2	Team Participation
1.3.2.1.02.3	Teaching Advisor
1.3.2.1.02.4	Student Teaching
1.3.2.1.02.5	Paraprofessional Training
1.3.2.1.02.6	Counseling
1.3.2.1.02.7	Supervision
1.3.2.1.02.8	Auxiliary Services (*e.g.,* Library aide etc.)
1.3.2.1.02.9	Tutoring
1.3.2.2.	Clinical Experience in a Community Agency (*e.g.,* Model Cities Board, Welfare Agency, etc.)
1.3.2.2.01.	Observation
1.3.2.2.02.	Participation
1.3.2.3.	Clinical Experience in the Community at Large
1.3.2.4.	Individualized Clinical Program
1.3.3.	RESEARCH STUDIES (the participant interacts with the community in such a fashion as to extract data to answer a question or test a hypothesis)
1.3.3.1.	Seminar Based Research (*i.e.,* research conducted and presented before a group of participants)
1.3.3.2.	Degree-required Research
1.3.3.2.01.	Masters Thesis
1.3.3.2.02.	Dissertation
1.3.4.	INSTRUCTIONAL TECHNIQUES
1.3.4.1.	Individualized instruction
1.3.4.2.	Micro-teaching/Video Tape recording
1.3.4.3.	Computer aided Instruction
1.3.4.4.	Other
1.3.5.	CURRICULUM CONSTRUCTION
1.3.5.1.	Selection
1.3.5.2.	Adaptation
1.3.5.3.	Development
1.3.6.	GROUP DYNAMICS
1.3.6.1.	Role-Playing Techniques
1.3.6.2.	Encounter Group-sensitivity Training
1.3.6.3.	Brainstorming
1.3.6.4.	Unstructured ("rap") sessions
1.4.	STAFFING ARRANGEMENTS
1.4.1.	EXPERIMENTS IN JOINT APPOINTMENTS
1.4.1.1.	Interdisciplinary within an Institute of Higher Education
1.4.1.2.	Between IHE's
1.4.1.3.	Between IHE and Public Schools
1.4.1.4.	Between IHE and Community
1.4.1.5.	Between Public School and Community
1.4.2.	EXPERIMENTS IN SUPERVISION
1.4.2.1.	Team of Participants supervises a project
1.4.2.2.	Team of Participants supervises pre-service training
1.4.2.3.	Team of Participants supervises in-service training

Element Taxonomy (cont'd)

1.4.3.	EXPERIMENTS IN STAFFING IN THE CLASSROOM
1.4.3.1.	Team Teaching (peer team)
1.4.3.2.	Team Teaching (Team made up of different ranks)
1.4.3.3.	Instruction with availability of consultant team
1.4.4.	EXPERIMENTS IN JOINT PROBLEM SOLVING
1.4.5.	EXPERIMENTS WITH FACILITIES
1.4.5.1.	Teaching Field Centers (*i.e.*, places where Institute of Higher Education, Local Education Agency, and Community people may interact)
1.4.5.2.	Resource Centers (*i.e.*, places where hard-to-get materials and media may be obtained, studied and demonstrated)
1.5.	MANAGEMENT AND COORDINATION OF TTT
1.5.1.	DIRECTING BOARD ARRANGEMENTS
1.5.1.1.	Parity Board which Directs
1.5.1.2.	Parity Board which has advisory powers only
1.5.1.3.	Other Directing body
1.5.2.	COORDINATING ALL INTER- AND INTRA-AGENCY COOPERATION
1.5.3.	RESPONSIVENESS TO OUTSIDE AGENCY CONTROLS
1.5.4.	MAINTAINING ADEQUATE SUPPORT SYSTEM ARRANGEMENTS
1.5.5.	RECRUITMENT AND PLACEMENT
1.6.	EVALUATION AND ASSESSMENT

2. Individual Taxonomy

INDIVIDUAL
CATEGORY

2.1.	TTT-LEVEL
2.1.1.	Actual:
2.1.1.1.	School district superintendents
2.1.1.2.	Graduate faculty in education
2.1.1.3.	Other Graduate faculty
2.1.1.4.	Public school supervisors of cooperating teachers
2.1.1.5.	Institute of Higher Education Administration
2.1.1.6.	Other (specify)
2.1.2.	Potential:
2.1.2.1.	Graduate students in education preparing to teach in graduate school
2.1.2.2.	Other graduate students preparing to teach in graduate school
2.1.2.3.	Other (specify)
2.1.2.4.	Other (specify)
2.2.	TT-LEVEL
2.2.1.	Actual:
2.2.1.1.	Student teacher supervisors in the University
2.2.1.2.	Cooperating teachers who supervise student teachers
2.2.1.3.	Public School principals

Individual Taxonomy (cont'd)

2.2.1.4.	Local Education Agency department chairmen
2.2.1.5.	Local Education Agency curriculum supervisors
2.2.1.6.	Leaders of teacher teams
2.2.1.7.	Resource colleague (*i.e.*, a person who is trained to provide expertise in a specific area to his colleagues)
2.2.1.8.	Undergraduate faculty in education
2.2.1.9.	Other undergraduate faculty
2.2.1.0.	Other (specify)
2.2.2.	Potential:
2.2.2.1.	Graduate students in education preparing to teach undergraduates
2.2.2.2.	Other graduate students preparing to teach undergraduates
2.2.2.3.	Graduate students preparing for supervisory roles in the public schools
2.2.2.4.	Teachers preparing on a part-time basis for supervisory roles.
2.2.2.5.	Other (specify)
2.2.3.	Other (specify)
2.3.	T-LEVEL
2.3.1.	Actual:
2.3.1.1.	Classroom teachers
2.3.1.2.	Paraprofessionals in fixed positions
2.3.1.3.	Public School counselors
2.3.1.4.	Other
2.3.2.	Potential:
2.3.2.1.	Undergraduates in education
2.3.2.2.	Other undergraduates
2.3.2.3.	In-service paraprofessionals in a career ladder
2.3.2.4.	Pre-service paraprofessionals in a career ladder
2.3.2.5.	Graduate students preparing to teach in public schools
2.3.2.6.	Other (specify)
2.3.3.	Other (specify)
2.4.	ULTIMATE CONSUMER
2.4.1.	Students
2.4.2.	Adult trainees
2.4.3.	Other (specify)
2.5.	COMMUNITY LEVEL
2.5.1.	Community Leaders
2.5.1.1.	Public Officials
2.5.1.2.	Community organization leaders
2.5.1.3.	Community Agency personnel
2.5.1.4.	Other (specify)
2.5.2.	Private citizens
2.5.2.1.	Parents of public school students
2.5.2.2.	Representatives of minority groups
2.5.2.3.	Other (specify)
2.5.3.	Outside Resources
2.5.3.1.	Evaluation Staff

Individual Taxonomy (cont'd)

2.5.3.2.	Government agency staff
2.5.3.3.	State Department of Education staff
2.5.3.4.	Other (specify)
2.5.4.	Other (specify)

3. Institution Taxonomy

*INSTITUTION
CATEGORY*

3.1.	GRADUATE INSTITUTION (Undergraduate and Graduate degrees granted)
3.1.1.	Education Department or School
3.1.2.	Arts and Sciences Department or School
3.1.3.	Administrative Unit of University (specify)
3.1.4.	University Board or other formal Public Support Base
3.1.5.	Special structures (specify)
3.2.	FOUR-YEAR COLLEGE (No graduate degrees granted)
3.2.1.	Education Department or School
3.2.2.	Arts and Sciences Department or School
3.2.3.	Administrative Unit of Institution (specify)
3.2.4.	College Board or other formal Public Support Base
3.2.5.	Special structures (specify)
3.3.	TWO-YEAR INSTITUTION (Degree-granting or non-degree-granting)
3.4.	LOCAL EDUCATION AGENCY (preschool through High School)
3.4.1.	Preschool
3.4.2.	Elementary School
3.4.3.	Secondary School
3.4.4.	Adult Education
3.4.5.	Administrative Unit of School System (specify)
3.4.6.	School Board or other formal Public Support Base
3.5.	COMMUNITY
3.5.1.	Formal Structures (specify)
3.5.2.	Informal structures (specify)
3.6.	STATE
3.6.1.	Department of Instruction
3.6.2.	Board, Governor, and Public Support Base
3.7.	REGIONAL EDUCATION AGENCIES
3.8.	TTT PROJECT STAFF
3.9.	FEDERAL AGENCY (specify)
3.0.	CONGRESS AND PUBLIC SUPPORT BASE

4. Individual Change Variable Taxonomy

INDIVIDUAL
CHANGE VARIABLE
CATEGORY

4.1.	KNOWLEDGE
4.1.1.	History
4.1.2.	Concepts
4.1.3.	Values
4.1.4.	Theory
4.1.5.	Problems
4.1.6.	Research Findings
4.1.7.	Current Practice
4.2.	SKILLS
4.2.1.	Professional skills
4.2.1.1.	Teaching skills
4.2.1.2.	Counseling skills
4.2.1.3.	Team Participation skills
4.2.1.4.	Administrative skills
4.2.2.	Problem-solving skills
4.2.2.1.	Research skills
4.2.2.2.	Analytical skills
4.3.	ATTITUDES
4.3.1.	Toward students
4.3.2.	Toward educators
4.3.2.1.	Public School Teachers
4.3.2.2.	University Professors
4.3.3.	Toward members of the community
4.3.3.1.	Minority groups
4.3.3.2.	Other
4.4.	RELATIONS
4.4.1.	With Students
4.4.2.	With Educators
4.4.2.1.	Public School Teachers
4.4.2.2.	University Professors
4.4.3.	With members of community
4.4.3.1.	Minority groups
4.4.3.2.	Other

5. Institutional Change Variable Taxonomy

INSTITUTIONAL
CHANGE VARIABLE
CATEGORY

5.1.	PURPOSE
5.1.1.	To facilitate training of Educational Personnel
5.1.1.1.	New Program or structure
5.1.1.1.1.	New Degree
5.1.1.1.1.1.	Ph.D.
5.1.1.1.1.2.	Ed.D.

Institutional Change Variable Taxonomy (cont'd)

5.1.1.1.1.3.	Doctor of Arts (D.A.)
5.1.1.1.1.4.	B.A. or B.S.
5.1.1.1.1.5.	M.A. or M.S.
5.1.1.1.2.	Other formal training
5.1.1.1.2.2.	Post-Masters certificate of competency (specialist degrees)
5.1.1.1.2.3.	Instructor's aide program
5.1.1.1.2.4.	Formal program without certificate for community representatives
5.1.1.1.3.	Formation of a special temporary task force
5.1.1.1.4.	Participation in a consortium or other cooperative arrangement
5.1.1.2.	Revision of content of existing instructional programs
5.1.1.2.1.	New or revised course
5.1.1.2.1.1.	Academic discipline course
5.1.1.2.1.2.	Education course
5.1.1.2.1.3.	Vocational or technical course
5.1.1.2.1.4.	Behavioral science course
5.1.1.2.1.5.	Special minority group course
5.1.1.2.2.	Practicum component
5.1.1.2.3.	Change in degree requirement
5.1.1.2.3.1.	Competency examination
5.1.1.2.3.2.	Research requirement
5.1.1.2.4.	Admissions policy
5.1.1.2.5.	Placement policy
5.1.2.	To facilitate institutional conditions conducive to the effectiveness of Educational Programs
5.1.2.1.	Change Certification standards
5.1.2.2.	Change conditions or work
5.1.2.3.	Change administrative support
5.2.	INTERNAL MAINTENANCE
5.2.1.	Strengthen staffing arrangements
5.2.2.	Change staff recruitment and hiring policy
5.2.3.	Imporve policy-making procedure
5.2.4.	Improve internal communication
5.2.5.	Improve staff training
5.2.6.	Increase member rapport and commitments (morale)

Project Codes

Name	Code
Appalachian State University	APP
Auburn University	AUB
Berkeley Unified School District	BUD
City University of New York	CUW
Clark University	CLU
Cleveland State University	CSN
Colorado Commission on Higher Education	CCE

Project Codes (cont'd)

Columbia University . . . . CBY
Fordham University . . . . FRU
George Peabody College for Teachers . . . . GPC
Harvard University . . . . HAU
Indiana University . . . . INU
Michigan State University . . . . MSU
New York University . . . . NYU
Northwestern University . . . . NRW
Portland State University . . . . PSV
San Fernando State College . . . . SFS
San Francisco State College . . . . SSC
San Jose State College . . . . SAJ
Southeastern State College . . . . SCL
Southern Illinois University . . . . SIU
State Department of Education (W. Va.) . . . . SDE
State Department of Public Instruction (Wash.) . . . . SPI
State University of New York (Buffalo) . . . . SNY
Syracuse University . . . . SYR
Temple University . . . . TEM
Texas Southern University . . . . TXU
University of Chicago . . . . UCH
University of Illinois . . . . UIL
University of Miami . . . . UMI
University of Minnesota . . . . UFM
University of Nebraska . . . . UKA
University of North Dakota . . . . UND
University of Pittsburgh . . . . UPT
University of South Florida . . . . USF
University of Texas . . . . UTX
University of Washington . . . . UWS
University of Wisconsin (Madison) . . . . UVW
University of Wisconsin (Milwaukee) . . . . URK
Washington University . . . . WUN
Wayne State University . . . . WST
Wesleyan University . . . . WEU

Appendix B: User's Guide to the National Drug Education Training Program Assessment

This is the user's guide that was prepared by E.F. Shelley and Company for the evaluation of the National Drug Education Training Program under the Discrepancy Evaluation Model. In this document is a glossary of terms, along with procedures and taxonomies for use in the evaluation.

Table of Contents

Introduction

Regardless of whether you work with a school, district, county or state, you are involved in a program which aims at conveying information and influencing people in connection with drug abuse.

This guide is designed to do two things:

1. Help you gather information about your program, and

2. Assist the National Action Committee (NAC) in collecting information to assess the National Drug Education Training Program.

The guide asks you to focus attention on the following information gathering tasks:

1. Identify the members of your immediate staff.

2. Identify the training program participants reached directly by your staff.

3. For each type of audience to be trained directly by your staff:

    a. Identify how they are to be reached (training method);

    b. Identify how they are to be affected by training (training purpose).

This will make it possible for the states and Federal goverment to determine what has happened and to plan for the future.

There are three response forms to be completed:

Form 1: Description of your staff—LEA commitment obtained—Format of your state's "multiplier effect"

Form 2: LEA's and institutions contacted directly by your training team

Form 3: Purposes served and methods used by your training team

Kindly fill in the incomplete portions of Form 1. (Note: Form 1 need only be completed once at each training level of your state's "multiplier effect".)

Complete Forms 2 and 3 for each training program conducted by your training team through November 30, 1970. Please return all completed forms by December 1, 1970 to:

Dr. James Spillane
Division of Program Resources
Bureau of Educational Personnel Development
U. S. Office of Education
Washington, D. C. 20202

A self-addressed, franked envelope is included for your convenience.

For training programs conducted after December 1, 1970, kindly complete Forms 2 and 3 for each. You will receive our request for mailing the next batch approximately February 1. Please wait for this request which will be accompanied with another self-addressed, franked envelope.

Please, do not send us Forms 2 and 3 after completion of each training program. We are attempting to minimize slippage and loss of data, and, thus, are calling for periodic bulk mailings on December 1, 1970, February 1, and April 1, 1971.

You may find these forms useful in planning and executing your state's training programs throughout the current school year.

Glossary of Terms

INSTITUTION, AGENCY, GROUP, SCHOOL DISTRICT, AUDIENCE. All of these terms refer to the "target group" of the National Drug Education Training Program, including those who participate in training programs and other community agencies and organizations from whom commitment to the program is sought.

TRAINING TEAM, TRAINERS. Persons responsible for actual training as distinguished from supportive or administrative personnel in your state/county/local drug education training programs.

TRAINING PROGRAM. Actual program conducted by the Training Team for the Trainees.

TRAINEES, AUDIENCE, PARTICIPANTS. Persons receiving the training.

PROGRAM. Both the information and the process or vehicle by which the information is conveyed to the trainees.

INFORMATION. The subject matter—"what" the group (traninees and trainers) is talking about, *e.g.*, lecturing about group process. In this program the subject matter being explored is drug education. The kinds of information which can be disseminated are outlined in a rather extensive "encyclopedia-type" format in Section 4 of the *Purpose Index* (See Appendix B).

PROCESS. The method of communicating the subject matter and the skills necessary for the trainees to become effective trainers. This includes:

(1) "How" the trainers transmit the subject matter to the trainees, *e.g.*, trainees participating in role playing, problem-solving, site visits, etc. These training program processes are depicted in the *Methods Index* (See Appendix C).

(2) "How" the trainees will carry out their own drug education training programs when they become the trainers at the next level. When describing this "how", think of outcome—the enabling objectives or "skills" taught the trainees to enable them to become effective trainers. These skills, because of the time constraints of your training programs, are somewhat specific and limited. They are outlined in Section 3 of the *Purpose Index* (See Appendix B).

Instructions for Form 1

This form is to be completed and/or approved by:

(person responsible for administration of your state program)

Form 1 is provided as a sample. (The actual forms to be executed by you or members of your staff are enclosed under separate cover marked Appendix D.) Items 1 through 4 request identification of your program and information about yourself. Fill in *either* Item 3 *or* Item 4 as it applies to your personal situation.

Item 5 requests information about all other members of your state Drug Education Training Program staff, including all state training team members and consultants. Only the State Team Leader's mailing address and telephone number is requested (Item 5.A.). For all other staff members, list *only names* and whether each is administrative staff, training team staff or outside consultant to the training team; and whether each is full-time or part-time; temporary or permanent through June 1971; volunteer or paid, *e.g.*, a fulltime, permanent, paid training team member. Give each member's functional title in the Drug Education Training Program and identify his or her background using the *Background Index* (See Appendix A). This index lists five areas where these individuals may regularly work or focus their interests. These areas are divided into: (1) national; (2) state; (3) county, township, or intermediate level; (4) community; and (5) school.

Within each of these five major categories, one or more different kinds of people and/or their associations are listed with identifying "Background Codes." In the last column of Item 5, please identify each of your staff members and consultants by background affiliation. (Note: if the appropriate background description is not listed, add it to the appropriate category under "OTHERS" and insert the appropriate code on Form 1.) For example, if a member of the training team is a "recent high school graduate, not currently enrolled in higher education," use Background Code 4E8—or, if a member is a "public school, secondary level, guidance counselor," use Background Code 5A2D1.

Item 6 of Form 1 requests the *number* of LEA's in your state, territory, or, in the case of Washington, D.C., district. And Item 7 asks your to give the number of LEA's which have given their commitment to participate in your state Drug Education Training Program by sending trainees to one of the training programs.

Item 8 of Form 1 asks you to describe the model of "multiplier effect" which your state/territory is employing.

Glossary of Terms Relative to Form 1

FULL-TIME. Individual has been released from his regular job to allot 35 hours/week (or more) to this position.

PART-TIME. Individual has been released from his regular job or has elected to allot *less than 35 hours/week* to this position.

TEMPORARY. Individual cannot serve in this capacity through June 1971.

PERMANENT. Individual is committed to serving in this capacity through June 1971.

VOLUNTEER. Individual serves on a time available/on-call basis with the training program staff in a non-paying position.

FUNCTIONAL TITLE AS A STAFF OR TEAM MEMBER. Job description on the Drug Education Training Program staff, *i.e.*, Training Team Member, Administrative Coordinator, Clerk Typist, etc.

CONSULTANT (Outside the Training Team). Individual paid to contribute special expertise on an on-call hourly or daily basis with the Training Team.

YOUR STATE / TERRITORY

FORM 1
Section 1
DESCRIPTION OF YOUR STAFF

1. The Name of Your Program: _____

2. Information About the State Program Director:

_____   (Area Code / Telephone Number)

(Name)

_____   _____   _____

(Mailing Address)   (City)   (State)   (Zip Code)

COMPLETE EITHER ITEM 3 OR ITEM 4, WHICHEVER IS APPLICABLE:

3. The Name of Your Previous Employer and Position, if you left this position to become State Drug Education Program Director:

_____

4. The Name of Your Employing Institution and Your Regular Position (i.e., State Director of Health):

_____

5. A. Information About The State Team Leader:
Give Name – Address – City/State – Phone No.

Check Whether He/She Is: Identify His/Her Background
                                Using Appropriate Background Code
___ Full-time or ___ Part-time   from Appendix A :

___ Temporary or   _____
___ Permanent through June 1971

_____

_____

_____

5. B.   List All Other State Program Staff By:

NAME ONLY

Name	Administrative Staff	Training Team	Outside Consultant	FULL-TIME	PART-TIME	TEMPORARY	PERMANENT	VOLUNTEER	PAID	Functional Title as a Staff or Team Member	Background Code from Appendix A
										Check Appropriate Boxes To Describe Each Member's Status	
1)											
2)											
3)											
4)											
5)											
6)											
7)											
8)											
9)											
10)											
11)											
12)											

YOUR STATE / TERRITORY

FORM 1

Section 2

LEA COMMITMENT OBTAINED

6. List the Number of LEAs in Your State/Territory: _____
                                                    (Total Number of LEAs)

7. Of These, How Many LEAs Will Participate in Your Drug Education Training Program: _____
                                                                                     (Number Participating)

Section 3

FORMAT OF YOUR STATE'S "MULTIPLIER EFFECT"

8. A. Describe the "Multiplier Effect" Training Team Format Which Your State/Territory Is Using. Samples Are Shown in Examples 1, 2, 3 and 4. In the Space Provided Below These Examples Fill in Your State's "Multiplier Effect" Format, Showing Numbers of Team Members at Each Level and Projected Numbers of People To Be Trained at Each Level:

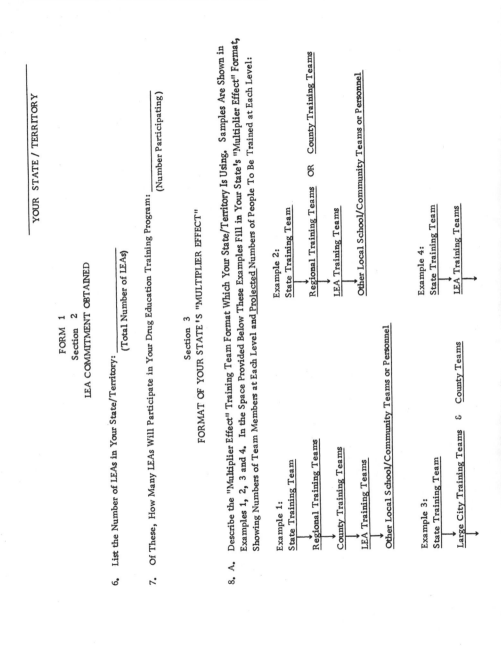

Example 1:
State Training Team

Regional Training Teams

County Training Teams

LEA Training Teams

Other Local School/Community Teams or Personnel

Example 2:
State Training Team

Regional Training Teams   OR   County Training Teams

LEA Training Teams

Other Local School/Community Teams or Personnel

Example 3:
State Training Team

Large City Training Teams   &   County Teams

Example 4:
State Training Team

LEA Training Teams

LEA Training Teams

Other Local School/Community Teams or Personnel

Other Local School/Community Teams or Personnel

FORMAT OF YOUR STATE'S "MULTIPLIER EFFECT"

Numbers of Team Members	ON	(fill in blank)	Training Teams	REACHING	(fill in blank)	Number Trained
_____ Team Members	ON	STATE	Training Team	REACHING	_____	Number Trained
_____ Team Members	ON	_____	Training Teams	REACHING	_____	Number Trained
_____ Team Members	ON	_____	Training Teams	REACHING	_____	Number Trained
_____ Team Members	ON	_____	Training Teams	REACHING	_____	Number Trained
_____ Team Members	ON	_____	Training Teams	REACHING	_____	Number Trained
_____ Team Members	ON	_____	Training Teams	REACHING	_____	Number Trained
_____ Team Members	ON	_____	Training Teams	REACHING	_____	Number Trained

(If you have more than one format, use supplemental FORM 1s to explain)

8. B. Estimate the Total Number of Teachers, Youth and Others Working with Youth that Will Have Been Trained in Your State/Territory by June 30, 1971:

_____ (Estimated Total Number Trained)

Your Name (Typed) _____   Title: _____   Date: _____

Your Signature _____

Instructions for Form 2

Form 2 is provided as a sample. This form should be completed for each
training program.

Column 2a requests that you identify the program trainees by background
affiliation, association or occupation. Again, use the appropriate "Background
Code" from Appendix A to describe the "types" of trainees in the training
program. Column 2b asks for a description of these types of trainees—note, you
do not need to repeat the *Background Index* description, *e.g.*, "public schools,
secondary level, teacher," but, kindly number or name the school districts these
teachers represent. And in Column 2c give the number of each type of trainee,
e.g., 20 public school secondary level teachers from districts etc. The total of
Column 2c should total the number of trainees trained per training program.

Glossary of Terms Relative to Form 2

DATES OF TRAINING. The beginning and ending dates of each training
program.

HOURS OF CONTACT. Total number of hours in training.

BACKGROUND. Description of an individual trainee's—or a group of trainees'—
affiliation—association—occupation vis-a-vis your Drug Education Training
Program. The *Background Index* (See Appendix A) is one evaluative standard
by which the National Drug Education Training Program is attempting to
codify "who" this program reaches.

TYPE of Trainee of Group Represented in the Training Program. A category
from the *Background Index* identifying the trainee or a group of trainees—the
distinguishing feature which describes why the individual is participating in
your Drug Education Training Program—his qualification for participation.

INSTITUTIONS

(1)

a) Name of Group (i. e. , School District) Contacted for Training
b) Name of Administrative Officer
c) Mailing Address – City – State – Zip Code
d) Area Code and Telephone Number of Administrative Officer
e) Beginning/Ending Dates of Training Program For This Group
f) Hours of Contact (Total Number of Hours in Training)

(a)
Background
Code from
Appendix A
Describing
Each Type

Descrip-

a) _____

b) _____

c) _____

_____

_____

d) _____   _____

e) _____ TO _____

f) _____

YOUR STATE / TERRITORY

Training Program # _____

(NOTE : LIST ONE (1) TRAINING PROGRAM PER PAGE)

FORM 2

CONTACTED DIRECTLY BY YOUR TRAINING TEAM

(2) TYPE OF AUDIENCE CONTACTED IN EACH TRAINING PROGRAM:

(b) tion of Each Trainee or Group of Trainees Represented in This Training Program (If Trainees Are From Various School Districts, List School District Name or Number beside Each Type Described in Item 2a)	(c) Number of Each Type Represented in This Training Program
	(TOTAL)

Instructions for Form 3

The National Drug Education Training Program has as its purpose the changing in some way of your training program audience. Form 3 is intended to describe how your training team's contact with various kinds of audiences achieves specific purposes.

The purposes can be listed under four (4) major enabling objectives.

1. Secure Institutional and/or Agency Commitment to an Action Program at the State and/or Local Level

2. Secure Individual Trainee Motivation for an Action Program at the Appropriate Level

3. Increase Trainee's Skills Useful to Implementing an Action Program

4. Increase Trainee's Knowledge Useful to Implementing an Action Program - Kinds of Information Explored

A *Purpose Index* (Appendix B) provides a variety of sub-objectives under three of the major program objectives. You must bear in mind that these are *enabling* objectives which will enable your trainees to become effective trainers at the next level of training. Do not confuse these enabling objectives with the "methods" used to teach them skills and impart to them drug education information.

For each major objective or sub-objective, one or more methods for achieving the stated objective may be required. A *Methods Index* (Appendix C) outlines 10 major categories of methods which may be used to achieve program objectives. These are:

1. Orientation
2. Factual Presentations
3. Dramatic Presentations
4. Site Visits
5. Program Visitations
6. Group Dynamics
7. Leadership Training
8. Use of Media
9. Planning and Implementation
10. Testing and Evaluation

By way of clarifying what is meant by asking you to state the methods used to achieve certain objectives, depending upon the type of audience you are trying to affect, think for a moment of the following situation:

Your theatre group has 5 or 6 scenarios in its repertoire—each with its impact/objective built around a certain level of anticipated audience response. Knowing your audience, you present the scenario which will deliver the message most effectively.

Form 2 describes the make-up of the audience of this training program. Form 3 asks you to outline the purposes you are trying to achieve with this group of trainees—and to give us the blueprint of the method(s) you use in attempting to achieve each stated purpose.

A sample of Form 3 is shown on the following pages. Using your schedule of training program activities, describe first, the purpose to be achieved, second, the method(s) used to achieve each purpose and, third, the approximate number of hours spent on each method used.

Glossary of Terms Relative to Form 3

PURPOSE. The enabling objective or goal you are trying to achieve by incorporating each educational component in your training program. The *Purpose Index* (See Appendix B) is the second evaluative standard by which the National Drug Education Training Program is attempting to identify "for what purposes" each state program is mounted.

METHOD. Vehicle by which the training program (content and process) is conveyed to the trainees. The *Methods Index* (See Appendix C), is the third evaluative standard by which the National Drug Education Training Program is attempting to discover "how" your training purposes and objectives will be attained.

APPROXIMATE HOURS OF CONTACT FOR EACH METHOD USED. Breakdown of the total hours of contact for each training program (refer back to Item 1f of Form 2) into approximate number of hours spent on the various methods used to train program participants.

YOUR STATE / TERRITORY

Training Program #_____

(1) PURPOSE OF CONTACT:

Purpose Code   Description of Purpose or Objective You Were Trying to Achieve Through
    from   Each of the Training Activities Undertaken in This Training Program
Appendix B

FORM 3

(NOTE: LIST ONE (1) TRAINING PROGRAM PER PAGE)

AND METHODS USED BY YOUR TRAINING TEAM

(2) METHOD OF CONTACT:

(3) HOURS OF CONTACT:

Method Code from Appendix C	Description of Methods Used to Achieve Each of the Stated Purposes in Item 1	Give Approximate Number of Hours Spent on Each Method Used in This Training Program

Background Index (Appendix A)

BACKGROUND CODE	INDIVIDUAL'S BACKGROUND DESCRIPTION

1   NATIONAL DRUG EDUCATION TRAINING PROGRAM

1A1   OE Drug Education Branch Staff

1A2   National Action Committee Personnel

OTHERS:

1A3

1A4

1A5 (etc.)

1B   National Training Center Personnel

1B1   Adelphi University

1B2   San Francisco State College

1B3   University of Texas

1B4   University of Wisconsin

OTHERS:

1B5

1B6 (etc.)

2   STATE LEVEL PROGRAMS

2A   State Agency Personnel

2A1   Attorney General's Office

2A2   Bureau of Alcoholism and Drug Abuse

2A3   Department of Corrections

2A4   Department of Education/Public Instruction

2A5   Department of Health/Public Health/Health & Welfare

2A6   Department of Juvenile Services

2A7   Department of Mental Health/Hygiene

2A8   Department of Narcotics and Dangerous Drugs

2A9   Department of Social Services

2A10   State Department

2A11   State Police/Highway Patrol

2A12   State University System

OTHERS:

2A13

2A14

2A15 (etc.)

2B   State Inter-Agency Coordinating Councils

2B1   Drug Control Committee

2B2   Governor's Task Force

2B3   Governor's Office of Drug Education

BACKGROUND CODE	INDIVIDUAL'S BACKGROUND DESCRIPTION
2	STATE LEVEL PROGRAMS
2B	State Inter-Agency Coordinating Councils
	OTHERS:
2B4	
2B5	
2B6	
2B7	
2B8 (etc.)	
2C	Resource People (Consultants/Specialists)
	IDENTIFY BY TITLE:
2C1	
2C2	
2C3	
2C4	
2C5 (etc.)	
3	COUNTY, TOWNSHIP OR INTERMEDIATE AGENCY PERSONNEL
3A1	County Superintendent of Schools (Not an LEA)
3A2	County Superintendent of Schools (Which is an LEA)
3A3	Community Action Program (countywide)
3A4	County Health Department
3A5	County Hospital
	OTHERS:
3A6	
3A7	
3A8	
3A9	
3A10 (etc.)	
4	COMMUNITY LEVEL PROGRAMS
4A	Local Agency Personnel
4A1	City Superintendent of Schools (Not Decentralized)
4A2	City Superintendent of Schools (Decentralized)
4A3	Community Action Program (citywide; not countrywide)
4A4	City Health/Sanitation Department
4A5	City Hospital
4A6	Community Mental Health Program
4A7	Narcotics/Drug Treatment Center
	OTHERS:
4A8	
4A9 (etc.)	

BACKGROUND CODE	INDIVIDUAL'S BACKGROUND DESCRIPTION
4	COMMUNITY LEVEL PROGRAMS
4B	Formal Groups Personnel (Professional Organizations, Service Clubs, etc.)
4B1	American Legion/American Legion Auxiliary
4B2	American Red Cross
4B3	Altrusa Clubs
4B4	Big Brother Clubs/Big Sister Clubs
4B5	B'nai B'rith
4B6	Boys Clubs of America
4B7	Boy Scouts/Girl Scouts of America
4B8	BPOE (Elks Clubs)
4B9	BPW (Business and Professional Women's Clubs)
4B10	Campfire Girls
4B11	Chamber of Commerce of USA
4B12	CORE (Congress on Racial Equality)
4B13	CYO (National Catholic Youth Organization Federation)
4B14	Delta Sigma Theta Sorority
4B15	DAR (Daughters of the American Revolution)
4B16	4-H Clubs
4B17	Fraternal Order of Eagles
4B18	Hadassah
4B19	Junior League
4B20	Kiwanis International
4B21	Knights of Columbus
4B22	League of Women Voters
4B23	Lions International
4B24	Loyal Order of Moose
4B25	Masonic Orders/Eastern Star
4B26	Metropolitan Police Boys Clubs
4B27	NAACP (National Association for the Advancement of Colored People)
4B28	National Council of Churches
4B29	National Council of Negro Women
4B30	National Jewish Welfare Board
4B31	Optimist International
4B32	ORT (Organization for Rehabilitation and Training)
4B33	PTA (Parent-Teachers Associations)

BACKGROUND CODE	INDIVIDUAL'S BACKGROUND DESCRIPTION
4	COMMUNITY LEVEL PROGRAMS
4B	Formal Groups Personnel (Professional Organizations, Service Clubs, etc.)
4B34	Rotary International
4B35	Salvation Army
4B36	Sisterhood
4B37	Urban Coalition
4B38	U.S. Jaycees
4B39	U.S. National Student Association
4B40	VFW (Veterans of Foreign Wars)
4B41	WICS (Women in Community Service)
4B42	YMCA/YWCA/Tri-Hi-Y/ Hi-Y/ Y-Teens
	OTHERS:
4B43	
4B44 (etc.)	
4C	Informal Groups Personnel
4C1	Local Civic Associations
4C2	Local Church Groups
	OTHERS:
4C3	
4C4	
4C5 (etc.)	
4D	Resource People (Consultants/Specialists) *Identify by Title*
4D1	Psychiatrist/Psychologist
4D2	Judge/Attorney
4D3	Scientist
	OTHERS:
4D4	
4D5 (etc.)	
4E	Individuals
4E1	Ex-Drug Addict
4E2	TV/Media Professional
4E3	Clergyman
4E4	Community Leader
4E5	Young Adult Working with Youth
4E6	Concerned Community Layman

BACKGROUND CODE	INDIVIDUAL'S BACKGROUND DESCRIPTION
4	COMMUNITY LEVEL PROGRAMS
4E7	Current Drug User
4E8	Recent High School Graduate (not currently enrolled in higher education)
4E9	Recent College Graduate (not currently enrolled in higher education)
4E10	Housewife
	OTHERS:
4E11	
4E12	
4E13	
4E14	
4E15 (etc.)	
5	SCHOOL LEVEL PROGRAMS
5A1	Public Schools - Elementary Level
4A1A	Administration
5A1B	Teacher
5A1C	Student
5A1D	Pupil Support Personnel
5A1D1	Guidance Counselor
5A1D2	Social Worker
5A1D3	School Nurse
5A1D4	School Physician
5A1D5	School Psychologist
5A1D6	Public Information Officer
5A1D7	School Custodian
5A1D8	School Bus Driver
5A1D9	School Truant Officer/Attendance Officer
	OTHERS
5A1D10	
5A1D11	
5A1D12	
5A1D13	
5A1D14	
5A1D15 (etc.)	
5A2	Public Schools—Secondary Level
5A2A	Administration

BACKGROUND CODE	INDIVIDUAL'S BACKGROUND DESCRIPTION
5	SCHOOL LEVEL PROGRAMS
5A2	Public Schools—Secondary Level
5A2B	Teacher
5A2C	Student
5A2D	Pupil Support Personnel
5A2D1	Guidance Counselor
5A2D2	Social Worker
5A2D3	School Nurse
5A2D4	School Physician
5A2D5	School Psychologist
5A2D6	Public Information Officer
5A2D7	School Custodian
5A2D8	School Bus Driver
5A2D9	School Truant Officer/Attendance Officer
	OTHERS:
5A2D10	
5A2D11	
5A2D12 (etc.)	
5A3	Public Schools - Junior College Level (includes technical schools, vocational schools, etc.)
5A3A	Administration
5A3B	Teacher
5A3C	Student
5A3D	Pupil Support Personnel
5A3D1	Guidance Counselor
5A3D2	Social Worker
5A3D3	School Nurse
5A3D4	School Physician
5A3D5	School Psychologist
5A3D6	Public Information Officer
5A3D7	School Custodian
5A3D8	School Bus Driver
	OTHERS:
5A3D9	
5A3D10	
5A3D11	
5A3D12 (etc.)	

BACKGROUND CODE	INDIVIDUAL'S BACKGROUND DESCRIPTION
5	SCHOOL LEVEL PROGRAMS
5A4	Public Schools - College/University Level
5A4A	Administration
5A4B	Teacher (Professor, Assistant, Associate, and Instructor)
5A4C	Student
5A4D	Pupil Support Personnel
5A4D1	Guidance Counselor
	OTHERS:
5A4D2 (etc.)	
5A5	Public Schools - College/University Graduate Level
5A5A	Administration
5A5B	Teacher
5A5C	Student
	OTHERS:
5A5D (etc.)	
5B	Private Schools
5B1	Parochial - Catholic
5B1A	Administration
5B1B	Teacher
5B1C	Student
5B1D	Pupil Support Personnel
5B2	Parochial - Protestant
5B2A	Administration
5B2B	Teacher
5B2C	Student
5B2D	Pupil Support Personnel
5B3	Parochial - Jewish
5B3A	Administration
5B3B	Teacher
5B3C	Student
5B3D	Pupil Support Personnel
5B4	Non-Sectarian
5B4A	Administration
5B4B	Teacher
5B4C	Student
5B4D	Pupil Support Personnel
	OTHERS:
5B5 (etc.)	

BACKGROUND CODE	INDIVIDUAL'S BACKGROUND DESCRIPTION
5	SCHOOL LEVEL PROGRAMS
5C	Parents of Students
5C1	Mother
5C2	Father
5C3	Guardian
	OTHERS:
5C4	
5C5 (etc.)	

Purpose Index (Appendix B)

PURPOSE CODE	PURPOSE - ENABLING OBJECTIVE - GOAL OF TRAINING PROGRAM
1	SECURE INSTITUTIONAL AND/OR AGENCY COMMITMENT TO AN ACTION PROGRAM AT THE STATE AND/OR LOCAL LEVEL
1A	ESTABLISH PROGRAM ACTIVITY
1B	DEFINE AUDIENCE (TARGET GROUP)
1C	SELECT KEY PERSONNEL NEEDED TO SUSTAIN PROGRAM
1D	INSURE CONTINUING SUPPORT
2	SECURE INDIVIDUAL TRAINEE MOTIVATION FOR AN ACTION PROGRAM AT THE APPROPRIATE LEVEL
3	INCREASE TRAINEE'S SKILLS USEFUL TO IMPLEMENTING AN ACTION PROGRAM
3A	BY IMPROVING SKILLS NEEDED TO ORGANIZE PEOPLE AND GROUPS
3A1	By Improving Ability to Secure Commitment
3A2	By Increasing Empathy
3A3	By Increasing Self-Awareness
3B	BY CREATING TASK-ORIENTED TEAMS
3C	BY IMPROVING TEAM PARTICIPATION SKILLS
3D	BY SHARPENING PROBLEM-SOLVING SKILLS
3E	BY IMPROVING COMMUNICATION SKILLS
3F	BY IMPROVING ADMINISTRATIVE SKILLS
3G	BY IMPROVING EVALUATIVE SKILLS
3G1	Skills in Materials Evaluation
3G2	Skills in Program Evaluation
3H	BY DEVELOPING SURVEY TECHNIQUES
3J	BY DEVELOPING CONSENSUS IN SUPPORT OF A PROGRAM
3K	BY DEVELOPING INFORMATION NEEDED TO ORGANIZE AT THE STATE/REGIONAL/LOCAL LEVEL
3K1	By Conveying Knowledge of Existing State Agencies, Programs and Personnel
3K2	By Conveying Knowledge of Existing Local Agencies, Programs and Personnel
3K3	By Conveying Knowledge of Support Personnel Within the State/Area

PURPOSE CODE	PURPOSE - ENABLING OBJECTIVE - GOAL OF TRAINING PROGRAM
4	INCREASE TRAINEE'S KNOWLEDGE USEFUL TO IMPLEMENTING AN ACTION PROGRAM - KINDS OF INFORMATION EXPLORED
4A	MAN'S CHEMICAL ENVIRONMENT
4A1	Agents - Types of Drugs
4A1A	Variety - Classification of Drugs
4A1A1	Prescription Drugs
4A1A2	Non-Prescription Drugs for Medical Use
4A1A3	Illicit Drugs
4A1A4	Legal Non-Medical Drugs (Alcoholic, Caffeine, Nicotine)
4A1B	Principles of Pharmacological Actions
4A1B1	Non-Drug Influences and Effects
4A1B2	Dose Response
4A1B3	Methods of Drug Administration (Ingestion, Injection, Inhalation, Absorption)
4B	THE INDIVIDUAL AND DRUG USE
4B1	Biological Man
4B1A	Drug Effects on Users
4B2	Psychological Man
4B3	Social Man
4B3A	Family Influences
4B3B	Subcultures as Reference Groups
4B3B1	Drug Culture Jargon (Glossary of Terms)
4B3B2	Peer-Group/Personal Identity
4B3B3	Peer-Group Values (The "In-Thing To Do")
4B3C	Society Influences
4B3C1	Social Standards/Value Conflict
4B3C2	Lack of Stimulation Due to a Sterile Environment
4B3D	Response of the Individual
4B3D1	Personal Decision-Making Style
4C	EXPLANATIONS OF DRUG USE
4C1	Characteristics of the Individual
4C1A	Personality Theory
4C1B	Dependency Needs
4C1C	Psychopathic Personality
4C1D	Sociopathic Personality
4C1E	Arrested Development
4C2	Results of Social-Psychological Factors
4C2A	Peer-Group Pressures
4C2B	Boredom
4C2C	Deprivation

PURPOSE CODE	PURPOSE - ENABLING OBJECTIVE - GOAL OF TRAINING PROGRAM
4C	EXPLANATIONS OF DRUG USE (cont'd)
4C2	Results of Social-Psychological Factors
4C2D	Child-Rearing
4C2E	Identity Crisis
4C3	Sociological Factors
4C3A	Counter Cultural Responses
4C4	Excessive Availability
4D	RESPONSES OF SOCIETY TO THE INDIVIDUAL AND TO GROUPS OF INDIVIDUALS
4D1	Individual
4D1A	Prevention Programs
4D1A1	Knowledge of Prevention Agencies
4D1B	Social Service Agencies
4D1B1	Availability of Service Agencies for the Treatment of Disorders
4D1C	Treatment Programs
4D1C1	Knowledge of Community/Private Treatment Programs
4D1D	Selection of Program Alternatives
4D1D1	References to Literature
4D1D2	Locating and Utilizing Information Centers
4D1D3	Utilizing Local (Community/Private/Service Agency), State or National Facilities
4D2	Group
4D2A	Prevention Programs
4D2A1	Knowledge of Prevention Agencies
4D2B	Social Service Agencies
4D2B1	Availability of Service Agencies for the Treatment of Disorders
4D2C	Treatment Programs
4D2C1	Knowledge of Community/Private Treatment Programs
4D2D	Selection of Program Alternatives
4D2D1	References to Literature
4D2D2	Locating and Utilizing Information Centers
4D2D3	Utilizing Local (Community/Private/Service Agency), State or National Facilities

Methods Index (Appendix C)

METHOD CODE	METHODS BY WHICH TRAINING WAS IMPLEMENTED
1	ORIENTATION
1A	Overview of National Drug Education Training Program
1B	Outline of "Multiplier Effect"—Discussion of Program Participants' Role as Next Level Trainers
1C	Briefing on Training Program Activities
1D	OTHER:
2	FACTUAL PRESENTATIONS
2A	Lectures
2A1	With question and answer period
2A2	Without question and answer period
2A3	With time allotted for personal conversation with lecturer
2B	OTHER
3	DRAMATIC PRESENTATIONS - To Expose Participants to Drug Users and Their Social Environment
3A	Panel Discussion (*e.g.*, with ex-addicts/current drug users)
3B	Film Presentation (*e.g.*, 1 minute vignettes of drug user in his subculture purchasing drugs, experiencing a 'bad trip', stealing to support his habit, going through 'cold turkey')
3C	Monologue (*e.g.*, parent describes his fear and panic upon discovery of his son/daughter's use of heroin)
3D	OTHER:
4	SITE VISITS
4A	To Prevention/Treatment Facilities
4A1	Tour of facility only
4A2	Tour of facility with interaction among center personnel and/or residents and outpatients
4B	To Drug Education Facilities
4B1	Museum/Library/Institutional display of drug education reading materials, photographs, films, and other audio-visuals
4B2	Information Center for Drug Education
4C	To Youth Culture Sites
4D	OTHER:

METHOD CODE	METHODS BY WHICH TRAINING WAS IMPLEMENTED
5	PROGRAM VISITATIONS
5A	By Prevention/Treatment Agencies and/or Groups
5A1	Talk to audience
5A2	Question and answer interaction with audience
5A3	Time allotted for personal conversation with visitors
5B	OTHER:
6	GROUP DYNAMICS
6A	General Discussion
6A1	Full group exchange—all program trainees in 1 group
6A2	Training program subgroup exchange
6A2A	Staff/Subgroup communication (*i.e.*, to discover participants' expectations, allay self-doubt, etc.)
6A2B	Youth-to-Youth communication
6A2C	Youth-to-Teacher communication
6B	Group Exercises
6B1	Role Playing
6B2	Psychodrama
6B3	Rap Sessions
6B4	Fish Bowl
6B5	Simulation
6B6	Micro-Lectures
6B7	Skits by Program Participants
6C	OTHER:
7	LEADERSHIP TRAINING
7A	Problem-Solving
7B	Community Analysis
7B1	Assessing Scope of Community Drug Problem
7B2	Techniques for Motivating the Community
7B3	Identifying and Marshalling Community Resources
7C	Teamwork
7D	OTHER:
8	USE OF MEDIA
8A	Reading Materials (Books, Pamphlets, Bibliographies of Drug Education Materials)
8A1	Recommended reading
8A2	Required reading during training program
8A3	Required reading with follow-up question and answer period discussing material

METHOD CODE	METHODS BY WHICH TRAINING WAS IMPLEMENTED
8	USE OF MEDIA (cont'd)
8B	Films and Other Audio-Visuals
8B1	Recommended viewing
8B2	Required viewing during training program
8B3	Required viewing with follow-up question and answer period discussing subject
8C	OTHER:
9	PLANNING AND IMPLEMENTATION
9A	Outline objectives of next level of training to be carried out by program trainees
9B	Outline activities (methods) to be used to implement next level of training
9C	Outline involvement of youth, educational personnel, parents and community groups
9D	OTHER:
10	TESTING AND EVALUATION
10A	Pre-training general knowledge assessment
10B	Pre-training attitudinal survey
10C	Periodic quizzes during training program to assess level changes in information and attitude
10C1	Test of information retention (Cognitive)
10C2	Test of attitudinal change (Affective)
10D	Post-training general knowledge assessment
10E	Post-training attitudinal survey
10F	Formal Training Program Evaluation (Written)
10G	Informal Training Program Evaluation
10G1	Team Reaction
10G2	Participant (Trainee) Reaction
10H	OTHER:

Footnotes

1. Following the completion of the bureau design as described, the Office of Education awarded a contract to an independent, commercial company to mount a bureau-wide evaluation. Unfortunately, in the author's opinion the contractor has not achieved an understanding of the conceptual structure required to implement the design successfully, nor has it been forced to do so by the Office of Education.

12

Implications

Evaluating Student Performance

The raison d'etre of the model is to estimate the effect of school programs on student performance. This performance may take many forms, such as academic achievement, incidence of disease, frequency of library book selection, musical accomplishment, and interest in school. Many others come to mind. All of these are change variables that may be affected by the establishment of some school-based program.

Under the model these variables will be subject to measurement depending on three conditions: (1) Some change in student performance is expected, (2) the degree of change can be specified at some level of precision, and (3) it is possible to select or create instruments to measure change at the level of specificity indicated. The problem of adequate instrumentation has long confronted educators interested in the effect of their programs on clients. In nonacademic areas, little reliable work has been done, and even in the well-charted fields of achievement and aptitude testing, existing instruments for measuring individual performance leaves much to be desired.

The Discrepancy Evaluation Model does not provide a methodology for instrument design and validation, but it does contribute to the resolution of noxious validity problems, and it increases the likelihood that appropriate instruments will exist to measure student performance as a function of program exposure once programs have been thoroughly debugged. Under Stage 3 of the model, there is continuous investigation of the relationship between student performance and repeated, sequential aspects of program treatment. The study of these relationships begins with crude instruments at the practitioner's level of understanding of the process he is using to produce changes in students. Initially, student behavior must be analyzed, content refined, learning situation dissected, and the necessary student preconditions to behavior better undertstood through empirical study using ad hoc, available instruments. Later, as the complexity of "process" is unraveled, more refined instruments can be selected or fashioned on the basis of both practical experience with initial instruments and greater conceptualization of function, conditions, and purpose of treatment.

If, for example, at the outset of a reading program one wanted to measure change in a student's phonetic ability, then halfway into the evaluation of the program (at Stage 3) it would be possible to achieve a new awareness of the importance of the subauditory pronunciation of phonems, the visual discrimination of paired letter shapes, and the analytic ability to dissect consonant blends, all of which would eventually be incorporated in an instrument with powerful face validity and very likely with considerable construct (internal consistency) validity as well.

The existence of a data base of continuous, valid measures on students makes possible a record of continuous student progress that has obvious utility for the diagnosis and remediation of individual student learning problems. Further, because this data has been created and completed by the student's teacher, its use is most obvious to the person who is most motivated and in the best position to help the student. Remediation need not be left to some stranger.

Evaluating Program Performance

The existence of longitudinal student data is as critical to the success of program development as to the success of individual students. The purpose of Stage 3 work is to permit the systematic revision of program "processes" in accordance with empirical findings. Once this has been done, a broad new basis exists for evaluating the program created. Because student program performance can now be measured, and the complexity of program processes has been understood and charted, the program can be installed and its effects measured over time in accordance with the revised program design. Just as in an industrial operation samples of indices of performance may be taken at various points in time to determine whether the anticipated level of output or quality of fabrication is maintained, so the formative evaluation suggested by Bloom[1] serves to confirm or deny the periodic effectiveness of programs. It is only when a series of these measures exist that one can be reasonably sure that the measured ultimate effects of a program are in fact a consequence of that program rather than of other factors not understood or controlled in a typical experimental design of the pre post variety. Causation, the established relationship between program and performance, process and output, can only be reasonably inferred from time series data. Any evaluation that lacks instruments to provide periodic measures of effect and fails to establish consistent relationships between enabling sequences of treatment and interim effects as predicted in program design is a spurious evaluation, doomed to an endless attack and artless defense.

Ultimately, acceptable proof of a school program's effects depends not on the experimental method but on the historical or case method. As the historian studies trends in events over time, to establish pervasive relationships, so the evaluator must build a precise record of a series of connections between program events and enabling objectives to "prove" the value of a program.

Better Program Management

The evaluation of student performance and program effect are generally the benefits of the model that are of greatest interest to the public and funding authorities. However, of equal importance are the model's influence on the development of program and the power it gives program management to support the staff's creative development work.

On analysis, the work to be performed in almost any educational program (even the serving of a hot lunch) consists of a surprisingly large and complex number of tasks. Some of these tasks are unknowable until the moment of their execution, and some resist analysis even after execution. It follows that the manager of an educational program is not in a position to "direct" activity like a plant manager. He must maintain a sensitive human apparatus for identifying and solving problems experientially so that a record of workable procedures can be constructed and used under new conditions subject to further human, exploratory adaptation.

The model ensures staff autonomy and operations flexibility while at the same time providing management and all decision makers (including staff) with all the available information about what a program should look like at any point in time, what minimal staff activity should be occuring, and what minimal conditions are necessary to staff success. Hence, the model provides management with a road map of ongoing operations so that support needs may be readily identified, resources provided, and consequences of management intervention verified. Beyond this level of information and control, managers of program operations cannot and should not want to go.

Another benefit to management is the clarity with which research and development tasks are identified during the program installation and debugging process. Too often, the enthusiasm of management to "make a program work" blocks an awareness of the program's operational deficiencies, and corrective action is not taken. Even when action is taken to bring performance into accord with program design, all the management energy and conviction in the world cannot compensate for a faulty design. Only when management realizes that its ideal version (criterion model) of a reading program is internally inconsistent, incompatible with the existing milieu, or based on untenable learning theory, will it be able to launch the necessary research to devise a more promising alternative. This more formal research, generally speaking, should not be the work of management and operations staff, and under no conditions should it be the work of an evaluation unit.

Finally, those interested in the evaluation of students and programs, must recognize that for the time being at least there is no point in evaluation without program improvement and quality management, just as management is not likely to improve a program without evaluation and feedback.

To insist that we separate successful from unsuccessful remedial reading programs without considering the causes of success and failure is a bit like buying an icebox in Alaska because it worked so well in Texas. For a long time yet we are going to have to build educational program models and their many component parts, and study them in context before we generalize about their effectiveness. In this sense, every school program is experimental, developmental, and in need of changing levels of management and research support, continuous assessment, and deferred judgment about generalizable successes or failures.

Use of Computers

The use of high speed electronic data processing is obviously essential to the kind of evaluation that has been described in this book. The microscopic examination and comparison of multiple events at client, practitioner, manager, project, program, and funding system levels of operation at repeated points in time, as well as the storage of the results of these comparisons, is only possible under conditions of modern information monitoring and retrieval. The hardware and programming techniques required to implement these information systems exist. Some technical problems remain to be worked out when information systems are very large, but the major problem facing most systems today is the inadequacy of information, not the inability to process information. Because the model confronts the "criterion" and "levels" problems of information, it makes a special contribution to the construction of a data-processing system while at the same time being dependent on the system.

The model goes one step beyond the maintenance of a client data base—the most common form of data-processing support for currently operational evaluation systems. It also uses computers to keep track of organizations and their programs so that a record of institutional decisionmaking becomes as available for analysis as the progress of students or the behavior of teachers. Evaluation therefore includes a history of decisions made and models and values used, as well as the criteria on which decisions were based, the actions taken, and the consequences. Computers can scan tables or indices of knowledge to search out suitable models and extant techniques, to identify assumptions of these models, and ultimately to test the consequences of a program against the sum of value preferences of decision makers. However the computer's essential and primary contribution is the collection and analysis of program data to identify discrepancies with minimum error and lay out decision alternatives with precision. The TTT Program described in Chapter 12 already makes use of a "red flag" technique to monitor discrepancies and a "design update" technique to facilitate the decision makers revision of any aspect of a program's recorded design, through the electronic computer.

Staff Training and Development

The feedback loop of the model is no different from the feedback that makes self-directed, experiential learning possible. A model of performance is conceptualized, and the learner experiments with his own behavior, studying and modifying its effects until a reasonably good approximation of the model is achieved in reality. From the child who learns to draw a crude stick figure of a man or the letter A, to a teacher using video-tape to improve his teaching effectiveness, the modeling and modification of learning requires cycles of feedback, comparison, experimentation, and more feedback. It is just this cycle of learning process that is fostered in a staff seeking to evaluate and improve its program. When evaluative information shows inadequacies in staff competence and the need for training (as is so often the case), the model provides the general remedy at the same time it identifies the problem. What is required is a subsystem training program design that makes explicit the standards of teacher competence to be reached, the level at which they begin the program, and the effects on their behavior of all the process steps in the training design. Hence, the Discrepancy Evaluation Model is not only a management and evaluation tool but a training device as well.

The Present Role of Nonprofit Foundations

Educational Testing Service (ETS) was instrumental in an effort by Pennsylvania to define goals and the American Institute of Research is presently involved in the translation of these goals into measurable objectives. The role of nonprofit institutions in nationwide evaluation activity is perhaps best exemplified by these efforts. Both organizations appear to be executing specific evaluation tasks without considering the requirements of a comprehensive evaluation system. It can be argued that as contractors they have done what was asked of them by clients with limited resources. But it may be in the interest of these nonprofit organizations to counsel clients to proceed piecemeal in the absence of a comprehensive design. Educational Testing Service has been a party to numerous conversations at the Office of Education about the evaluation of federal programs. In those meetings attempts were made by all parties to plan for the development of a national evaluation system controlled by the federal government. When political and practical obstacles to such a system arose, the ETS representatives giving "technical advice" were unable to suggest viable alternatives.

The formulation of a national evaluation strategy predicated on sound theory, hard technology, and social and political reality has repeatedly been neglected by nonprofit foundations and institutions. Only when advisors to national policy makers work from assumptions of the value and purpose of evaluation in a rapidly changing society, will imaginative, broadly conceived decisions be made. However, dependent as they are on educational institutions as clients, it is not in the interests of most nonprofit organizations to advocate evaluation systems that will have their greatest utility and political support at the local level. Local evaluations generate highly volatile information of great importance for changing local institutions. And in the aggregate, state institutions may be changed as well. Therefore, most chief state school officers and local superintendents will not support bona fide evaluation systems on philosophical grounds, and the nonprofit institutions dare not risk opposing this consensus of educational opinion. The notable exceptions to this professional bias are a few courageous city and state school administrators and some public-service-minded federal officers who have no professional reference group and no organization with sizable contracting capacity to turn to. As a result, a demonstration, which could be launched by a few of these educators, of the benefits of sound evaluation to a public concerned with more effective educational programs, has not been forthcoming.

The position of other foundations regarding evaluation has not been studied. Recently, the Ford Foundation rejected a proposal from a reputable investigator to fund a modest evaluation planning effort. Other foundations have periodically proclaimed an interest in supporting the evaluation of institutional change, but they have not funded any effort.

A New Agency

The ultimate application of the model is a national evaluation system. A new kind of national institute is needed to make local education agencies strong in the theory and practice of self-evaluation through the cooperative assistance of local institutions, state agencies, and federal bureaus. If there was an impartial institution with professional credentials to coordinate such an effort, it is likely that government agencies, as well as local school boards, would rely heavily on it.

It is unrealistic and wasteful to imagine that each local school system can muster an independent capability for developing its own evaluation procedures. A much more feasible plan is the initial demonstration of a national evaluation system in a selected number of communities in close cooperation with their state departments of public education, followed by nationwide installation under a national institute.

The advantage of this approach is that the satisfaction of the short term information needs of both a local district or city and a state would be used as the basis for their involvement in the design of an evaluation system to obtain their long term information needs. City and state would therefore combine their resources to fashion a theoretically sound evaluation system, useful to both parties and capable of evolving to meet the changing information needs of both parties. Such a city-state alliance would be voluntary, born of mutual need. It would create a self-determined evaluation system to which both city and state staffs would be committed. Trade-offs between city and state, essential to the success of any state system, would be assured.

The success of such an institute would depend on combining the interests, efforts, and funds of local, state, and federal offices concerned with program improvement and assessment. The proposed strategy for funding would be to establish a long term capital or endowment base for the institute, to which would be added city, state, and federal funds on a project unit basis. Each party would receive unique benefits beyond those he could buy alone. No party would be asked to give an inordinately large amount. As new kinds of services were provided under new contracts and the reputation of the institute was secured, income would increase to the point where sophisticated theoretical work as well as the service work of the institute could be supported on a self-sustaining basis.

One approach to development of an institute is to provide a series of conferences on which to build a national consensus about the purpose and methods of evaluation. Another is to broaden the theoretical work that has already been done by securing new concepts as well as reactions to extant work from new contributors. Obviously, both approaches could be taken at the same time. However, the ultimate success of the institute will depend on its demonstrated power to effect changes in educational programs regardless of the academic acceptability of its methodology. Therefore, the sooner the potential for this power is demonstrated or even intimated, the greater the public support for the institute will be and the more likely its establishment.

It is therefore recommended that during its early life the institute emphasize field development programs supported by applied research and facilitated by the discussions and deliberations of theoreticians meeting in private and public sessions. One of the first objectives of the institute will be to secure the joint cooperation of a coterminous city and university and their state department of education in the establishment of an evaluation system that also serves the federal government's information needs. Several such evaluation units can be linked and launched simultaneously.

The activity carried on under field development projects would provide participants with immediate evaluation benefits. It would facilitate the testing and development of new evaluation ideas and techniques. In addition, it would gradually result in the development of one or more prototypes—comprehensive systems having an impressive capability of responding to professional and public inquiries.

The Social Utility of Evaluation

As never before, our public institutions are being held accountable to the people they serve. Part of this trend is a growing concern about the quality of the public schools. The public has insisted that these schools be subject to rigorous evaluation. This insistence usually takes the form of demanding to know what is "wrong" and insisting that it be made "right." As we have seen, this process is not simple.

The battle for our schools is one of good intentions. Many see the schools as the critical ingredient required to solve our nation's problems. The United States is on a problem-solving kick, and its schools have become an instrument for social change because they are one of the few institutions that affect many families on a daily basis. Our schools, the great equalizers of disparate social classes for the last three generations, are still perceived by many as our society's major apparatus for social revision.

There is a practical basis for this conviction: The budgets of most school systems surpass those of city governments. As a result, city planners and a growing clutch of social engineers view the schools as a cure for the city's pox of problems. It is believed that integration can be achieved through the schools if not through fair housing practice laws and that delinquency, drug addiction, physical health, and even the creation of "model cities" can be dealt with through new school programs. At the same time, there is a large group of people for whom the schools represent power, knowledge, and resources that might be better used directly to make inner city existence bearable. For these people, family survival may appear more important than a child's education, and facilities such as a dependable bus line and day care centers will certainly have more value than good penmanship. In view of this situation, it is understandable that methods of evaluation, whether for school improvement or social revision, can become a focal point of public attention, particularly if they reflect values that are not responsive to public needs.

Public institutions and their managers have always been responsive to special interest groups; private, privileged influence; and the spur of self-perpetuation. They have been responsive to all but the broadly based constituents served by their institutions. The managers in federal agencies feel mainly responsible to the standards and expectations of their professional colleagues on whom they must depend for support when their period of service ends. In the Office of Education, key positions are for the most part held by school superintendents or college professors who serve short stints in Washington and then inevitably move to some academic position. Leadership drawn from industry is no exception. Office of Education executives from industry have, after leaving Washington, returned either to industry or to the university community serving that industry. As a result, the influences that sway policy making in the Office of Education are lodged in the relatively small professional reference groups that originally spawn federal managers, support them while in office, and then stand ready to embrace them on their demise.

What is true in Washington is generally true in state capitals and large city school systems as well. Public school superintendents and chief state school officers prepare in advance for the day when a fickle and misinformed public or powerful and unanticipated interest group may remove them from office. They know they will then have to turn to their colleagues for the support they have earned by upholding the standards and expectations of their professional reference group—expectations that may be vastly different from the expectations of those who are served by the public schools. Therefore, as our client population becomes more demanding, school officials feel more compelled to embrace the values and standards of their colleagues rather than those of the general public. The university then becomes both the depository of the values of and the custodian of the economic lives of the members of professional interest groups that have increasingly less currency in the world of public affairs. It is ironic that when public institutions to date have been evaluated, they have usually been forced to submit to the judgment of "experts" drawn from the collegium of the university.

Those few selfless managers who are "sensitive to the people" (and a few OE staffers actually come to mind) pay the price of alienating special interest groups and their own colleagues who eventually turn on them with that special fury reserved for the outcast. Given these pressures within any large public organization, it is unrealistic to expect managers to hold themselves accountable to the public. Instead, an accountability system must be mounted that defines for managers the groups they will reference and the source of the values they will serve. We will have viable public institutions only when a manager is responsive to his client population, holds their values as his own, and uses their values as the basis for evaluating his own work. Public school evaluation then becomes a mechanism essential to the establishment and maintenance of participatory democracy. Seen in this light, public school accountability is not a bookkeeping system for aggregating performance scores and school description statistics, it is a public inquiry into the purpose and worth of any school's educational program.

The "Value" in Evaluation

As part of the growing concern for the quality of our schools, the public has insisted that schools be subject to rigorous evaluation. Only a comprehensive and formalized evaluation system can ensure that these voices will be heard, that standards will be set and performance measured, and that decisions will be made on the basis of discrepancy.

The evaluation of any institution involves two major steps: (1) adequately defining the standards that must be adhered to, and (2) comparing the actual performance of the institution with the standards. Evaluation in the public schools consists of determining whose expectations will constitute performance standards; comparing student, teacher, or program performance against these standards; and feeding this information back to determine if expectations are in fact being met. This process is not as simple as it sounds in outline. One area that deserves particular attention, because it has often been neglected in the past, is the process of defining appropriate standards.

Standards are derived from knowledge and value, and value is the determinant factor. Value determines what portions of a vast possible supply of knowledge will be used as a standard and then confers authority on that standard. Value also determines what factors or materials are to be judged. Evaluation therefore requires that someone or some group apply a value both to what is being judged and to the standard used to make the judgments. The rationale for choosing the standard and the material to be judged by it should be made public before the conduct of any evaluation.

Although value judgments are a necessary part of educational evaluation, their presence has not always been made explicit and standards have been used in a slipshod manner despite appearances to the contrary. Boards of experts have often been convened, authorities have been installed, and citizens' panels have embarked on inquiries, investigations, and studies; but these groups have seldom revealed, and sometimes have not been aware of, the values influencing their judgments. Trying to judge the worth of a particular program on the basis of these separate, value-influenced judgments is similar in effect to trying to judge the worth of an automobile by looking at the testimony of a race car driver, a truck driver, and a little old lady in tennis shoes. Each of these "experts" is qualified to make judgments on the aspects of the car that he is familiar with, but none can supply an overall judgment of its value. The worth of any individual's judgments to an outsider will depend on whether they have considered the criteria the judge views as important and have assumed values he would accept. Unless the criteria are drawn before the evaluation, it is unlikely that an appropriate expert will be chosen to render a judgment.

The evaluation of a social institution like a public school requires a careful decision about whose values are to be applied to what. This decision should be made before any evaluation, because to evaluate something while at the same time deciding on a standard is like judging a defendant's guilt while gathering evidence. One day he may appear to be guilty, the next not, depending on what evidence we have found at the moment. Further, judging a defendant without a set of values about the rules of evidence and acceptable judicial procedure exposes him to the whims of his judge's value system.

In public school evaluations we have often convened a few educators to observe some of the characteristics of a school. These characteristics have sometimes been predetermined. They might include the condition of a building, the number of books in a library, and the training and experience of teachers. The standards generally do not include the performance characteristics of students. Schools have been judged not in terms of what students can do but in terms of what schools appear to be. This is a bit like judging the performance of a driver by the size of his car's engine and the number of years he has been driving rather than by his track record.

Another problem in education, of course, has been that resources as well as expectations vary. Some districts prefer students with mechanical aptitude rather than verbal fluency. Some wish to teach the young no more than the fundamentals. More important, schools are not machines. Dollar costs that seem exorbitant for one district may seem low for another, yet, the constituents of both districts may be dissatisfied with similar levels of student performance. Obviously, nonmonetary resources also vary; there are differences in